The Diplomatic Corps
under Charles II and James II

The Diplomatic Corps

under Charles II & James II

BY PHYLLIS S. LACHS

Rutgers University Press

NEW BRUNSWICK, NEW JERSEY

The type used in the composition of this book is Granjon, with Caslon Old Style No. 337 as display. It was printed by letterpress on 60# Publishers' Imperial Text, and bound in Columbia's Natural Finish Fictionette with endpapers of Lindenmeyr Schlosser's Multicolor. The book was designed by JoAnn Randel.

To My Husband

Preface

England's great experiment in republican rule ended in May 1660, when Charles II accepted the invitation of Parliament to assume the English throne. Charles II inherited, along with his father's crown, some unpleasant bequests of the Cromwellian era: an exhausted treasury, an unpaid army, and widespread disagreement over the proper religious settlement. Moreover, if the restored monarchy was to continue without interruption, the choice of a bride for the young King was a decision of national importance.

Charles II returned to England on a wave of strong royalist sentiment on the part of most of his subjects. Charles came back without the aid of foreign arms, and he came back as an absolute monarch without any restrictions imposed upon his sovereignty. The King's own program, embodied in the Declaration of Breda, was formulated by Edward Hyde, later earl of Clarendon, who had earned the position of Lord Chancellor by guiding Charles during the trials of his exile. The King's promises were general. They proposed a general amnesty to the rebels, property settlement according to the will of Parliament, discharge with payment of arrears to the army, and "liberty of tender consciences" in religion.

The Convention Parliament turned its attention to the work connected with the Restoration. Some of the regicides who had taken part in the trial and execution of Charles I were themselves executed. The legislative achievements of the Convention included the restoration of crown and church lands to original owners; the discharge of the army; and the settling of £1,200,000 annual income upon the King. Feudal tenures were abolished, a post office was established, and a Navigation Act was passed to foster English overseas trade.

The Convention was unable to solve the thorny question of religious settlement, and this was left to the first or Cavalier Parliament of the reign which convened in the spring of 1661. This Parliament consisted of a group of zealous Anglicans who ranged themselves solidly behind church and King. The bishops returned to their seats in the House of Lords, and the two Houses succeeded in passing a series of laws which firmly established the Anglican Church and excluded the Presbyterians from the Establishment and from the government.

In the sphere of foreign policy Charles II inherited the hostilities and alliances which had been formulated during the Protectorate. Cromwell had bequeathed a war

with Spain and the tradition of friendship with France
and enmity with the United Provinces. Although the
King was himself not hostile to Spain and the Anglo-
Spanish war was ended in 1660, Charles did not ally himself with the Spanish house. Clarendon, acting in concur-
rence with the diplomatic machinations of Louis XIV,
saw to it that Charles married the Portuguese princess
Catherine of Braganza. The alliance with Portugal was
popular in England. It brought with it Tangier and Bom-
bay and the promise, if not the ultimate payment, of a substantial dowry. The marriage of Henriette Stuart to the
Duke of Orléans and the sale of Dunkirk to France were
further links in the union between Stuart and Bourbon, a
union which was to grow more and more displeasing to
the English as time progressed and Charles's Catholic
and autocratic tendencies became more manifest.

In March 1665, England and the United Provinces entered a second war born of commercial rivalry. The war
was one of Parliament's choosing, and the King and the
Lord Chancellor gave their consent with reluctance. As
the original war fever subsided, parliamentary grants for
the successful waging of the war were neither prompt nor
adequate. Maladministration, corruption, and the disaster
of the Plague in 1666 combined to limit English achievements.

Meanwhile a sporadic effort to offset French influence
by alliance with Spain produced little lasting result. A difficult mission, which set forth in 1664, had as its purpose
the negotiation of a commercial treaty whereby England
would secure from Spain advantages then enjoyed by the
French and the Dutch. Although England had been at
peace with Spain since 1660, the peace was considered to
apply only in European territories, and hostilities between

the two powers continued in Jamaica, Cuba, and Mexico. After three years of negotiations, England acquired a treaty applying to colonial trade in Spanish ports. France tried unsuccessfully to prevent the Anglo-Spanish entente, but managed to keep Portugal from accepting an English invitation to be party to the treaty.

The leading minister during the early years of the Restoration was Clarendon, who was on intimate terms with the King and allied to the royal family through the marriage of his daughter Anne to James, Duke of York, who became James II in 1685. Clarendon constantly upheld his ideals of a monarchy working in harmony with Parliament and an established Anglican Church. He had the professional lawyer's respect for the law, but his long exile from active affairs in England left him unprepared to cope with the altered situations in his native country. As time passed he lost favor with the King as a result of his annoying disapproval of Charles's personal conduct. Because Clarendon's name was attached to the religious settlement, he was hated by the Dissenters. Clarendon fell from power in 1667, the victim of various aspects of national discontent. Old royalists blamed him for introducing rebels into the government. The populace expressed its displeasure with his conduct of foreign affairs and his apparent corruption in financial matters during a time of economic distress.

Clarendon's place in the direction of affairs was taken by the five ministers of the cabal: Thomas Clifford; Henry Bennet, earl of Arlington; George Villiers, duke of Buckingham; Anthony Ashley Cooper, later earl of Shaftesbury; and John Maitland, duke of Lauderdale. These men possessed no political cohesiveness amongst themselves and no joint control of Parliament. Despite its failings, the cabal ministry witnessed some success in foreign affairs. The Triple Alliance of 1668, effected by Sir William Temple, allied England, the United Provinces, and Sweden against the designs of Louis XIV. The negotiations, begun in 1667, were ostensibly designed simply to obtain a defensive agreement with the Dutch to guarantee the borders of the Spanish Netherlands. As concluded, the treaty offered in its public clauses to guarantee the terms that France had already offered to Spain. Secretly, the three parties to the treaty promised that if Louis XIV failed to conclude peace with Spain according to these terms, the signers would wage war against France on Spain's behalf.

The alliance, which never found favor in Charles's eyes, was soon betrayed by the English government. Clifford and Arlington were party to the secret Treaty of Dover of 1670 in which Charles II promised to support France against the United Provinces and to declare for Roman Catholicism in England in return for a subsidy from Louis XIV that would help to keep him independent of parliamentary grants. Since the agreement at Dover placed no time limit on the English King's public conversion, which never took place, and French payments began almost immediately in substantial sums, Charles emerged the diplomatic victor.

The only real common purpose of the cabal ministry was a desire to do away with the penal codes against the nonconformists, for not one of the five was an Anglican. In 1672, on the eve of renewed hostilities with the United Provinces, Charles issued a Declaration of Indulgence relaxing the persecution of the nonconformists. National resentment of the Duke of York's Catholicism and of the current negotiations for his marriage to the Catholic princess Mary of Modena was intensifying. The church party refused to extend toleration to the recusants, and Parliament withheld the supply until the declaration was withdrawn. The Test Act, designed to exclude all Catholics and Protestant nonconformists from civil and military office, passed quickly through both Houses. The King's French policies were by now so unpopular that Charles decided to make a separate peace with the United Provinces in 1674. The period of the cabal ended without the achievement of the ends for which Charles had been striving.

As an alternative to future dependence on parliamentary grants, Charles II chose the solution of dependence on French subsidy. By 1677 it was apparent that he did so in defiance of popular opinion. To assuage national anti-French feeling and English fears of a change in the religious settlement, Charles consented to a marriage between William of Orange, later William III, and the princess Mary, Protestant daughter of the Duke of York. When the Glorious Revolution of 1688 brought this royal pair to the throne, William combined his own Dutch forces with those of England to effect a diplomatic revolution which took England out of the sphere of French domination and into the forefront of the anti-French coalition.

The primary purpose of this book is to examine the English diplomatic corps from the Restoration to the Revolution of 1688. It encompasses a description of the location and regularity of embassies sent abroad, the routine of business and ceremonial duties, the appointment of ambassadors and their households, the cost of the service, diplomatic privileges, and literature that the diplomats produced as a result of their service. The study is not concerned with foreign policy during this period except for those ways in which policy influenced the techniques of diplomacy, as in the selection of ambassadors and the treatment afforded foreign ministers in hostile territories.

The limits set to this study are not meant to suggest that England's foreign policy was lacking in incident, or that new patterns of alliances were not emerging. The institutions of diplomacy, however, merit particular attention. The Restoration was not a time when English interests were able to dominate the affairs of states, but the end of the seventeenth century was a time when the techniques of diplomacy were developing and changing. The literature on international law, no longer a new field when Hugo Grotius published his influential *De jure belli ac pacis* in 1625, continued to grow in the works of Richard Zouche, Samuel von Pufendorf, and Samuel Rachel. Zouche, like one of the earliest authorities in the field, Alberico Gentili, taught and wrote in England. Along with texts on international law, which revealed an increased awareness of the role of the sovereign state in the affairs of Europe, many manuals on the ideal diplomat were being published. These guides to the qualifications and training of prospective ministers were rarely honored in practise, but they show that men were interested in the best way to achieve national goals through diplomatic representation. The forms that this representation assumed were also changing. The story of the transformation of occasional embassies to permanent ones belongs to an earlier period. The diplomatic method that was new in the seventeenth century was the general congress. The first large assembly of diplomats, held in Westphalia in 1648, settled the Thirty Years War. During the period of the Restoration England participated actively in three more: Aix-la-Chapelle (1668), Cologne (1673), and Nimeguen (1675 to 1679). Delegates to congresses were considered

ministers of more than ordinary importance. This importance was reflected in the organization of their households
and in the new forms of etiquette that evolved.

The most important body of source material for this
book was the correspondence between the ministers
abroad and the Secretaries of State in London. When
quoting directly from these sources, I have chosen to maintain the original spelling. This, I believe, conveys a sense
of the time and the nature of the material without sacri-
ficing clarity. In the spelling of proper names I have followed the preferred usage of the *Dictionary of National
Biography*. For names which are not listed in the *Dictionary* and which appeared in various forms in the seventeenth century, I have indicated alternate spellings in
parentheses at the first mention of the person.

English diplomats dated their letters in different ways.
Some used the Old, or Julian calendar, followed in England. Others used both the Old and New Style, or Gre-
gorian calendar, followed by all Catholic and some Protestant countries on the Continent. All dates are given here
according to the Old Style, and can be adjusted to the
other usage by adding ten to the dates of days.

Whereas the translation of dates from one calendar to
another is fairly simple, the task of determining the seventeenth century equivalents of various national currencies
in terms of the English pound is in many cases very difficult and in others impossible. The ministers of Charles II
and James II naturally received their salaries in pounds,
shillings, and pence, but when they drew up their expense
accounts or made statements concerning their indebted-
ness abroad, they frequently made reference to the coinage
of the other country. Wherever possible I have translated
the foreign currency into the English equivalent. Appen-

dix I includes some expense accounts which are helpful in determining seventeenth century prices and, by implication, the purchasing power of the diplomatic salary.

I want to express my gratitude to Professor Caroline Robbins of Bryn Mawr College, who directed this study, and who has tirelessly helped and encouraged me at every stage of my work. I benefited from the assistance of Mary Maples Dunn during my stay in London and after my return, and from the suggestions of Professor David Herlihy. Dean Hartley Simpson of Yale University kindly made available to me the Denzil Holles papers collected by the late Alexander Thomson. Financial assistance from the American Association of University Women made possible a year devoted to uninterrupted work on the doctoral dissertation which formed the basis of this book. A grant from the Research Council of Rutgers, the State University, contributed to the cost of publication.

PHYLLIS S. LACHS

Oreland, Pennsylvania
January, 1964

Contents

TABLES

*The Diplomatic Corps
under Charles II and James II*

The Structure of
the Diplomatic Corps

*"The Embassador is oblig'd . . . to act according to Forms
. . . whereas the Resident . . . being less incommodious and
less formal than the Embassador . . . has his Business dispatch'd with much more Expedition."*
ABRAHAM DE WICQUEFORT, The Embassador and His Functions

A good way to gauge the maturity of a seventeenth century diplomatic corps is to discover the number of permanent embassies the government maintained abroad. The
permanent, or resident, embassy developed slowly from
the custom of sending ambassadors to heads of state for
special purposes. They negotiated treaties or conveyed
good wishes on royal birthdays, weddings, and other family events, and then returned. Venice, in the late fifteenth
century, followed by the Pope and other Italian rulers, led
the way in establishing permanent diplomatic representation in the capitals of Europe and in Constantinople. In

the course of the next hundred years the permanent diplomatic mission gradually became a familiar part of the
European scene. Certainly the resident embassy was no
novelty by the middle of the seventeenth century, but
neither was it a universally established institution. France,
under Louis XIV, had the most fully developed and widespread system of permanent embassies in Europe. Louis
XIV maintained resident ministers of varying ranks in
twenty-one states.[1] Judged by these standards, the English
diplomatic corps under Charles II and James II was a
youthful, rather irregularly developed organization.

The English service during these years had so developed
as to maintain some permanent embassies, and it recognized the four main grades of rank in service which seventeenth century secular powers used: ambassadors, envoys,
residents, and agents, in descending order of importance
and dignity. The ambassadors of the Pope were called
nuncios. The title ambassador extraordinary, or "ambassador *pro tempore*" as he was sometimes styled, signified
one sent abroad for a special occasion, usually a birth, marriage, accession, or death in a royal family. He travelled
with more pomp than his fellow diplomats and was permitted to return as soon as he had accomplished the purpose of his mission, unless his commission contained a re-
straining clause. The ambassador in ordinary was obliged
to remain at his post until he received letters of revocation.
The agent, at the other end of the ladder, was concerned
almost exclusively with mercantile affairs. Governments
maintained agents at courts where their political interests
were small, but where commercial advantages might be
gained by having a public minister on the scene. The in-
termediary titles are of later origin. A resident originally
meant an ambassador in ordinary, but by the beginning of

the seventeenth century it came to mean a minister who did not have the power to represent his sovereign in the first degree. The envoy, a rank more modern than that of resident, served on a mission which by its nature was less complicated or less important than one calling for an ambassador. An envoy was usually designated "extraordinary" to insure that he receive treatment above that due a resident.[2] The term plenipotentiary did not signify a special grade but simply indicated that the minister had full powers to negotiate on behalf of his sovereign. When a minister plenipotentiary and an envoy were both present at one court, the former outranked the latter.[3] The first time one person held both these titles was at the Congress of Nimeguen in 1678.[4] Seventeenth century commentators usually divided diplomats into two main categories: ministers of the first order, meaning ambassadors; and ministers of the second order, meaning envoys, residents and agents.

The crown sent diplomatic missions to thirty rulers between 1660 and 1688 but maintained permanent embassies in only five places: France, Spain, Portugal, the United Provinces, and the Hanse Towns of Hamburg, Bremen, and Lübeck (see Tables I and II *).[5] The permanence of

---

* Tables I and II indicate public missions only. In addition to embassies listed in Bittner and Gross, *Repertorium,* and the *Calendar of Treasury Books,* a few secret agents were abroad: 1664: Sir Bernard Gascoigne in Florence arranging for intelligence from Rome (S.P. 98/5). 1665: Theobold Taafe sent to Flanders to treat with the Marquis of Castel Rodrigo (*C.S.P.V.* XXXIV, 195, 208 and notes). 1668: Gascoigne in Spain carrying secret papers empowering him to negotiate (*C.S.P.V.* XXV, 278 and notes; H.M.C. *Fifteenth Report,* "Hodgkins MSS.," p. 132), and in Portugal on confidential affairs ("Hodgkins MSS.," p. 129). 1674: Walter Vane with the Prince of Orange at the behest of Danby to keep him informed of the Prince's attitude toward the prospective marriage alliance with Princess Mary (Browning, *Danby,* I, 133).

TABLE I

English Embassies in the Southern Province, 1660–1688

Year	France	Spain	Spanish Netherlands	Portugal	Savoy	Genoa	Tuscany	Venice	Modena	Pope	Morocco
1660	Ia x	IIb	IIb	x			IIc				
1661	Ia x	IIb	IIb	Ia, IIa			IIc				
1662	IIa x			Ia, Ib, IIc			IIc				
1663	Ia x	Ib		Ib			IIc			x	
1664	Ia x	Ib		IIc			IIc				
1665	Ia	Ia		IIc							IIc
1666	Ia	Ia, Ib, IIa	IIb x	Ia, Ib, IIa			IIb				
1667	Ia	Ia, III	IIb	IIb			IIb				
1668	Ia, IIa	IIa	IIb	Ia, IIb			IIb				x
1669	IIc	IIa	x	IIb	x		IIb				Ia
1670	Ib, IIc	IIa	IIa	III	x	x	IIa, IIb	Ia, III		x	
1671	Ib, IIc	IIa	IIa	III	x		IIb	III			
1672	Ia, Ib, IIa, IIc	Ib	IIa	IIc	x			III			
1673	Ia, Ib, IIa, IIc	Ib		IIc		x			Ib		
1674	Ia, Ib, IIa, IIc	Ib	IIa	IIc	x			IIa			
1675	Ia, Ib, IIa, IIc	Ib		IIc	x			IIa			
1676	Ia, IIc	Ib	IIb	IIc		IIa		IIa			
1677	Ia, IIc	Ib	IIb	IIb		IIa		IIa			

Year												
1678	Ia, IIc	Ib	IIa, IIb, x	IIb	IIa	IIa		IIc	IIa			
1679	IIa, IIc	Ib	IIb	IIb	IIa	IIa		IIc	IIa			
1680	IIa	Ib	IIb	IIb								Ib
1681	IIa	IIa	IIb	IIb								
1682	IIa	IIa	IIb	IIb								
1683	IIa	III	IIb	IIb								
1684	IIa	III	IIb	IIb								
1685	IIa	IIa, III	IIa	IIb							Ib	
1686	IIa*	IIa	IIa	IIb							Ib, IIc	
1687	Ib	IIa	IIa	IIb							Ib, IIc	
1688	Ia	IIa	IIa	IIb							Ib	
Total number of men sent	36	11	14	13	3	5	3	6	3	1	7	4

KEY:

I Ministers of the first order
  Ia — Ambassadors extraordinary
  Ib — Ambassadors in ordinary
II Ministers of second order
  IIa — Envoy or envoy extraordinary
  IIb — Resident
  IIc — Agent

III Secretary or *Chargé d'Affaires*
 x diplomatic visit of no special character

*Tabulation for the embassy in France in 1686 follows *C.T.B*, VIII, part 2, 949, 975, 1010, which lists Bevil Skelton as envoy extraordinary, and Jusserand, *Instructions*, II, 338, which names him in this character, although Bittner and Gross describe him as an ambassador.

TABLE II

English Embassies in the Northern Province, 1660–1688

Year	United Provinces	Denmark	Sweden	Poland	Empire Vienna	Empire, Diet of Regensburg	Lower Saxon Circle	Hanse: Hamburg, Lübeck, Bremen	Mainz	Frankfort-a-M.	Cologne	Münster	Palatinate	Saxony	Brandenburg-Prussia	Brunswick-Lüneburg-Celle	Brunswick-Lüneburg-Wolfenbüttel	Hesse-Cassel	Hanover
1660	IIb			x				IIc							IIa				
1661	IIb				x			IIc											
1662	IIb							IIc											
1663	IIb	Ib, IIa						IIc											
1664	IIb	IIa	Ia, IIa		IIa			IIb	IIa	IIb					IIa				
1665	IIb	IIa	Ia, IIa					IIb		IIb		IIa				IIa		IIa	
1666			IIa, IIc					IIb		IIb			x						
1667	PP		IIa					IIb		IIb									
1668	IIa	Ia	IIc					IIb		IIb				IIa	IIa	IIa			
1669	Ib	Ia, IIa	Ia	Ib				IIb		IIb			IIa	IIa	IIa	IIa			IIa
1670	Ib	IIa	IIa					IIb		IIb									
1671	Ib	Ia, IIb	Ib, IIa					IIb					x						
1672	Ib	IIa, IIb	IIa		IIa			IIb							IIa	IIa	IIa		IIa
1673		IIa, IIb	IIa		IIa			IIb								IIa		IIa	
1674	Ia	IIb	IIa					IIb										IIa	
1675	Ia		IIa					IIb											

Year																		
1676	Ia	IIb	IIa	Ib	IIa													IIa
1677	Ia, IIa, pp	IIb	IIa															IIa
1678	Ia, IIa, pp	IIb	IIa															
1679	Ia	IIb, x	IIa		IIa													
1680	IIa	IIa	IIa	IIa				IIa										
1681	IIa, IIc	IIa	IIa					IIa										
1682	IIa, IIc		IIa	IIa		IIc		IIa										
1683	IIa	x			IIb		IIa		IIb									
1684	IIa	IIa	IIb		IIb		IIa		IIb		IIa			IIa	IIa	IIa	IIa	
1685	IIa	IIa	IIb		IIb		IIa		IIb		IIa	IIa	IIa		IIa	IIa	IIa	
1686	IIa	IIa	IIb		IIb		IIa		IIb		IIa		IIa		IIa	IIa		
1687	IIa	IIa	IIa		IIb				IIb		IIa	IIa	IIb	IIa		IIa	IIa	IIa
1688	IIa	IIa	IIa		IIb				IIb		IIa		IIb			IIa	IIa	IIa
Total number of men sent	13	14	10	3	7	2	1	4	3	1	2	4	4	8	4	3	6	3

KEY:

I Ministers of the first order
  Ia — Ambassadors extraordinary
  Ib — Ambassadors in ordinary

II Ministers of second order
  IIa — Envoy or envoy extraordinary
  IIb — Resident
  IIc — Agent

III Secretary or *Chargé d'Affaires*

pp plenipotentiary

x diplomatic visit of no special character

these embassies reflected the importance of the countries in the foreign affairs and commercial interests of England. There was a fluctuation in rank at every capital, for the service was not so formal that any post invariably received a minister of a certain grade. France, Spain, Portugal, Venice, the United Provinces, Denmark, Sweden, and Poland all received ambassadors at one time or other, but the procedure was not regularized. Even Louis XIV, the most powerful sovereign in Europe and the favorite ally of Charles II, received ministers varying in grade from ambassador extraordinary to agent, although when an agent assumed charge of the Paris embassy, higher ranking diplomats came on frequent short missions so that no year passed without at least one ambassador or envoy at the French court. Two examples show the tentative manner in which rank was established at Paris. Ralph Montagu, duke of Montagu, intended at first as an envoy, received accreditation as an ambassador when the government found sufficient funds. Sir John Trevor left London as an envoy, carrying instructions that if he were well received he would be promoted to ambassador.[6]

The Spanish post was usually entrusted to an ambassador or an envoy, but at times it was left to an ungraded member of the clerical staff who acted as a *chargé d'affaires,* or, as from 1662 to 1664, left vacant. Spain never received a resident after Henry Bennet, later earl of Arlington, left Madrid in 1662, because the Spanish considered the title out of date and suitable only for a backwater such as Denmark.[7] The customary grade assigned to the Portuguese mission was envoy extraordinary, although the ministers charged with making arrangements for the marriage alliance between Charles II and Catherine of Braganza were honored with the title of ambassadors extraordinary. The Portuguese post was left to an embassy secretary in 1670 and 1671. This caused Queen Catherine, anxious for England to send an ambassador to her native land, to support the Portuguese ambassador in London, Dom Francesco de Melo, out of her private funds, in the hope that England would reciprocate by sending a minister of the first order to Portugal.[8] The only result was that the secretary in Lisbon was promoted to resident.

The assignment of rank sometimes depended upon the efforts of the ministers themselves. Sir Thomas Higgons, accredited to Venice in 1672 as resident, delayed his departure for almost two years until he succeeded in getting his status changed to envoy extraordinary, which carried with it a higher salary.[9] Sir William Temple was able to influence the assignment of his rank in the other direction. The embassy at The Hague ranked officially as a residency[10] until after the Second Dutch War (1665–1667). When the winds of Anglo-Dutch friendship blew warmer following the Peace of Breda, Arlington wished to send Temple, his personal choice for the position, as an ambassador. Temple, ever intent on business and shy of protocol, declined, informing his patron that he did not wish a higher title than envoy extraordinary. "In this [the envoy's office]," Temple wrote to Arlington, "I am pretty confident to acquit myself well enough, both in these and other circumstances; whereas the other is a thing I know nothing of, and enough to make a poor Man's head turn round, that was always brought up in shade and silence till your lordship brought me out upon the stage."[11] Arlington acquiesced in Temple's wishes until after the conclusion of the Triple Alliance of 1668. Then the King raised Temple's rank to ambassador, in which character he remained until he left the United Provinces in 1671.

After the Treaty of Westminster (1674), which ended the Third Dutch War, Temple returned to the Hague as ambassador extraordinary, so that he outranked other English ministers sent to the Prince of Orange during this period. Lest Temple's rank and seniority give him a dominant voice at the Congress of Nimeguen, Honoré Courtin, seigneur de Chantereine, French ambassador in London, used his influence with Charles II to have John Berkeley, baron Berkeley of Stratton, "a man well disposed towards France," named chief of the embassy. The title was an empty one, which Courtin soon realized, and Temple played the principal role at the Congress.[12]

The Scandinavian countries, too, received ministers of varying grades. Here an envoy was considered sufficient for ordinary business, but an ambassador came to Denmark in 1669 and 1672 to lend greater dignity to the signing of treaties. The King promoted the minister to Sweden from envoy to ambassador in 1671 because France and Holland had ambassadors in Stockholm and he wanted his minister to be of equal rank.[13]

Neither statute nor custom fixed a time limit on service at one post, and England had no system of rotation in service. A suggestion that three years was a proper period to remain in one place before replacement was put forth as a reason for recalling Temple from the Hague in favor of Sir George Downing in 1671.[14] Thomas Belasyse, earl Fauconberg, learned on his mission to Venice that the Republic did not expect an ambassador extraordinary to stay longer than three months.[15] In general, terms of service depended more on the availability of replacements and the state of the Treasury than on any definite pattern. Tenure varied from a few months to several years, with no relation to grade or country.

Only two generalizations can be made about the structure of the diplomatic service. The Empire, the German States, Savoy, Genoa, and Tuscany never received a diplomat above the grade of envoy, and from 1680 to the end of the reign of Charles II no diplomat of the first order was accredited anywhere. A general downgrading of rank beginning in 1679 affected posts in France, Spain, and the United Provinces (all reduced from ambassador to envoy) and Sweden (reduced from envoy to resident). The Italian embassies came to an end, as did the practise of maintaining an agent in France in addition to higher ranking ministers. The reduction in service was part of a broad effort on the part of the commissioners of the Treasury [16] to reduce government expenditures, and the ministers who were recalled were considered to be of little or no use.[17] A royal commission reduced the English delegation at Nimeguen by two-thirds, leaving Temple to ponder the reason with Prince William of Orange. "All we could guess was the design of sparing so much money, by ending Mr. [Laurence] Hyde's and Sir Lyonell's [Jenkins] embassy now the peace was so near concluded, and continuing mine only, for the decency of mediation till the assembly should break up." [18] The government gave serious thought to recalling the resident in Brandenburg-Prussia, but Edmund Poley wrote from Berlin that England should keep her embassy with Frederick William, who was such a strong supporter of the Protestant religion. The commissioners decided that an embassy must have more to justify its existence than support for the reformed faith, and Poley's commission expired a few months later. In Portugal, ambassador Francis Parry hoped that the efforts at economy would relieve him of an unwanted assignment,[19] but Parry's job was to collect overdue payments on the Queen's dowry and he was held at his post until 1682, when an envoy replaced him.

The accession of James II brought a few changes that reflected the rule of a Catholic King. Unlike his brother, James II maintained an ambassador at the papal court,[20] and he raised the grade of the service in three Catholic courts: France (envoy to ambassador), Spain (secretary to envoy), and the Spanish Netherlands (resident to envoy). Even with these promotions the service was smaller under James II, who sent the German and Italian princes no representatives. Diplomats travelled to twenty-five countries between 1660 and 1685; to ten between 1685 and 1688.

Two posts, Turkey and Russia (Table III), were in a special category.[21] The ambassadors to Turkey came in the name of the King, but were in fact the paid servants of the Turkey Company (a joint-stock organization of merchants), which made this embassy independent of government funds and, to some extent, of government policy. The ambassador and the company concluded a private contract which stipulated salary, duties, tenure of service, and embassy personnel.[22] In addition, Heneage Finch, earl of Winchilsea, pledged himself in a secret agreement never to do anything at the Porte without the consent and approval of the company, binding himself with a promise to pay the merchants £10,000 if he should break the agreement.[23] Under these circumstances, the ambassador's obligations to the King could not weigh as heavily upon him as his duties toward his employers. Independent of the erratic fiscal policies of the crown, the embassy in Constantinople was the first permanent embassy to be established following the Restoration, and the only post that was served by an ambassador for the entire twenty-eight years of the Restoration.

TABLE III

Embassies of the Trading Companies, 1660–1688

Year	Turkey	Russia
1660	Ib	
1661	Ib	
1662	Ib	
1663	Ib	Ia
1664	Ib	Ia
1665	Ib	
1666	Ib	
1667	Ib	
1668	Ib	IIa
1669	Ib	IIa
1670	Ib	
1671	Ib	
1672	Ib	
1673	Ib	
1674	Ib	
1675	Ib	
1676	Ib	IIa
1677	Ib	IIa
1678	Ib	
1679	Ib	
1680	Ib	
1681	Ib	
1682	Ib	
1683	Ib	
1684	Ib	
1685	Ib	
1686	Ib	IIa
1687	Ib	
1688	Ib	
Total number of men sent	5	4

KEY:
Ia — Ambassadors extraordinary
Ib — Ambassadors in ordinary
IIa — Envoy or envoy extraordinary

The Russian embassy, too, was a commercial expedition, but not so successful as that maintained by the Turkey Company. Because of financial difficulties, the Russia Company was not able to keep up constant representation abroad. The company underwrote the greater part of the expenses of the missions of 1663 and 1667, while the crown paid for the cost of equipping the men. In 1676, when the government wished to send a congratulatory mission to the new Czar, Theodore III, they asked the company to pay, but the merchants were unwilling to assume the burden of an embassy which promised no profit.[24] John Hebdon, in the hope of personal gain, offered to pay for his expenses in Russia out of his own purse if the government would provide him with transportation and £600 for equipage. He secured the agreement, but it proved unprofitable. His money was quickly gone and he desired to return to England, but was not permitted to do so without express permission of the King; this he finally received, at the advice of the company, late in 1677. In 1686 the crown again assumed the cost of maintaining the embassy.[25]

During the intervals when England had no organized mission in Russia, communications between the King and the Czar were entrusted to English merchants settled in Moscow who received, translated, and passed on all necessary messages. One of these merchants, Thomas Brejn, received the semiofficial title of vice-agent after the departure of Charles Howard, earl of Carlisle,[26] but he received no remuneration from the crown.

The English diplomat of the seventeenth century was the personal representative of his King to a foreign head of state. Although expressions such as the envoy at the

Hague, or the ambassador in France were common usage, the precise and legal designation for these men was the envoy of Charles II to the States General, or the ambassador of James II to the Most Christian King. All diplomatic papers described foreign ministers in this way, showing that the King, at least in theory, chose, accredited, instructed, and recalled all the diplomats who served him.

The King usually did not act alone in formulating policy, although Charles II was able to carry out secret designs when he wanted to, notably the secret Treaty of Dover (1670), which was negotiated without the knowledge of leading ministers of state. For advice the King turned to the special committee of the Privy Council concerned with foreign affairs, which included the two Secretaries of State, the Chancellor, and the Treasurer, although he was not legally bound to consult them or to accept their opinions.

Although the King assumed the responsibility for directing foreign affairs through his ambassadors, neither Charles II nor James II was so industrious as to attempt to take into his own hands the management of day to day business in the various embassies. Unlike Louis XIV, who ordered all his ambassadors to maintain a constant correspondence with himself as well as with his Secretaries of State, and who personally read all incoming mail,[27] the English King rarely exchanged letters with his ministers abroad. The despatches that came to the sovereign were usually petitions for a change in appointment, an increase in salary, or some other personal favor. The enormous task of receiving and evaluating diplomatic correspondence, advising ministers in difficult situations, and keeping them abreast of affairs at home and at neighboring courts fell to the office of the Secretaries of State.

Two principal Secretaries of State shared these responsibilities. At the Restoration Secretary Edward Nicholas had charge of Spain, Flanders, Italy, the Empire, the Catholic principalities of Germany, Turkey, Barbary, and the Indies. Secretary William Morice directed affairs with France, the Netherlands, the Protestant German states, and the Hanse Towns, Denmark, Sweden, Russia, and Poland. He also assumed charge of relations with Portugal at the request of the Portuguese ambassador in England, who feared that Nicholas was too Spanish in sympathy. When Arlington became Secretary of State in 1662, he redistributed the countries so that France, Spain, and Portugal were united in the southern province, together with Flanders, the Italian states, Turkey, Barbary, and the Indies. The southern province, because it included France, was the more important of the two, and the Secretary of the southern province was the senior Secretary of State. When the senior Secretary left office, the junior Secretary moved up to direct the southern province. The divisions, however, were not hard and fast. Ambassadors wrote to both, or to either Secretary, for personal reasons, a failure to get a quick reply, or because a delicate or difficult matter in the northern province required the attentions of the more important Secretary.[28]

Ordinarily the Secretaries and the Foreign Committee worked together to draw up diplomatic instructions.[29] The documents appeared in their final form with the King's signature, countersigned by the Secretary of the province where the mission lay, but the Secretary did not necessarily have the influential voice in framing them. Temple drafted his own instructions in 1668 because the Lord Keeper, Sir Orlando Bridgeman, did not want the task to be left to Morice. In 1674 the King directed Arlington to tell Henry Coventry, Secretary of the northern province, exactly how Temple's instructions for his embassy to the Hague were to read.[30]

For embassies concerned primarily with commercial affairs, the Committee for Trade and Plantations helped frame the instructions. John Brisbane, sent as agent to France to defend the grievances of English merchants against French privateers, received his instructions from this committee and wrote his despatches to it. Laurence Hyde, later earl of Rochester, ambassador to Poland to negotiate for trading privileges for the Eastland Company, attended a meeting of the committee with the Eastland merchants to discuss the instructions for the mission.[31]

Ambassadors to Russia and Turkey received their instructions from the directors of the companies. They dealt with specific business ventures and efforts to establish the trading privileges of the merchants. The crown required ministers in Moscow and Constantinople to send reports to the Secretaries of State, but detailed descriptions of commercial activities were directed to the companies.[32]

The English diplomatic instructions were businesslike documents. They had a reputation for being clear, exact, and plain,[33] and they reveal more about aims in foreign policy than the structure of the diplomatic corps. They said nothing of the working staff the minister was to have, with the exception of an "orthodox, learned divine" who was sometimes, although not always, formally required at the embassy in Paris.[34] Unlike the French, the English documents told the recipient little of the political leanings and personal characteristics of the men he was likely to meet during his mission.

Instructions always began with a superscription indicating the name, title, and rank of the diplomat and the name of the sovereign who was to receive him. If a minister was to negotiate a treaty, the name of the place of the conference replaced the name of the sovereign. Knights received the appellation "trusty and well beloved" before their names, while a peer's instructions were addressed to "our right trusty and well beloved cousin ———." The date and place where the instructions were given, followed by the King's signature, appeared sometimes at the end of the superscription, sometimes at the end of the instructions themselves.

The body of the instructions was broken down into numbered paragraphs, each dealing in precise terms with the matters that were to engage the minister's attention. Very often they began with a command to proceed with "all convenient speed" to the destination, sometimes indicating that a royal yacht was provided for the diplomat's convenience.[35] They might also indicate the route the ambassador was to take, as part of the obligation of the mission. Fauconberg complained to Arlington that his instructions to pass from Turin to Leghorn by way of Villa Franca (Piedmont) without a stop at Genoa were unwise. "I collect that is with a Prospect of my Passing from Villa Franca by Sea, wch I am very well Informed is not only 500 miles the further and worse way but very unsafe both in regard of Accommodations and Pyrates. Howbeit . . . I shall pass by any Private Inconveniences of my owne, to serve his Matie as becomes my duty." [36]

The rest of the paragraphs for the most part concerned specific points of policy, maximum and minimum demands that the ambassador was empowered to make, and directions on how to conduct himself with ministers of other powers. Rules of protocol[37] and duties of correspondence appeared in most instructions.

Regular instructions habitually omitted any point that might compromise the mission or throw suspicion upon the good intentions of the diplomat. Although a minister did not have to show his instructions to his host, he was supposed to be able to do so if he thought it was desirable. When necessary, the government provided ministers with a second, secret set of instructions which he was obligated to guard more closely than the first. Bevil Skelton received two sets of instructions on his mission to Vienna in 1676, the secret one empowering him to offer bribes to members of the Imperial Court.[38] The instructions to Denzil Holles, baron Holles of Ifield, and Coventry, ambassadors at Breda, contained twenty-three paragraphs concerned with the negotiations for peace, followed by a special page inscribed "The following Article being of a more private nature was written by itself." [39] The secret section advised the ambassadors to confer with Franz Paul von Lisola, the delegate from the Empire, in order to establish friendship with the House of Austria, but to keep this activity unknown to the French. In at least one case instructions were so confidential that even the Secretaries knew nothing of them. "Mr. [Sidney] Godolphin went this day to the Prince of Orange, as some say, but others to the French camp, he taking his last instructions from my Lord Treasurer [Thomas Osborne, earl of Danby], who seems to be alone in the secret of what is now transacting with France, and was, they say, called out of his bed at one of the clock on Saturday night to attend his Majesty and the Duke, who had been at a long conference with the French minister." [40]

Before a minister left for his destination, he was provided with other papers necessary for his mission. The

King gave him letters of credence addressed to the sovereign who was to receive him. Credentials indicated the name and rank of the bearer, the trust that the King placed in him as a man of prudence and confidence, the general purpose of the mission, and a request to the addressee to give full credit to whatever the minister said on behalf of the government. Credentials were impressive documents, written by professional scribes on pieces of parchment about eighteen inches square, bearing the signatures of the King and a Secretary of State and an official seal decorated with a ribbon.[41] The form varied according to the quality of the receiving power. Credentials addressed to a fellow monarch included all the titles of the receiver and were signed *"Bonus frater et consanguineus";* those to a republic were addressed to the governing powers and were signed *"Vester bonus amicus."* [42] Because a diplomat was accredited to a head of state and not a nation, the death of either sovereign invalidated his letters and he needed a new set in order to proceed with his mission.[43]

Ministers charged with negotiating a treaty received letters of full powers as well as credentials. Those accredited to a congress took only full powers instead of letters to a specific sovereign, and presented their full powers to the mediators of the congress.[44] Sometimes, as in the case of the instructions to Sir William Lockhart to France in 1674, full powers were incorporated into the instructions themselves in an additional clause.[45] All ministers carried, in addition to their other papers, passports for all the territories they were to pass through in the course of their travels. The passport enumerated the number of persons, animals, and pieces of baggage that were making the journey.

If a King wished one of his ministers abroad to proceed directly from one post to another without coming back to London, he forwarded recredentials to the sovereign of the place. These documents told of the new assignment and expressed confidence that the good will between the two countries would continue after the departure of the diplomat. Not all diplomats were familiar with these formalities. Berkeley, who received recredentials when he left Paris for Nimeguen in 1676, wrote to Coventry that before his letters *"de recréance"* arrived he had never heard the word.[46] Before a diplomat could leave his post to return home, he needed an official letter of recall. A letter announcing the recall, and the ostensible reason for it, went also to the head of state in the place of the mission. These letters were phrased so as to conceal the real motive for the recall if the truth would have affected the good reputation of the minister. When complaints came to London in 1684 that Thomas Chudleigh, the envoy in Holland, had offended William of Orange by stirring up the officers of the city of Amsterdam against the Prince, James II wrote to the States General that he was recalling Chudleigh because he needed him for employment at home.[47]

Official diplomatic papers never indicated that anyone but the King was responsible for the contents, although in some instances the King was implementing wishes other than his own. Occasionally Parliament succeeded in having ministers recalled. In 1678 the House of Commons urged the recall of the delegation at Nimeguen because it was costing £50,000 to £60,000 to maintain ambassadors at a congress where no visible progress in negotiations was being made.[48] Later in the same year the Commons forced Charles II to terminate the mission to Spain of Sir William Godolphin, who was a Catholic. During the

investigations of the Popish Plot, rumor had it that Godolphin was planning to lead a Spanish army of ten thousand
men into England, and that he was to become Privy Seal
in a new Catholic government. Parliament asked the King
to recall Godolphin to London to answer the accusations.
The King revoked Godolphin's commission and appointed another to succeed him, but Godolphin chose to
remain safely in Spain, where he was created a grandee
and lived in great style.[49]

If, however, Parliament tried to step between the King
and his foreign ministers to direct the affairs of a mission,
it crossed the limit of its authority. Certain members
wanted to prevent the marriage of the Duke of York to
Mary of Modena by forbidding Henry Mordaunt, earl of
Peterborough, the ambassador charged with making the
marriage arrangements, to bring the Princess to London
unless she became a Protestant. Secretary Coventry answered the objections with, "The Earl of Peterborough
had his several instructions and commissions from the
King, and his orders." [50]

Although the House of Commons urged the Second
Dutch War upon the reluctant Charles II and Lord
Chancellor Clarendon and brought about a speedy conclusion to the Third Dutch War, which had been under-
taken at the King's decision, the King guarded his prerogative jealously. When he encountered sharp objections
from Parliament in 1677 and 1678 to his francophile tendencies, Charles II gave them stern words and asserted that
Parliament could not encroach upon the fundamental
powers of making peace and war. Member John Swynfen,
ordinarily an opponent of the court, expressed the same
viewpoint when he urged that Parliament should abstain
from giving advice on policy and "leave it to the King and

Council, who correspond the world over." [51] The final authority in the direction of foreign affairs was the King, and the primary responsibility of the diplomat was to implement the King's policy.

II

Duties and Responsibilities

"The Secretaries of State never remembered one Day, what had been done the Day before, or never cared what would be done the next; so as to leave very often, for many Months together, an Embassy of the Greatest Importance, without any Instructions at all."

WILLIAM WYNNE, The Life of Sir Leoline Jenkins

The whole duty of the diplomat, summarized neatly by the political commentator James Howell in his handbook on ambassadors, was to fulfill the obligations inscribed in his instructions.[1] Although Arlington remarked in 1668 that he believed it best to "Send a wise man on an errand and say nothing to him," [2] the general practise was to furnish ministers with a list of specific duties. A minister was supposed to accomplish the political aims of his mission, gather intelligence, maintain a regular correspondence with the Secretaries of State, and give a report to the King at the conclusion of his embassy.

Because a minister was not supposed to improvise policy,

the King advised him in his original instructions to be ready to receive further directions in any unexpected situation. Ordinarily subsequent orders came as part of the regular correspondence from the Secretaries' office, although they could arrive as separate, formal documents from Whitehall, as they did for Edward Montagu, earl of Sandwich, in Portugal and again in Spain.[3] Sir Robert Southwell, on his mission to Brandenburg-Prussia, was directed to turn to the Prince of Orange for additional instructions connected with his embassy.

The government insisted that each minister act within the limits prescribed, and men engaged in a mission were reluctant to assume personal responsibility in matters where they had no authorization to do so. An extract of a letter from Henry Coventry in Stockholm expressed the dependence of the diplomat upon specific advice from London: "The King must give him power, and fresh Instructions how to use it:—the Swedes themselves have proposed a league defensive, and offered to receive his Master as garenty betwixt the two Crowns, and Coventry has Instructions to try them upon these points, but no power to conclude upon it. If he shall return with their bare word, he believes it will be one of the worst accounts Sir Phil. Warwick will give in to the Parliament of the King's money spent; and if he stay there without the capacity of doing any service it will be a worse." [4]

Acting without instructions, or disobeying them, was a serious offense. At the least it led to political disgrace, as Coventry learned when he returned from Breda in 1667 to receive accusations of showing undue favoritism to the French at the negotiations for peace.[5] Coventry did not suffer more than the loss of his office of the bedchamber, but other diplomats faced more serious punishments.

Charles II ordered Sir George Downing to the Tower in 1665 for disobeying a warning that he was going too fast in precipitating a quarrel with the Dutch. "I would have you use your skill to amuse them," the King wrote to Downing, "that they might not finally despaire of me, and thereby give me time to make myselfe more ready and leave them more remisse in there obligations." Because Downing pushed ahead on his own to break diplomatic relations, he spent six weeks in prison after his return.[6] James II imprisoned Bevil Skelton, minister at Paris in 1688, for sending a warning to the Prince of Orange that Louis XIV would interpret any action taken by the Dutch against the English as an infraction of the peace. Although Skelton was motivated by zealous devotion to the King, he went to the Tower for writing an unauthorized letter.[7]

Ralph Montagu's diplomatic career came to an end in 1678 because he left his post at Paris without waiting for permission to do so. Montagu's relations with the Countess of Sussex, who was living in Paris, became the subject of scandal, and he hurried back to defend himself before the King. He obtained an interview, but Charles II was so displeased by his unofficial return that he struck him off the Privy Council and ordered Robert Spencer, earl of Sunderland, to Paris as a replacement.[8] The incident coincided with the investigations of the Popish Plot, and Montagu determined to use the agitations of the moment to reinstate himself in good favor. His plan was to discredit Treasurer Danby by producing in evidence letters in which Danby had instructed him to take 6,000,000 livres (£300,000) from France in return for English neutrality for three years. Danby countered by exposing a rumor that Montagu had been in secret and unauthorized conferences with the papal nuncio at Paris. The King ordered Montagu's papers seized, to see whether he had acted contrary to instructions. Montagu would have been arrested, had he not secured election to Parliament. The House of Commons were reluctant to infringe upon the privileges of a member, although they were intent on unearthing anything that smacked of Popery. Sir William Coventry told the House, "It is a great fault in an Ambassador, an omission to give the King an account of public transactions that have passed through his hands. It may be through forgetfulness; but unpardonable, if the King calls for it, and the person does not give it." [9] Montagu's papers were finally brought before the House, and the incriminating letters about the French subsidy were used to initiate charges of high treason against Danby.[10]

Few diplomats had to face official reproof for overt disobedience. Most went about their duties in an acceptable fashion, receiving occasional rebukes from Whitehall if they did not carry out the responsibilities of their embassies to the satisfaction of the Secretaries. The Secretaries, on their part, were obligated to keep ministers informed of domestic events and intelligence coming into Whitehall from other countries. One way this was accomplished was by furnishing the diplomats with handwritten newsletters, or *gazettes à la main,* compiled in the office of the Secretaries. Their purpose was to keep government officials and other select persons abreast of news more confidential than material published in the regular newspapers.[11] Those diplomats who received newsletters were well informed of current events at home. Sir Richard Bulstrode, agent at Brussels, received daily gazettes which included news of court appointments, proceedings in parliament, military and naval manoeuvres, affairs of the Exchequer, and intelligence gathered from the embassies. Sir Joseph Williamson, while he was plenipotentiary at the Congress of Cologne, received letters from his friends in the Secretary's office, the City, and Parliament, which were nearly as frequent, although not as ample in the coverage of foreign news, as those Bulstrode received.[12]

Not all the embassies, however, received this news service. A list of fifty-four men who obtained the gazettes between 1667 and 1669 [13] shows that twelve diplomats, representing England at ten courts, were regular subscribers. Ministers in Morocco, Frankfurt-on-Main, and Sweden during these years did not receive the gazettes. Another list of subscribers for 1674 [14] indicates that only six ministers, out of ten who were abroad, received the gazettes. Embassies in Venice, Denmark, Sweden, and the Hanse Towns were without newsletters in that year.

The Secretaries also kept diplomats instructed and informed by writing them individual letters concerned with the specific affairs of the embassies and including news of the moment. The frequency of letters sent out from Whitehall is difficult to gauge, since the State Papers Foreign at the Public Record Office consist almost entirely of incoming mail. In a register kept by Bevil Skelton at Hamburg of the number of letters he received from Secretary Edward Conway, earl of Conway, in 1681, the average was five a month,[15] and other diplomatic correspondence indicates that a week was the normal interval between letters arriving from London.

When too long a time elapsed without advice from Whitehall, ministers were quick to point out that they were unable to correspond with their colleagues because they did not know who they were, and they could not negotiate intelligently when they were ignorant of affairs

at home. Complaints were frequent enough to suggest
that the Secretaries often fell behind in their correspondence. Godolphin at Madrid wrote reproachfully in 1670,
"10 or 12 lines a week is no hard Task, unless there be
many Ministers abroad, of whom you have more care." [16]
Even the important embassy at Paris was neglected. Denzil Holles complained in 1663 that he learned more about
England from the Portuguese ambassador in France than
he did from his own mail,[17] and in 1665 that the priests
in Paris told him of the mission of Theobold Taaffe, earl
of Carlingford, to Vienna three months before he heard
it from London.[18] Henry Savile confessed his impatience
with the Secretary's office to his brother: "I am sometimes
out of countenance to be told things by Mons[r] de Pompone, which I did not know, and asked questions which I
cannot answer, so that I am reduced to the truest part of
wisdom, which is silence, and upon that foundation must
I build my reputation here; in a word, I am fain to nibble
in my discourses of England like the asse mumbling
thistles." [19] The most frequent charges of neglect on the
part of the Secretaries of State came from the ministers in
the Scandinavian countries, who sometimes went for
months without receiving news from England or other
embassies.[20]

One of the most important responsibilities incurred by
a minister engaged in the King's business abroad was to
provide the government with a constant supply of intelligence. He had to report on the progress of his own negotiations, and also to procure and pass on news from the
place of his assignment. The method of obtaining news
depended on the location of the mission and the resources
of the minister himself.

Consuls, who did not have diplomatic rank or status at

this time, in those countries where they were stationed, were an important source of news. Their value as intelligencers led the government to establish more consulates than overseas merchants thought necessary, for the consuls drew their livelihood from the profit of trade at their posts and were of greater service to the Secretaries of State than to the men of business. Intelligence from consuls came directly to the Secretaries except in France and Spain, where the consuls supplied their reports to the ministers to be forwarded to Whitehall as part of the diplomatic correspondence. The Scandinavian countries had no English consuls, and intelligence from Denmark and Sweden was consistently inferior to the information arriving from other European courts.[21]

In addition to sending news to the government at home, consuls received and passed on mail from London intended for the various embassies, and advised diplomats about conditions in neighboring courts. Ministers at Paris depended on consuls in southern French cities for information on shipping and military manoeuvres in Spain and Italy, and complained of any irregularity in their news supply. "You may be pleased to give a line of rebuke to ye Consul at Marseilles for not corresponding with us," William Perwich wrote to Arlington in 1669, "or appoint some other person there that may be punctuall, it being a Principall Post from whence all the intelligence from ye Mediterranean is most commonly sent to Court here." [22]

Gazettes à la main sent by foreign governments to their embassies provided another source of intelligence. Diplomats usually contracted to buy the gazettes and petitioned the Treasury for reimbursement in their quarterly bills of extraordinary expenses, but occasionally they were able to secure the sheets by trading news items with their source of supply.[23] Some men, because of lack of funds or lack of initiative, did no more than enclose printed gazettes with passages of special interest underlined.

More expensive, but considered the best means of securing confidential news, were arrangements to buy information from private parties. Perwich sent Arlington a *gazette à la main* from Paris which cost 100 pistoles a year, and news bought from an individual informer, he warned, would be considerably dearer. He received orders to continue with the more expensive intelligence. Savile, told by Secretary Sunderland, "Your intelligences are the worst informed in the world, noe one word of haveing been ever spoke of like what you mention," defended himself on the grounds that he was trying to avoid extravagant expenditures. "There is nothing soe easy as to furnish you with men who shall send you the ordinary occurrences wch are onely the materialls of a Gazette," he answered the Secretary, "But for things more difficult & necessary to bee knowne, it will bee hard to find a fitt instrument and when found, are not to be gayned but by such temptations as would perhapps bee above your reache, for that ware would bee sold by small parcells & at great rates." [24] Savile finally made arrangements to hire an intelligencer for £100 per annum.[25]

The value of news obtained by private contract depended on how highly placed the informer was, and men vied to secure the best source of supply. Philip Warwick the younger, envoy at Stockholm, informed the Secretaries that he did not buy his intelligence from an ordinary necessitous man who, for £5, would be likely to betray him or give him false information, but had the good fortune to purchase news from leading Swedish businessmen. Francis Parry in Portugal mentioned an amanuensis of a

Secretary of State in Lisbon who sold state secrets to anyone willing to pay 500 doubloons, although Parry felt the
Secretary's intelligence was overpriced and more of a bargain at 50 doubloons. Once a good intelligencer was
secured, it became desirable to keep him employed by successive diplomats at that court. Fauconberg, the only ambassador who came to Venice during these years, asked
indulgence for the inadequacies of his reports because he
lacked "the usual help of other ambassadors, who stand
upon the shoulders of their predecessors." [26]

Some men secured their intelligence by hiring spies. Sir
George Downing bragged of his success with spies who
brought him papers from the files of Pensionary Jan de
Witt and reports of private debates of the Dutch ministers
within two or three hours after they had taken place.[27]
Downing complained that no one in London valued his
intelligence, but he overestimated the worth of his reports.
The Venetian ambassador pointed out that although
Downing often boasted there was no secret in the state
that he could not find out, in 1664 he failed to write about
a public decision to send Admiral Michel van Ruyter to
the Guinea coast,[28] a move which contributed to the outbreak of war in 1665.

Richard Graham, viscount Preston, envoy at Paris from
1682 to 1685, had at least two spies in his employ. One of
Preston's men, Roger Tilley, served his master by drink-
ing informants into a stupor and picking their pockets
for confidential information. Preston's agents did not reveal whether they received a regular salary, although one
expressed gratitude for 2 louis d'or which Preston was
pleased to give him for his efforts.[29]

The government did not ordinarily hire spies directly,
but left these arrangements to be made by the ministers

themselves, who submitted their bills for intelligence to the Treasury. Exceptions to this rule were Downing's agents, who received their remuneration of £25 per quarter directly from the office of the Secretaries of State, as did Edward Riggs, employed in Holland by Arlington and Williamson. Riggs complained to Arlington that his salary was too small for him to perform his duties usefully: "The £35 you gave me only found me in lodgings and diet during the 6 months I was there, and I wore out my clothes in the service. A house of 3 or 4 rooms costs £15 a year, business expenses £10, and that would leave only £15 for a years victuals; £100 a year is as little as it can be done for, and £6 or £7 for transport. I must have some trade for a show, but the work would take most of my time, and other business would have to give way." [30] Others who received their salaries from the secret service funds of the office of the Secretaries of State were better paid than Riggs. Edward Everard, employed in Holland and France from 1686 to 1688 for Bevil Skelton, and named as a source of information by one of Preston's informers, received a total of £321 9s. 2d. for three years work. Another agent, Francis Benson, received £250 in 1679. [31]

Intelligence from the Levant was sparse because neither the crown nor the Turkey Company was willing to assume the expense of buying political information. Winchilsea wished to use his position in Constantinople to keep the King informed of affairs between Turkey and the Empire, and even to secure for England the place of mediator in settling disputes between the powers in the East. He did not even receive money to post his letters carrying political intelligence because Secretary Nicholas thought Constantinople was too remote to provide any news of value. Win-

chilsea considered that Nicholas had made a "grosse mis-
take, and the interest of his Majestie might as well have
been promoted here as in the more neere parts of Christendome." He complained to Secretary Morice, of the northern province, to the Treasurer, and later to Arlington and
the King, but without result. He received no funds to buy
news and rarely received any communications from the
Secretaries. The whole year of 1666 passed without one
letter from London. Sir William Trumbull, who came to
the Levant in 1687, tried to get the company to spend
money for public affairs in Constantinople, but the merchants turned down petitions that were for matters of state
and unrelated to trade.[32] Winchilsea and Trumbull alone
of the English ambassadors in the Levant tried to establish Constantinople as a center for English intelligence.
The others ignored the potential political value of the embassy or agreed with the Secretaries that the government
had nothing to gain in that quarter. "'Tis now more than
a full year, that I have bin in this remote part of the world,"
Sir John Finch wrote to Secretary Coventry from Turkey
in 1674, "and the matters that relate in this place to Publick concern have bin so few, that they scarce afforded
matter enough to warrant the directing Persons of your
weighty affayres, from their important businesse." [33] James
Brydges, baron Chandos, wrote only seven letters from
Constantinople in two years.[34]

The Secretaries expected ministers who were stationed
near courts where England had no diplomatic representation to arrange for intelligence from those parts. News
came to England from Rome by way of Tuscany. For
£100 per annum, a man with connections at the papal
chancery sent information to Sir John Finch in Florence,
who forwarded the news to London in his own des-

patches.[35] Sir Bernard Gascoigne, a Florentine who entered the service of Charles I and Charles II, came to his native city in 1664 to arrange for intelligence from Venice and Vienna, where there were no English ministers at that time. Father Nicholas Donellan, Gascoigne's contact at the imperial court, reported from the Empire until Carlingford arrived as envoy in 1665. Donellan then joined the embassy as secretary and interpreter. After Carlingford left Vienna in 1666, Donellan remained as intelligencer at Vienna until Gascoigne assumed charge of the embassy in 1672.[36] While Sir William Temple was in Brussels, he was a regular purchaser of Dutch and German news.[37] The agents in Hamburg, the only German city with a permanent embassy, were responsible for sending intelligence to London from German courts where representation was only occasional. Despatches coming in from Hamburg included items bought from travelling merchants, printed gazettes from different parts of Germany, and intelligence received from English ministers at Copenhagen and Stockholm, who found it quicker to send their mail via Hamburg than by the alternate route by the Ostend post.[38]

The government received information from the Polish court from Du Moulin, formerly employed as intelligencer by the Paris embassy. Though he lost his job because he displeased ambassador Montagu, Du Moulin appealed to the Secretary's office for continuation of his employment, and made arrangements to stay on in France to forward reports from Poland to London.[39]

One of the hazards incurred by entrusting instructions and intelligence to the mails was that information might be intercepted by another country. The French were notorious letter openers, and the English knew it. Holles hoped to protect his despatches by impressing two wax wafers at each end and covering the seals with a paste of boiled starch. He described his methods to Arlington and urged him to take the same precautions in writing to Paris. Even with these preventive measures, the French intercepted and copied letters to and from Holles. Jean-Baptiste Gaston, comte de Comenges, the French ambassador in London, wrote to Louis XIV that it would be wise to make a show of shocked surprise if Holles registered another protest. Montagu and Preston suspected foul play because their mail arrived in batches after long intervals. They believed that men at the French post office read the letters before releasing them for delivery.[40] Sometimes the French made no efforts to conceal their designs. Trumbull wrote to Sunderland on 19 December 1685, "Yo^r Lo^{ps} of 7/17 Instant came not to my hands until the 17/27, And the other letters of ye 10/20 . . . not till yesterday. Both ye Pacquets have been opened. And ye former was brought to me all in pieces, ty'd onely together with some pack thread." The ministers had strong reason to believe that the French intercepted English mail to and from Spain and Portugal as well. Letters to Florence were usually opened and read by the Inquisition, unless they came by way of Venice, and mail from Denmark and Sweden arrived with broken seals.[41]

England had subtler methods of her own to learn the contents of foreign mail. A device invented by Sir Samuel Morland opened letters in a way that left no trace, and made rapid facsimiles of any document. Charles II was fascinated by the machine, as were the foreign ministers in London who knew of its existence. The Spanish minister, baron de Batteville, tried to bribe the clerks in the post office to tell him the contents of the French despatches, but when the King heard of it, he ordered the guilty clerks to be hanged. The machine was destroyed in the Great Fire of 1666 and was never rebuilt, but England continued to intercept and read most incoming mail.[42]

In order to prevent the loss of state secrets to another power, the Secretaries instructed diplomats to use ciphers for writing confidential information.[43] Each minister received his own cipher, and, if he expected to write regularly to both Secretaries, he received two sets. Samuel Pepys, then a clerk in the navy office, devised Downing's cipher, and had a hard time pleasing him, for Downing continually sent samples back until he received one that appeared satisfactory.[44] Efficient use of intricate codes could have maintained secrecy, but most of the codes were simple cryptograms, with letter or number substitutes, which could be broken by anyone who secured a large sample. Sometimes a cipher consisted of no more than the substitution of pseudonyms for important proper names. One diplomat received a code requiring him to use, among other keys, "Mr. Church" for the King, "Mr. James" for the Duke of York, "Mr. Bridge" for the Lord Keeper Bridgeman, "Mr. Gorgis" for Buckingham, "Mr. Thomas" for Danby, and "Mr. Bird" for Heneage Finch.[45] Such a cipher would have been transparent to anyone familiar with the leading figures at court. The French codes could not have been much more difficult, for Henri de Massue, marquis de Ruvigny, guessed that the code was broken during his mission to London, and had to request a new one from Paris.[46]

Moreover, if ciphers were too complicated, they confused the correspondents more than they confounded the enemy. Letters of the diplomats contain repeated instances of men receiving the wrong cipher, losing their keys, or deciding to use some one else's code because it was simpler and easier. Edmund Poley's cipher required him to form his words in broken syllables, but because clerks in the Secretary's office found it difficult to transcribe his letters he obliged them by underlining whole words, and explained what he was doing in an uncoded letter sent through the regular mail. Holles had coded messages returned to him by Arlington with marginal corrections, and two passages underlined with the comment, "I cannot guess at this . . . nor this." Temple had such difficulty in decoding his advices from London that he enlisted the aid of De Witt. "I very frankly pulled out my letter, and my key, and my paper with the rules, and upon it we fell to work together for two hours, and all to as much purpose as picking straws." [47]

The government found it wiser and safer to use other means to safeguard official communications. Ministers frequently made use of private couriers to avoid the risks of the regular post. This method was highly favored for secret transactions, and was used exclusively for the negotiations in 1669 leading up to the secret Treaty of Dover, because neither Charles II nor Louis XIV trusted the regular channels of diplomatic communication. [48] Louis XIV sometimes appointed men to permanent positions in the embassies who did nothing but carry despatches and instructions between Paris and his ministers. During the negotiations at Breda the French did not have to risk communicating anything to writing. [49]

The Secretaries in London liked to send letters to ambassadors under the cover of local merchants. This subterfuge helped to expedite mail through enemy countries, and lessened the chance of interception. [50] A Flemish merchant carried letters to Brandenburg-Prussia, businessmen in Marseilles took care of correspondence for Constantinople, and a Bayonne merchant received letters for ministers in the Iberian peninsula.[51]

All instructions obligated ministers to write regularly to London, and to maintain a good correspondence with the diplomats at other embassies. Most of the men wrote to the Secretaries two or three times a week, unless special news required instant despatch by an express or private courier. Secretary Williamson frequently admonished his ministers to send a few lines by each post, even if the letter did no more than regret the absence of news, but obligations to write to colleagues in neighboring courts were less strict and diplomats wrote to each other only when they had something of moment to report. A failure in the duties of correspondence made the official of little use to his government. Berkeley had to defend himself against an accusation that "His Majesty has an Ambassador Extraordinary in France to his great charge, and it were as good to have none, as he held no correspondence with his Majesty's ministers either at home or abroad." [52]

As diplomatic correspondence reached the Secretary's office clerks prepared it for later attention by making interlinear transcriptions of all coded passages and writing summaries of the contents on the reverse sides. These summaries dealt briefly with every item in the letter, no matter how unimportant. Despatches, unless they were marked for the Secretary's private attention, were read and discussed at the meetings of the Foreign Committee. When Danby was directing foreign policy, many diplomats maintained a regular correspondence with him as well as with the Secretaries of State. Temple made a point of sending Danby copies of the letters he wrote to Williamson, so that the Treasurer would have time to digest the contents before Dutch affairs were brought up at the next committee meeting.[53] A minister could, of course, write directly to the King, as Preston did when he wanted to keep the contents of his letter secret from the Secretaries, but this was not the usual procedure. The Secretary recommended despatches to the King when he felt they were worth royal attention. Arlington complimented Sir Richard Fanshawe because Charles II chose to have all Fanshawe's letters from Portugal read to him, and considered them especially worthwhile.[54]

No matter how frequent and informative a diplomat's despatches were, he was expected to render to the King "a very perfect and ample narrative" of his mission after he returned to London.[55] The Russia Company required an account in writing at the conclusion of an embassy.[56] Instructions to Fanshawe and Southwell stipulated that the account had to be in writing,[57] but this was not a general rule. Secretary Williamson's papers contain a translation of a Dutch treatise on diplomatic reports which advises, "It is a custome in all well governed Governments that Amb^rs returned from their ambassage are to deliver over a verbal or written Relation of what they have negotiated." [58]

The Republic of Venice was the first to establish the custom of requiring a relation from every minister at the conclusion of his mission. Originally Venetian ambassadors presented oral reports, which, as early as 1268, were written out by a clerk of the Senate as they were delivered. A decree of 1425 made it obligatory for the ambassador himself to present a written relation of his mission.[59] Louis XIV began to require a written report at the suggestion of Hugues de Lionne, marquis de Berny, who thought it would be a good idea to follow the Venetian practise. The French report, like the Venetian *relazione*, included more than the specific accomplishments of the embassy. Courtin received instructions upon his departure for London in 1676 to give an account of his negotiations, the state of the court and the country, ceremonies of entry and audience, and a description of the King, principal ministers, and all the people with whom he negotiated.[60]

The general absence of written summaries of embassy affairs in the English diplomatic papers points to the conclusion that an oral report was the common custom. Moreover, references to the report indicate that it was given within a few days of the minister's return to London, which would have given him little time to prepare a formal paper.[61] Ministers delivered their reports to the King and the Secretaries, or to a special committee which was interested in the embassy. Sandwich reported to the Committee on Tangier when he returned from Spain in 1668. Pepys wrote that Sandwich spoke "so low and mean, and delivered in so poor a manner," that it appeared unlikely that he would be adequately reimbursed for the expenses of the expedition.[62] After 1680 the government required the report before they would allow the extraordinary expense accounts of the mission, but permitted ministers who were out of the country when this order went into effect to apply for payment immediately after their return.[63]

Some diplomats presented written reports because aspects of their behavior needed formal justification. Sir Henry Goodricke prepared a written narrative after he had his audience with the King upon his return, but this was due to his expulsion from Spain for criminal behavior. Sandwich had to write a letter in 1668 to justify his deportment in matters of protocol while he was in

Portugal. The King ordered Sandwich's letter to be read to the Board, and was so satisfied with the contents he kept it as a public memorial of Sandwich's actions. John Dodington gave a written report on Venetian trade to the Committee on Trade and Plantations.[64]

One account of an embassy, written by Fauconberg in 1670 after he returned from Savoy, Genoa, and Venice, indicates that it was composed to satisfy the requirements of a report on the general nature of the mission.[65] "Warranted as well by the generall practise of Ambassadors of the late and present age, as commanded by your Majesties instructions of the 10th of January in the twenty-first yeare of your Majestys most happy raigne, at such time as you were graciously pleased to honor me with the character of your Extraordinary Ambassador to divers of the princes and states of Italy, I most humbly prostrate at your Majesties feet, and doe with all submission and reverence offer to your Majesties consideration this following accompt of the observations I made in the severall places where I carryed that character."[66]

Fauconberg's relation is in the classic Venetian style. It begins with a few lines describing the particulars of his voyage through France, and devotes the remaining paragraphs to a description of the politics, national characteristics, natural resources, revenues, and foreign affairs of the places he visited. The account gives an admirable summary of the governments of the seventeenth century Italian states, but is most interesting for Fauconberg's personal opinion of the different people whom he met. He admired Charles Emmanuel II, duke of Savoy, "vigorous, active, amorous, free of discourse, a great lover of buildings," and his subjects "ingenuous, industrious, friendly, sociable and honest in their dealings." He found the

Genoese less sympathetic, because they "use all strangers very ill, and your Majesties subjects as bad as any. Their nobility are all traders, but when the merchants have any demands, however just, upon them, it is impossible to procure any right against them." Fauconberg liked the Venetians because they were careful to preserve their spiritual and civil liberties, but found little merit in the office of the doge, whom he described as "rather an honourable prisoner than a prince." [67] His conclusion on the political value of the Italian states to England was that "there are few of them to bee relyed upon in any league, so apt they are to play fast and loose, as it best suites with their humors and designes." [68]

Other ambassadors, who did not present a written account to the King, used the notes they made during their missions to produce literary works. Some of these books, modelled on the Venetian *relazione,* appeared within a few years after the ministers returned to England, and are discussed in chapter VIII.

Excluding the final report to the King, the execution of all diplomatic responsibilities rested on efficient communication between the government and the minister. The evidence shows that what system there was worked poorly. Some of the trouble was simply carelessness: haphazard ciphers entrusted to inadequately trained correspondents, or a casual indifference to the necessity of regular letter writing. Part of the trouble was economic. A diplomat who was hard pressed to pay for his food and lodging could not spare the cash to hire informers or purchase secret information. In general, the most reliable media were the gazettes sent abroad from Whitehall and the consular reports forwarded to London from the continent. Reliance on these two channels resulted in two difficulties. A minister was often in doubt as to how to solve specific problems of his own mission, and certain embassies, lacking the government newsletters and local consulates, were of limited use to the government.

III

Personnel

"I do not want him produced from the shades of the schools: I want him educated in practical politics and in the administration of high offices."

ALBERICO GENTILI, De legationibus libri tres

At the time of the Restoration, no country in Europe had a formal course of study to prepare men for diplomatic careers. The Republic of Venice had long followed the custom of sending prospective diplomats to accompany experienced men on their embassies,[1] but the idea for a school did not come until the eighteenth century, when Jean-Baptiste Colbert, marquis de Torcy, French Secretary of State, suggested that Joachim Legrand draw up a curriculum that would develop skills in negotiating and composing diplomatic correspondence. The program never received widespread support, and the English reaction was expressed by Joseph Addison, who scoffed at the plan as a "Seminary of Petticoat Politicians, who are to be brought up at the feet of Madame de Maintenon and to be despatched into foreign courts upon any emergency of state." [2]

Treatises on the qualifications of the ideal diplomat, on the other hand, were numerous. The custom of writing on the perfect ambassador had produced a sizeable body of literature by the sixteenth century,[3] and theorists continued to contribute ideas to this already venerable tradition through the succeeding hundred years. Francis Thynne, an ancestor of Thomas Thynne, who was envoy to Sweden from 1667 to 1669, dedicated a manual on the ideal ambassador to William Brooke, Lord Cobham, who was ambassador of Queen Elizabeth to Flanders in 1577. Thynne wanted his ideal minister to be well born, honest, highly esteemed by his fellow men, a skilled linguist, and an eloquent speaker. In addition to possessing these virtues of character, Thynne would have him tall, handsome, and blessed with a sweet voice.[4]

Legal theorist Jean Hotman recommended that ambassadors should have the worldliness acquired by foreign travel, practical experience in affairs of state, and a sure knowledge of history, which, he felt, was more useful for this career than any other study. Eloquence, some training in Roman law, and a familiarity with the laws of his own country were other prerequisites. Hotman's ideas were practical. Although it was admirable for a diplomat to know the language of the country to which he was sent, he should pretend not to understand it, for he could always gain a greater advantage by negotiating in his own tongue. With a keen sense of the realities of the diplomat's problems, Hotman wrote, "So also would I have him rich, not only in the goods of the minde, but also in the goods of fortune." [5]

Alberico Gentili preferred an ambassador to have political acumen rather than encyclopaedic knowledge. A good personal appearance was important, but not necessarily high birth, for a man of plebeian origin might be best able to accomplish a mission whose purpose was to influence the common people. The ability to make a swift and competent decision outweighed the skills of elaborate oratory. History, ancient and modern, and those branches of philosophy which deal with morals and politics were useful, but no abstract study could substitute for training in affairs of state. Fidelity, fortitude, temperance, and prudence were, to Gentili, the cardinal virtues in an ambassador.[6]

Abraham de Wicquefort's manual on ambassadors is the richest guide to the ideas of the seventeenth century on the qualities needed for success in diplomatic affairs. Wicquefort was a popular author, although his works had not yet been translated into English, and *L'Ambassadeur* formed part of the library that Sir George Etherege took with him on his mission to Vienna in 1685.[7] Wicquefort thought that an ambassador who was going to serve on a ceremonial mission should be of an illustrious family, but anyone who did not have a mean or sordid background could aspire to ordinary embassies of business. The prospective diplomat should prepare himself for employment by studying Latin, polite literature, particularly Horace, and civil law. Above all he should apply himself to the study of history, with special attention to the memoirs of Philippe de Comines and Niccolò Machiavelli, which had most to offer in knowledge of diplomatic skills. Wicquefort also recommended the study of the correspondence of able diplomats as a profitable pursuit. Yet, he believed, experience counted for more than birth or education. "I cannot tell whether the Men of Letters are fitter for Embassy than Tradesmen: but I shall not scruple to say, that an Embassador is not better form'd in the College than in the Shop." [8] Since experience came with maturity, Wicquefort preferred his ambassador to be between forty and sixty years old, although this was not so important in one being sent on a purely ceremonial mission. He thought the prince should choose men for diplomatic employment who would be agreeable to their hosts, and that it was best to avoid the clergy, because they had no posterity for whom to make patriotic efforts, and could not be punished for their misdeeds. [9]

In his catalogue of outstanding diplomats of his day, Wicquefort credits England with only one ambassador of note, Sir William Temple, whose success in negotiating the Alliance of 1667 (between England and the United Provinces) and the agreements at Aix-la-Chapelle in 1668 (to which Sweden also adhered) earned him the compliment of a "Minister of very Parts." [10] P. Ferdinand Galardi, a commentator on Wicquefort, agreed that Temple was one of the most illustrious ministers of the age, because the French held Temple, and not the Dutch, responsible for the anti-French coalition of the Triple Alliance. [11]

The paucity of men who earned a lasting reputation from their work in diplomatic missions shows that the English corps was not only unprofessional, but rarely provided a career to which men devoted most of their adult years. Temple spent only eight years in the service of Charles II, and his fame rests on two short periods of service in the United Provinces from 1668 to 1671 and 1674 to 1676. Temple always preferred the joys of his garden at Sheen to the rigors of the negotiator's table, and declined offers of a position as Secretary of State or ambassador at Madrid, both posts considered means by which he could have recouped his fortune, in order to retire to private life. Nor did Temple have any apprenticeship that would have qualified him for the title of a professional diplomat. He passed from obscurity to an envoyship at Münster without any experience in public life, and admitted that when he entered the diplomatic service all he knew about Dutch affairs was what he had gleaned from common conversation.[12]

Temple's record of service, admirable for its accomplishments in a limited sphere, cannot be compared to the career of Franz Paul von Lisola, a lawyer who entered the Austrian service when he was twenty-five years old and was a member of the Emperor's diplomatic corps for thirty-five years. Lisola is an example of a diplomat of high order who passed from court to court as his government decided a man of skill was needed. He came three times to London, and accomplished missions in Brandenburg-Prussia, Poland, Spain, Portugal, and the United Provinces. He was present at the negotiations at Breda in 1667, Aix in 1668, and Cologne in 1673 and 1674. Lisola's biographer describes him as a talented politician as well as a professional diplomat, whose vision, like Temple's, enabled him to see more clearly than most of his contemporaries the danger to Europe from an overpowerful France.[13]

England had no one who served in the diplomatic corps as long as Lisola, and only four who had more employment abroad after the Restoration than Temple. Of the diplomats who had extensive years of service to their record, three, Sir John Finch, Bevil Skelton, and Sir William Swann, spent most of the time at minor posts in Germany and Italy, while Sir Richard Bulstrode stayed at Brussels for thirteen years and was present at no major negotiations involving English interests.

One hundred and eighteen men served Charles II and James II on diplomatic missions,[14] and a composite picture of their careers shows that most of them lacked the experience in politics and diplomacy recommended by the theorists. Twenty-seven were of such small stature, either before or after they entered the corps, that no biographical material is available for them. Most of them who were men of note achieved their fame on the basis of accomplishments after they left the service.

In an age when it was not unusual for governments to employ foreigners on diplomatic missions, the English service was predominantly native, with only seven men who were not natural subjects of the King. Three were French. The Huguenot Henri de Massue, marquis de Ruvigny and earl of Galway, connected by marriage to the Russells and Wriothesleys, and whose father, the first marquis de Ruvigny, came on a congratulatory mission from Louis XIV to Charles II in 1660, became an English subject in 1688, six years after he had represented Charles II at Lisbon.[15] Louis Duras, earl of Feversham, the nephew of the great marshal Henri, vicomte de Turenne, was naturalized in 1661, three years before he received diplomatic employment. Sir Gabriel Sylvius, born in southern France and educated in Holland, served in the household of William of Orange as a young man. He travelled to England in 1665, where he came to the attention of Arlington's wife, the former Mlle de Nassau-Beverweert, daughter of a former Dutch ambassador to England who had expressed an interest in Sylvius' career. Through Arlington's influence Sylvius secured diplomatic employment in

Germany and received a grant of denization in 1679.[16]
The other foreigners were Sir Wilhelm Curtius, created a
baronet by Charles II in 1652;[17] Johann Hogius, who
served in Germany; the Florentine Gascoigne, an old
royalist soldier who was captured by the parliamentary
forces at Colchester in 1648 and had his life spared because he was a foreigner;[18] and Leontij Marselius, accredited to Russia in 1664.[19]

The largest single group of men were, like Gascoigne,
former royalists. Thirty-seven had either fought for
Charles I in the Civil War or were of families who had
taken up arms for the King. Seven had fought for Parliament, or had given their support to the Protector's regime:
Sandwich, Lockhart, Fauconberg, Downing, Holles,
Southwell, and Trevor.

Preparation for their work in the foreign service varied
widely. Their academic achievements may be rated high,
for thirty-seven received a university education: John Brisbane at Edinburgh,[20] James Douglas, duke of Hamilton,
at Glasgow, Downing at Harvard, Finch at Padua, and
the rest at Oxford and Cambridge. Eleven were lawyers,
including Sir Leoline Jenkins, who was professor of civil
law at Oxford following the Restoration. Charles II chose
Jenkins to go to France to negotiate the settlement of the
Queen Mother's estate in 1669 because he was impressed
with his command of legal knowledge.[21] Finch and Sir
Charles Scarburgh were physicians; the latter was personal physician to Charles II, James II, and William III
and was the author of several works on anatomy and
mathematics.[22] The clergy produced two diplomats: John
Robinson, later bishop of London, who served the embassy
in Sweden as chaplain in 1680 and became successively
secretary and resident at Stockholm; and Cardinal Philip

Howard, who represented James II to the Pope in 1685.[23] Sir Samuel Tuke and Sir George Etherege were dramatists. Finch, Gascoigne, Thomas Henshaw, Henry Howard, later earl of Arundel and duke of Norfolk, Sir Gilbert Talbot, Sir Peter Wyche, and Southwell were Fellows of the Royal Society.

To the seventeenth century mind, however, the ideal diplomat was not a man of letters, but one well born, experienced in travel, and a mature statesman. Charles II and James II chose important peers for ceremonial missions. The most illustrious was the King's cousin, Prince Rupert, Count Palatine of the Rhine and Duke of Bavaria, who announced the Restoration to the Emperor. Ambassadors were usually men of noble birth, such as Charles Stuart, duke of Richmond, and George Villiers, duke of Buckingham. Henry Howard received a baronetcy, the first of other titles, in order to increase the splendor of his embassy to Morocco,[24] and before Richard Fanshawe became ambassador to Portugal, the King felt it necessary to appoint him to the Privy Council because the Fanshawe family had a mercantile background.[25] On the other hand, most of the ministers of the second order were no more than knights, and it was not deemed important for a resident or agent to have any title at all.[26]

The exodus of royalist sympathizers during the Protectorate provided the crown with thirty-one men who had spent some time travelling on the Continent before they entered the foreign service. This experience undoubtedly gave them a degree of cosmopolitan polish, but few men gained reputations for being fine linguists. Sandwich used to conduct his negotiations at Madrid in an awkward combination of Latin, French, and Spanish, though by the time he left Madrid he spoke Spanish well.

TABLE IV

English Diplomats Who Drew Special Notice for
Their Language Skills

Diplomats	Latin	French	Spanish	Italian	Portuguese	Dutch
Arlington	X	X	X			
Blathwayt						X
De Vic		X				
Essex	X					
Fanshawe	X	X	X		X	
Finch				X		
Henshaw		X				
Jenkins	X	X				
Marvell	X	X	X	X		
Ossory		X				
Parry	X					
Perwich		X		X		
Poley	X					
Temple	X	X	X			
Wyche					X	

Hardest to find were men who could negotiate in German. Temple felt the want of German disqualified him from giving proper service in Münster, and asked to be recalled. Skelton and Wyche succeeded in learning the language after some years' service at the Hanse Towns.[27] The latter observed: "Though Germany is so neere England, a Learned man observed to mee that Arabick and Chaldee are better knowne in our University and Country then High Dutch, so that without arrogance, I may say, any other person that is not so qualified must be some yeares hard labour to be fitted to doe the same service."[28]

The men who entered the diplomatic service following the Restoration were younger than Wicquefort's ideal. Half of those for whom the date of birth is known had not yet reached their fortieth year. Of those who could claim experience in diplomatic affairs, some had entered the foreign service during the reign of Charles I: Joseph Averye, resident in Denmark, Sweden, and Germany for twenty years before 1660; John Berkeley, ambassador to Sweden in 1636; William Crofts, baron Crofts of Saxham, sent to Queen Elizabeth of Bohemia at the Hague in 1635. Wilhelm Curtius served Charles I, Elizabeth, Queen of Bohemia, and Frederick V, Elector Palatine.[29] Walter Montagu and Henry Jermyn, earl of St. Albans, attended embassies to Paris before the Civil Wars. Richard Fanshawe was secretary in Spain in 1636, and Talbot was secretary at Venice in 1628 and resident from 1638 to 1645. Sir Henry De Vic, appointed resident at Brussels by Charles I, remained there until 1661.[30]

Two had their first positions as ministers for the King in exile. Sir William Swann represented Charles II at Vienna in 1649, and Arlington was his resident at Madrid from 1658 to 1661. Sir John Hebdon and Sir Patrick Gordon represented Czar Alexis I in England before serving as English envoys in Russia.[31]

Three of the King's ministers owed their original employment to Oliver Cromwell. Although not all received accolades from commentators, each earned the respect of his contemporaries because of industry and skill. Sir George Downing, the Protector's ambassador to France and Switzerland in 1655, came to The Hague in 1658 and remained there until the outbreak of war in 1665. The French did not think highly of Downing's origins. Godefroy, comte d'Estrades, described him as "a man pushed up by Cromwell from being a schoolmaster to being an ambassador," [32] but Downing's ability, which brought him diplomatic employment by the Protector, the Parliament, and the King, earned him the admiration of Galardi, who praised him as highly as he praised Temple. Downing received his first appointment to The Hague because he was knowledgeable in the commercial affairs that occupied the interests of the two nations. After Cromwell's death, he offered to serve as secret intelligence agent in Holland for the benefit of Charles II. The King accepted the offer. He knighted Downing when he met him at The Hague on his journey to England in 1660, and decided to maintain him as resident because he was pleased with Downing's anti-Dutch sentiments. When Charles II needed an excuse to start the Second Dutch War, he called on him again, confiding to Colbert that he was convinced that no one else could create an issue to inflame the populace against the Dutch as cleverly as Downing.[33] Downing's diplomatic experience, his political foresight in deciding for the King on the eve of the Restoration, and his participation in domestic affairs as a commissioner of the Treasury between diplomatic missions give him claim to being closer to the ideal diplomat than Temple, a claim marred only by Downing's disobedience in 1672, which ended his career.

Lockhart, a Cromwellian soldier and the Protector's ambassador to France from 1656 until the Restoration, earned the good opinion of Charles II, who sent Lockhart to France again in 1673 because he thought his skill as a negotiator equalled his military experience. The diarist John Evelyn remarked that the newly accredited ambassador was "a gallant & a sober person," [34] while Louis XIV found him a man of great ability and personal worth. When Lockhart died in France in 1675, the Venetian ambassador at Paris wrote that England would have difficulty finding a replacement who would be as capable. He was right, for the French were dissatisfied with the intended successor, Sidney Godolphin, later earl of Godolphin, who, they thought, was too unimportant for so exalted a post as minister to Paris. The King had to alter his resolution to despatch Godolphin and chose John Berkeley, whom the French found more congenial.[35]

Fauconberg, Cromwell's ambassador to France in 1658, had enough initiative to secure the desirable position of ambassador to Venice in 1670. To do so he had to overcome the efforts of several competitors. Finch, who had the advantage of being in Italy, brought pressure upon the King through his brother, the Solicitor-General, and offered to defray part of the costs himself. The King favored Finch's suit, but the Republic objected to the candidate because they knew him as an anatomy lecturer at the University of Pisa and resident at Florence, and felt they deserved someone more noteworthy. Arundel also wanted the post, and accepted the embassy to Morocco in 1669 as a means of getting it, but the government was reluctant to send a recusant to a Catholic power. Even Temple indicated that he would be pleased to accept a mission to Venice, although his real desire was to get to Tuscany, "where wit and weather are equally clear." Fauconberg approached James, Duke of York, and promised that his wife, Cromwell's daughter, anxious to get away from court where she had not been well received, would pay for the entire embassy herself. The argument reached Arlington's ears, and the job went to Fauconberg. "He is of good house and remarkable parts," the Venetian Republic heard from their minister in England.[36]

The great majority of the King's ministers had no prior experience in the foreign service, a situation that Clarendon said caused Charles II some distress.[37] Before their employment abroad, twenty-three held honorary positions in the royal households, ten were members of the Privy Council, seven had been lords-lieutenant in the militia, five held commissions in the armed forces, three held civilian offices in the army or navy, and twenty had entered public life in some other governmental post, but no major office of state.

Many earned their employment abroad because of political sympathies rather than on records as statesmen. Forty-three were members of Parliament, of whom twenty-five appear on lists of the Court Party in the House of Commons.[38] Goodricke, member for Boroughbridge, joined the supporters of the Court in 1676, and came to prominence as a leader of the opposition to the impeachment of Danby in 1678. He had no thought of employment abroad until his activities in Parliament brought him to the King's attention, and he received an appointment to Madrid.[39] Sir Charles Bertie, member for Stamford and secretary to his brother-in-law, Danby, was called to account to the House for mismanagement of secret service funds in 1679. The members were dissatisfied with Bertie's explanations, so the King despatched him as envoy to various German courts to prevent further discussion of Bertie's activities.[40] Another polite exile was the assignment of Sandwich to Madrid. Clarendon was displeased with the way the admiral had distributed prize goods captured at Bergen, and it was deemed discreet to get Sandwich out of the country before his actions became a public issue.[41]

The King could, of course, choose anyone to be his ambassador, but different factors combined to limit the freedom of his choice. One was the availability of men who had, and were willing to spend, sufficient private income to undertake a costly embassy. Berkeley and Arundel seem to have received their positions primarily because they were rich.[42]

Another factor was the consideration of the political sensibilities of the host country. The choice of ministers to the Hague was a weather vane of current Anglo-Dutch policy, and Temple and Downing alternated at the post as England tried to conciliate or antagonize the Dutch. In 1679, when Henry Sidney, later earl of Romney, was departing for Holland, the King told him he received his appointment at the suggestion of the Prince of Orange. At the conclusion of Sidney's mission, Charles II wanted to send Bevil Skelton to succeed him, but the Prince and Pensioner Kaspar Fagel refused to accept Skelton, because he had exhibited pro-French tendencies at Vienna. Thomas Chudleigh received the Dutch embassy, and Skelton received an appointment to the Hanse Towns as compensation. Chudleigh did not make a favorable impression in Holland, where he was regarded as a "pitifull fellow pickt up to serve a turne, and when that is done, to be layd aside with disgrace." [43]

The King named Sir Peter Wyche for the Moscow mission in 1669 at the suggestion of the Swedish resident in London, and Coventry went to Stockholm in 1671 because the Swedes had expressed their approval of him. Talbot owed his appointment to Denmark to the fact that he was known and trusted by Frederick III. After 1670, the choice of minister to France involved the ticklish question of finding someone trustworthy to whom the intrigues of Charles II and Louis XIV could be confided. The French were displeased in 1672 with the choice of George Savile, marquis of Halifax, who was not only ignorant of the secret treaty but openly hostile to a French alliance.[44] In 1675 Arlington thought it would be wiser to send Dom Francesco de

Melo, the Portuguese ambassador in England, rather than risk extending the circle of those who knew about the pact,[45] but Charles II did not act upon his advice. James II chose John Churchill, later duke of Marlborough, to announce his succession to Louis XIV at the approval of the French ambassador in England, Barillon, who knew Churchill was party to the secrets of Anglo-French diplomacy.

Simple favoritism accounted for other selections. Observers noted that Crofts, Charles Berkeley, viscount Fitzhardinge, and James Hamilton became ministers because they were personal friends of Charles II.[46] Convenience, too, was a deciding factor. If a man was already on the spot, the cost of transportation was saved. When Hyde reached the Netherlands on his journey home from his embassy to Poland, he found a commission waiting for him which designated him mediator at Nimeguen. The oddest choice was Bulstrode, who had been taken prisoner as a debtor in Flanders. While he was in prison he got into the habit of writing newsletters to Arlington. Arlington showed the letters to the King, who was so pleased with them he had Bulstrode released, paid his debts, and installed him as his minister at Brussels.[47]

Connections at court or political patronage accounted for many appointments. Clarendon was responsible for suggesting Holles and Henry Coventry to the King when men were needed to negotiate the peace of Breda. The choice displeased Arlington, who had hoped to get the commission for Thomas Clifford, later baron Clifford of Chudleigh, and himself. When Arlington became Secretary of State, he used his influence to have Temple appointed to the United Provinces in 1668, and sponsored Finch for Florence, Ralph Montagu and William Perwich for Paris, Sunderland for Madrid, and Clifford for Copenhagen. The despatch of Clifford troubled Sir William Coventry who regretted "the absence of so considerable a man from parliament." [48] Poley owed his employment in Germany and Sweden to Arlington and Conway. Sir George Etherege went to Vienna because he had the favor of Sunderland. Charles Fanshawe, nephew of Sir Richard Fanshawe and envoy to Lisbon in 1679, was "a creature of Mr. Secretarie Coventrie's; a yong man, and though a great court politician yet unexperienced in southern affaires." Chudleigh and Skelton were dependent for favors on Jenkins, and Lockhart and Wyche acknowledged Williamson as their patron.[49]

If political influence passed from the Secretary of State to another office, so did the power to nominate ambassadors. When Danby was at the height of his power, he was in a position to offer embassies to his supporters. He sent Temple to the Hague in 1674, and, at Sunderland's suggestion, gave Savile the post at Paris in 1678. Philip Warwick, envoy to Sweden, was related by marriage to the Treasurer's family.[50] Preston enjoyed the protection of Halifax at the time of his French embassy, and Trumbull secured his appointment to Paris in 1685 through the influence of Rochester, although Sunderland would have preferred to send Savile or St. Albans.[51]

The embassy in Constantinople was a desirable position, because the Turkey Company paid more regularly than the crown, and there were numerous opportunities to invest in profitable business ventures while discharging regular duties. For this reason several claimants usually presented themselves every time the post fell vacant, with the King and the merchants each asserting the right to name the ambassador. Winchilsea was the King's candidate in 1660, but the company did not accept him without protests. In 1667, the King left the choice to the merchants, provided the man would be to his good liking, and accepted Daniel Harvey, who may have been a connection of the Harveys who were shareholders in the company at the time he received the appointment.[52] John Finch, related by marriage to Harvey, got the position in 1668 through the intervention of his brother-in-law, Conway.[53] In 1680, when Coventry was hoping to secure the post for his nephew Thynne, the choice reverted to the merchants. They elected Chandos, who was related to the governor of the company, after the King rejected Sir Paul Rycaut because Rycaut had already been in the Levant as secretary to Winchilsea and would not make a fitting ambassador. Charles II was displeased with the election of Chandos, who was a signer of a petition for the sitting of Parliament, but Chandos recanted and the company received the royal assent to the election.[54] James II named Trumbull in 1686, ignoring vigorous protests from the merchants who had recently chosen and equipped Sir William Soame. Soame died on his way to the Levant, and the merchants preferred to maintain Chandos rather than undertake again the expense of fitting out another man.[55]

An analysis of the criteria used in selecting members of the corps shows that practical politics rather than idealistic considerations accounted for the choices. Whereas the theorists urged that diplomats should be experienced statesmen, well read, fluent in many tongues, and mature in worldly wisdom, those who had to find men for the various positions were more likely to be influenced by the candidate's loyalty to the court, his family connections, his expendability, and the state of his pocketbook.

These methods of distributing diplomatic employment did not necessarily result in the selection of men of the first calibre. The old royalist Carlingford, who came to Vienna in 1666, impressed Emperor Leopold I as being an agreeable fellow, but not very clever.[56] Carlingford's own secretary wrote that his master's principal qualifications were that he was "a fattey man and a good Drinker, which is a condition very necessary in banquetts, where he is every day." [57]

On the other hand, a considerable number of men who were insignificant when they entered the foreign service went on to successful careers. William Godolphin, who began as one of the several secretaries in the suite of Sandwich at Madrid, rose to be envoy and then ambassador at the Spanish court. Industry, rather than patronage, accounted for his success. Pepys met Godolphin while he was still secretary to Sandwich and found him "a very pretty and able person, a man of very fine parts." [58] Godolphin's merit ranked high even in the sophisticated opinion of the Venetian ambassadors in Spain. One admired his skill in languages and his finesse, and another praised him because he was "a man of ordinary birth who has arrived at his present position by his remarkable talents and the skill with which he has conducted the most difficult transactions." [59]

A few men, Rycaut, Marlborough, Ruvigny, Poley, Robinson, and Trumbull, continued in the foreign service after 1689. It speaks well for their abilities, since William III was scrupulous in penetrating the character and skills of the men in his diplomatic corps, and patronage counted for less than ability.[60]

Nine men rose to be Secretaries of State for Charles II and James II: Arlington, Williamson, Henry Coventry,

Sunderland, Trevor, Jenkins, Sidney Godolphin, Preston, and Middleton. Sunderland had taken the Paris embassy in 1678 in the specific hopes of obtaining the Secretary's place.[61] This high percentage of Secretaries with diplomatic experience, for only three during the period of the Restoration had seen no service abroad, is greater than in succeeding periods of English history.[62] Clifford, Rochester, and Halifax were to come into political prominence after they had served the King abroad. Trumbull and Romney became Secretaries of State after the Revolution of 1688. The more brilliant record of the men after their diplomatic service implies that diplomatic employment was an effective stepping-stone to advancement at court. The large number of claimants for royal favor in the early years of the Restoration exceeded the number of positions available, and ambitious men accepted the relatively undesirable jobs away from home as a means of furthering their political careers.

IV

The Embassy Household

"But that which troubles me most is, that we have chosen a son of Secretary Morice, a boy never used to any business, to go . . . [as Secretary] to the Embassy, which shows how little we are sensible of the weight of the business upon us."

SAMUEL PEPYS, Diary, 1666

The concern with which Pepys viewed the choice of secretary to the embassy to Breda indicates that a clear distinction had emerged between the business staff of the embassy and the other members of the diplomatic ménage. At the turn of the seventeenth century the English embassy staff was still essentially the personal household of the ambassador, chosen and paid by him, and leaving the place of the assignment at the termination of the mission.[1] By the end of the century the government was appointing, and paying at a fixed salary, an official whose job was to take charge of embassy records, keep letterbooks, and assist in the work of preparing memorials and intelligence reports.

Official secretaries, as distinct from secretaries employed by the ambassador in a private capacity, were not yet constant members of every mission, but they were appearing regularly in the important embassies that England sent abroad during this period. An official secretary accompanied each delegation to negotiate a peace, at Breda, Cologne, and Nimeguen, and belonged to the staff for some or all of the years in which ministers were in France, Spain, Sweden, the United Provinces, Modena, the Papal States, Venice, and Morocco.[2]

The young man chosen to attend the embassy to Breda in 1667, Nicholas Morice, had no greater claim to the position than that his father was then Secretary of State. He was a member of Parliament for Newport, Cornwall, from 1667 to 1679, but never served any other mission in an official capacity. Morice was atypical, for most of the other embassy secretaries had extensive periods of service to their credit.[3]

Of the fourteen employed directly by the crown, Thomas Warren and Peter Wyche were former diplomats who accompanied ministers going abroad for the first time. William Godolphin, Robinson, Henshaw, and Chudleigh rose from the rank of official secretary to independently accredited minister. Chudleigh, who served as secretary of five different missions before promotion to the corps, appears as a forerunner of the professional civil servant on the embassy staff.[4] Secretaries Brisbane, John Litcott, John Dodington, and Roger Meredith acted as chargés d'affaires at their respective posts. A continuity in secretarial service, which provided a method of initiating a new minister in the nature of his assignment, was beginning to appear in the foreign service.

Ministers engaged their own clerical staff to supplement the service of the embassy secretaries, or to take their place if the crown had not supplied one. Diplomats at Paris regularly employed a special staff member for French correspondence. The ambassadors looked for men who had special skills to assist them. Carlisle chose Andrew Marvell, the poet and parliamentarian, to accompany him to Russia in 1663. Before his diplomatic employment Marvell was known for his linguistic skills, and had served with John Milton as Latin secretary under Cromwell's Secretary of State, John Thurloe. He had also spent some time travelling on the continent, and had been with Carlisle in France and the Netherlands. Marvell was responsible for all the general correspondence and formal documents connected with the mission. The Russians paid tribute to his special place in the embassy by presenting him with the head of a sturgeon at a formal banquet.[5]

Carlisle chose Francis Vernon to attend his embassy to Sweden at the end of 1668 because of Vernon's years of experience as a traveller. The next year Vernon went to Paris to become Montagu's private secretary at the ambassador's request. Vernon "was a school fellow of mine," Montagu wrote, "as witty and modest a man as ever I knew of his breeding and education. He has been the world over, and speaks French and Spanish and Italian better than ordinary Englishmen do." [6] Temple had several clerks on his mission of 1668 who served under embassy secretary Thomas Downton. One of these men, William Blathwayt, later Secretary of State under William III, was valuable as the only member of Temple's household who knew Dutch. He became official secretary at the Hague in 1671, and later attended embassies in Copenhagen and Stockholm.[7] Thomas Ross, the poet,[8] and René

Petit,[9] like Blathwayt, became official secretaries after serving some years as private clerks to different ministers.

In the case of the private staff employed by the diplomats, terms of service frequently overlapped the tenure of individual ministers. This pattern is especially noticeable in the Turkish, French, and Dutch embassies, where secretaries, clerks, and intelligencers served two or three successive ministers. James Vernon, who served Downing in Holland and Halifax and Sunderland in France, succeeded Trumbull as Secretary of State in 1697. Private secretaries John Werden, Francis Parry, William Loveing (or Loving, Loring), George Etherege, and Hugo Hughes became members of the diplomatic corps without intermediate service as official secretaries. Although England had not yet established a system of furnishing each diplomat with a trained staff, a nucleus of experienced secretaries working in the more important embassies is clearly visible.

In addition to secretaries and intelligencers, a minister usually had a chaplain in his household. Diplomats in Holland who did not have their own chaplain attended services in the chapel of the Princess of Orange. Chudleigh's expense accounts indicate that he paid 91 guilders for a velvet cloth and cushion for his own pew in the English church at the Hague.[10] Ordinarily the embassy chaplain returned to England at the conclusion of the mission, although Fauconberg's chaplain, Mr. Durham, remained in Italy to serve the factory at Leghorn, for which service the merchants agreed to pay him 600 dollars per annum.[11] Chaplains did not receive a salary from the government, but the King issued orders to insure that clergy who attended embassies should continue to receive the profits of their livings, and be eligible for all preferments, even though they were absent from their regular posts.[12] The embassy of Gabriel Sylvius to Denmark in 1685 provided employment for a French Protestant divine who had just fled from his native land.[13] One chaplain of note was Henry Compton, later bishop of London, who joined the embassy of Denzil Holles after the ambassador dismissed his first chaplain, Richard Pettys, "a roring swaggering & swearing man . . . so drunck as he could not reade prayers." [14] Chaplains could serve a dual purpose. Rochester's chaplain, Dr. Robert South (1634–1716), also acted as Latin secretary to the embassy to Poland,[15] and Bevil Skelton's chaplain served as tutor to the children of the diplomat's household.[16]

In Hamburg and Constantinople the chaplain was engaged and paid by the trading companies in the area.[17] To become eligible for the post in Constantinople, a clergyman had to secure a letter of recommendation from the Solicitor-General. The directors of the company listened to several candidates preach, paying each one £5 for his efforts, and selected the one whom they liked the best. Chaplains in the Levant served three or four years, shorter than the terms of the ambassadors. They received an annual salary of 200 dollars, plus a small sum for an outfit, and an additional 200 dollars as a gratuity. After 1668 the company paid in lyon dollars (Dutch Rix dollars) instead of weighty dollars. The ambassador in Turkey assumed the expense of feeding and lodging the chaplain, and paying for a chapel clerk.[18]

The staff of an embassy usually included one or more interpreters, a majordomo, a steward, coachmen, and other domestics. Menials could be hired locally, a procedure which many found easier and cheaper than transporting servants from England, but a nobleman, used to the comforts of a large staff, might elect to bring his whole household from England. References to embassy employees, however, usually indicate that the lowest ranking members of the staff were natives of the place.[19] In Russia the English could not employ subjects of the Czar without first obtaining formal permission. Couriers were not engaged as such. This service was performed by domestic servants or under-secretaries, as the occasion demanded. One man received a present of £60 for taking a message to envoy Gilbert Talbot in Copenhagen.[20]

The minister paid the salaries of all staff members except the official secretaries out of his own pocket, so the rate and manner of payment varied. Private secretaries in Germany received from £40 to £60 per annum. Fauconberg's secretary enjoyed an annual income of £10 as a Fellow of Magdalen College, but found it insufficient for his needs while abroad. He petitioned for an additional 10 shillings per week, which he did not receive.[21]

Wages, of course, depended on conditions in the place of the assignment.[22] Thynne paid his menials in Stockholm between 5 and 10 shillings a week. Dodington's Italian secretary received £13 a year, and six footmen, four gondoliers, and a cook cost him another £134. The minister furnished all the clothes for them at a cost of £130. William Swann's annual expenditure on staff in Hamburg was £22.[23] It must have been a meagre group, for when Swann was out of town, his wife had to take over his duties of correspondence. Savile advised Trumbull on the methods he used in France: "Considering the differences of our circumstances probably my rules of economy will not fit you, but I thought it turned extremely to account to keep all my servants in livery at board wages of 20 sols per diem and no wages, so that without further

counting they were easily dismissed in case of misde-
meanour." Fanshawe dismissed for insolence four Spanish
pages in his employ who petitioned that the 4 reales a day
and two suits of livery a year which they received were insufficient, since they had no money to buy white stuffs,
ruffles, gloves, and stockings.[24]

Not all the people in the diplomatic suite were working
members. The size of the entourage reflected the affluence
of the ambassador, and a brilliant embassy included musicians, several liverymen, gentlemen of quality who attended for their own pleasure, and young nephews of the
ambassador who came to gain the polish that comes with
foreign travel. Etherege's household included a dancing
master and a fencing master. The largest suite belonged
to Arundel, who travelled to Morocco with two hundred
persons, of whom sixty were in livery of gold cloth richly
trimmed with lace. A current newsletter reported, "It will
certainly be the most magnificent that has been seen in
Europe these many ages." [25] The company of Roger Palmer, earl of Castlemaine, on his mission to the Pope drew
notice for its size. Sandwich came to Madrid with a retinue
of sixty-six, including two secretaries, two under-secretaries, two chaplains, interpreter, steward, gentleman of
the horse, trumpeter, surgeon, and the rest relatives, gentlemen, and domestic servants.[26] Patrick Gordon, who
witnessed Carlisle's arrival in Russia, felt the ambassador's
group was "not so numerous as gallant," [27] yet Carlisle had
almost forty in his company: two secretaries, six pages,
two trumpeters, twelve footmen, chaplain, surgeon, six
musicians, interpreters, gentlemen, and tradesmen. The
tradesmen came to seek their own gain. "I might have had
a profitable employment from [Carlisle]," one wrote, "but
Russia is too cold for me." [28]

Travelling with a sizeable retinue added to the cost of an embassy more than to its efficiency, and most English households were much smaller. Southwell had thirteen attendants at Berlin: three gentlemen, steward, clerk, four lackeys, two pages, coachman, and postilion. Temple employed ten at Brussels, as did Goodricke in Spain; Fanshawe went to Spain with only seven. Preston's retinue on his journey to Paris consisted of four gentlemen, one page, six servants, one coach, and six horses, an entourage considerably less august than those the French habitually brought to London. Comenges came with thirty-six persons and sixteen horses, and Courtin brought thirty persons and thirty horses. During the Plague of 1666 the Célèbre Ambassade, an illustrious trio representing Louis XIV, sent most of their retinue back to France, keeping a skeleton staff of twenty-three men each.[29]

In Constantinople the ambassador had the service of an English secretary maintained by the Turkey Company. Winchilsea's secretary, Paul Rycaut, became consul at Smyrna from 1677 to 1678, and resident at Hamburg from 1689 to 1700. George Etherege was secretary to Harvey in 1670. Trumbull brought to Constantinople the same secretary, Jacques Dayrolle, and chaplain, William Hayley, who had served him in France.[30] Trumbull learned about the management of the staff in Constantinople in letters from the former secretaries. Etherege told him: "The Secretary of this Embassy at Constantinople is allowed 600 Lion Dollars a year which is paid by the merchants, the Company esteem him their servant and pretend a right to choose him; if you think fit to have a private secretary, you must pay for him yourself, but you may endeavour to get the Company to approve one whom you shall recommend; the man who enjoys the place at present is one

Mr. Cook; his principles and his countenance are both very odd. . . . I fear you will not find them turned toward your good liking." [31] Rycaut cautioned Trumbull to take few servants with him. For grooms, porters, and other servants below stairs it was best to hire local Greeks and Armenians. "The salary of common servants by the year is usually 30 Lion Dollars a man, the cellar-keeper 40, and the butler 50, besides liveries once a year." Rycaut advised that it was a good idea to take about twenty extra liveries from London to outfit men hired for special occasions, such as the day of audience. A coach was of little use in that part of the world; a chair and horse-litter would do better service. "Perhaps my Lady is so curious as to have her own chamber furnished after her own fashion, but as to other things, I would not have you carry anything besides linen, pewter dishes, and plate." [32]

The principal staff problem in the Levant was finding adequate and reliable dragomans [33] to act as intelligencers and translators. Louis XIV tried to solve this problem by creating the institution of the *jeunes de langues,* young boys sent to be educated in Oriental languages by the Capuchin fathers in Smyrna and Constantinople, in order to serve the French ambassadors who came to the Levant. The plan was in operation only from 1669 to 1671, and produced no successful results. [34] Rycaut wanted England to institute a similar program: ". . . it hath been known, that the Embassadour hath been forced to interpose his own Person, between the fury of the Visier and his Interpreter, whose offense was only a delivery of the words of his Master; some of whom have notwithstanding been imprisoned, or executed for this cause . . . and therefore it were very useful to breed up a Seminary of young Englishmen, of sprightly and ingenious parts, to be qualified in that Office; who may with less danger to themselves, and honour to their Master, and advantage to the publick, express boldly without the usual mincing and submission of other Interpreters, whatsoever is commanded and declared by their Master." [35] Since Rycaut's advice went unheeded, the ambassadors in Turkey had to depend on subjects of the Grand Seigneur. Most of them were of Italian extraction, related to dragomans who served other embassies, and likely to be more influenced by fear of Turkish officials or bribes from other ministers than the interests of their masters. The Venetian ambassador at the Porte wrote that Winchilsea confided in him that he had half a mind to stick a dagger into his treacherous dragoman. "I say nothing of the dragomans of the Republic; I try to keep them loyal." [36]

The company paid dragomans annual salaries from 200 to 400 dollars, depending on their seniority, and allowed them small sums for vests. Younger men who assisted the dragomans, called *giovanni di lingua,* received amounts up to 100 dollars. The merchants liked to limit the number of interpreters, whereas the ambassadors constantly complained that they needed more men. Chandos said he had three overgrown youths aged thirty as *giovanni,* and a staff of dragomans which was inadequate by any standards. "Old. Sig. Giorgio hath served me in my audiences as Drug. he speaking the best English of y^m all, but he is above 70 yeares old & hath ye stone wch much hastens his superannuaring. For Draco he is much given to wine, lives at Stambull or att home." Turkish protocol required that the dragomans wear special red and blue shoes, which cost twenty shillings, and had to be paid for by the ambassador. If the chaplain needed a dragoman, he employed his own.[37]

The lodging for the diplomatic household was, in most places, the responsibility of the ambassador, for governments were not yet maintaining overseas dwellings for their representatives. In London, York House in the Strand was a popular residence for visiting diplomats. Here the Spanish ambassador lived in 1661 and 1666, the Russian ambassador in 1662, and the French ambassador in 1670. D'Estrades lived in a palace in Chelsea in 1661 and 1665, and Comenges took up residence in Exeter House. Charles Colbert, marquis de Croissy, leased Leicester House from the Sidney family in 1668, for an annual rent of £700. Courtin built his own house on the north side of St. James Square in 1676. His successor, Paul Barillon, lived there in 1686 and on subsequent visits to London. The Dutch minister Johan Boreel stayed at Piccadilly House, and Lisola lived in Charing Cross.[38]

Of the English embassies abroad, only the delegation to Breda had their lodgings provided free of cost. The States General prepared a special residence for Holles and Coventry by breaking through the walls of two adjoining houses. The residence was given to them unfurnished.[39] The French had lodgings hired and ready for Jenkins when he came to Cologne, at a cost of £253. At Nimeguen each minister leased his own house. Temple's cost him £1,000 per annum; Berkeley paid £686; Hyde, who stayed a shorter time, paid £285.[40]

Ministers did not like to burden themselves with expensive dwellings, because they had to pay for them in advance, usually before they had received their salary. For this reason Fauconberg and Finch were grateful for the opportunity to live at the house of Bernard Gascoigne when they were in Florence. A minister in Venice was burdened with the cost of gondolas in addition to his rent. Dodington paid 40 shillings per month for his gondolas and £80 per year for a house on the Grand Canal.[41]

St. Albans resided with Henrietta Maria, the Queen Mother, at her palace at Colombes outside Paris, but all the other ministers to France had to make their own arrangements about housing. Holles took lodgings in the Rue Royale. Ralph Montagu's secretary secured a house in Paris before his master arrived, but Montagu was displeased with it and took another place in Saint-Germain, at £70 per annum, forfeiting a year's rent. Preston lived near the Hôtel d'Entrague. Trumbull wanted to lease the Hôtel d'Ecosse, but it was already taken. He found lodgings in the Hôtel de Beziers in the Rue Colombier for 30 pistoles per month, while waiting for a country house on the Versailles road. Later he lived in the Rue du Bac. Skelton took over Trumbull's furnishings, but not his house.[42]

When Temple was in Holland, he succeeded in finding "a little garden house just outside of town," maintaining another house in the capital for £200 per annum. Downing took over the same house in 1671, which saved Temple some expense. When Thomas Plott arrived in 1681, he rented a house on the Prince Gracht for 600 guilders.[43]

Lodgings in Russia were difficult to find, primitive, and uncomfortable. On their journey to Moscow, Carlisle and his retinue were forced to stay in little wooden cottages, "Black all over with smoak, so that to dissipate the stinks which are occasioned by the same, and the sweltering heat of their skins, which would be otherwise intollerable, we were forced to keep the Windows continually open." In the capital the company received a stone house near the Czar's castle, in the select Kitaigorod district. It had shutters and doors of iron, chambers hung with red cloth, and two great halls. Carlisle used one hall as a chapel and one to lodge part of his train. When he complained that the house had no beds, and the quarters for sleeping were too cramped to accommodate all in his retinue, his hosts told him it was "best for them to lye together, lest the Rats should run away with them being single." [44]

The most luxurious lodgings that English diplomats found were in Spain. In this country the King assigned vacant houses at his discretion, and the diplomat reimbursed the owner. Sandwich had a *quinta,* or country house, outside Madrid, and a grandee's residence in the city at Siete Chimeneas. Because one dwelling was not enough for his large retinue he obtained another nearby for his staff, and the Spanish King provided furniture for both houses. In the summer he had the use of a country estate which belonged to the King. Fanshawe stayed for a while at Cádiz, in a house so elegantly appointed that the worst chamber, given to the servants, was hung with damask. In Madrid, Fanshawe took a liking to the house occupied by the Venetian ambassador, the Casa de las Siete Chimeneas, 2 Calle de las Infantas, Plazuela del Ré. He secured it for himself by applying to the government and paying the owner a year's rent in advance, to the distress of the Venetian who wanted to keep it for his successor. When Southwell arrived he stayed at Fanshawe's house, and Sunderland lived at the estate of the Baron de Batteville, considered one of the best in Madrid, with a fine garden of orange trees and splendid fountains. [45]

Occasionally the Treasury reimbursed a minister for a second dwelling, if it was needed for him to reside near the sovereign of the place. Montagu received £60 for house and stable rent at Fontainebleau, and £70 for lodgings at Versailles. Edward Wood, when he was envoy in Sweden, received £50 for three months' rent at Upsala.[46] This practise was not a common one, for most ministers maintained only one permanent dwelling abroad.

Foreign embassies in Constantinople were in Pera, a hilly section of the city. The Turkey Company paid for the ambassador's house, which was assigned by the Turks. When the Grand Seigneur had to find lodgings for a visiting dignitary, he evicted a Christian or a Jew and then obtained the rent from the merchants. The dwellings were unattractive. Winchilsea called his "incredibly vile, confined and ruinous in every part," and Finch complained that his was "the damd'est, confounded place that ever mortall man was put into." Winchilsea ultimately bought his own house in Pera for £1,000, including furniture. He also had a villa at Belgrade, where he withdrew in times of plague. The Sultan lived at Adrianople, and when ambassadors had to stay in that city for formal occasions, the Turkey Company provided them with a pavilion.[47]

At the end of the seventeenth century the government was not yet assuming full responsibility for the management of its embassies abroad. Although important missions received an official secretary, most ministers had to assemble and support the whole staff, arrange for transportation, and find a suitable place for all to live. Their expenses began before they left England, and remained constant for the duration of the mission. The functioning of an embassy therefore depended to a great extent on the personal resources of the individual minister, supplemented by the financial support from the crown, which took several forms.

Remuneration

"The office of Ambassadors is most profitable, and most necessary; which makes the Spaniards call it Santo Officio y Ministerio de los Angeles, *the Holy Office and Ministry of Angells."*

JAMES HOWELL,
A Discourse Concerning the Precedency of Kings

Diplomats received their remuneration from the crown in three forms: an amount for equipage, a salary for entertainment which was to cover ordinary daily costs, and allowances for extraordinary expenses incurred during the course of the mission. The scale of payment for the first two items varied according to rank and place of assignment. Payment for entertainment was calculated at a daily, weekly, or monthly rate, and was paid quarterly, in March, June, September, and December. The prescribed method of payment was for a diplomat to receive his equipage money and the first quarterly payment for his salary in advance, the advance being deducted from his first year's salary.

In the early years of the reign of Charles II, the government had not yet established a formal scheme for rates of pay in different countries.[1] The crown used the scale of payments in the reign of the late King as a general precedent, with the rule of thumb that the allowance for an ambassador to Spain should exceed by one third the allowance for an ambassador to France. In 1663 Charles II decided that money for ordinary entertainment was to start thirty days before the diplomat took formal leave of the King, instead of forty days as had been done in the past.[2] Since remuneration was still being decided on an individual basis,[3] the procedure did not result in a uniform wage scale. Some ministers received salaries, while others received a lump sum which was supposed to cover all the expenses connected with the mission. Payment in this form was rendered after the diplomat returned to London. To cover his expenses while abroad he spent his own funds, or arranged to borrow money, and then submitted an itemized bill for all his expenditures to a Secretary of State, who referred it to the Treasury with advice to act upon it.

The salaries varied tremendously from court to court during the first eight years following the Restoration. Inequities in remuneration for ministers of the same rank to France, Spain, Portugal, Sweden, and the German courts are immediately apparent from Table V. Another obvious irregularity is the salary for the resident in the United Provinces. Downing, who ranked officially as a resident, although he designated himself an envoy in his correspondence, drew the same salary as the ambassador to France in 1663. A less obvious factor that led to disputes was the time basis on which salaries were calculated. Entertainment for Denzil Holles was to be £400 per month.

TABLE V

Remuneration of English Diplomats Abroad, 1660–1668

Rank	Assignment	Equipage	Entertainment
Plenipotentiaries	Breda	£3,000	£100 per week
Ambassadors	France	4,000 (1661)	400 per mensem
		3,000 (1663)	400 per mensem
	Spain	6,000 (1667)	11,000 *
		4,000 (1664)	1,000 per quarter
	Portugal	(1661)	5,000 *
		2,000 (1662)	6 per diem
	Sweden		525 *
Envoys	France		500 *
	Spain		100 per mensem
	Portugal	1,000 (1661)	4 per diem
		(1667)	100 per mensem
	Denmark	500	5 per diem
	Sweden	700 (1666)	5 per diem
		500 (1664)	5 per diem
	Empire		2,480 *
	Germany	300 (1668)	2 per diem
		200 (1668)	3 per diem
Residents	Spanish Netherlands		100 per mensem (166
			2 per diem (1661)
	Portugal		2 per diem
	Tuscany	500	1,000 per annum
	United Provinces	4,000	400 per mensem
			20s. per diem (1663)
	Hanse Towns		£2 per diem (1666)
	Germany		2,000 *
Agents	Morocco		5,500 * †

Compiled from *C.T.B.* I-III and *C.S.P.D.* 1660–1668.

* Lump sum paid in lieu of regular salary.

† This sum, paid to Thomas Warren for five years service at his post, was supposed to cover £1,700 paid to redeem English captives (*C.S.P.D.* 1660–1685, *Addenda*, p. 344).

Holles succeeded in convincing Secretary Morice that he should be paid on the basis of a lunar month of twenty-eight days, which brought his annual salary to £1,300, rather than the £1,200 paid to other ministers who had their pay assigned on a *per mensem* basis. The £3,000 that Coventry received for equipage when he went to Breda was not deducted from his regular salary, a favor resented by others.[4]

The situation that dramatized the need for a coherent scheme to settle diplomatic salaries was the inordinately expensive mission of Sandwich to Spain in 1667. Sandwich spent so much of his personal fortune, close to £10,000, on his grandiose embassy, that he had to borrow £500 from Pepys when he got back to London.[5] One of the causes of his personal debt was that payment was slow in coming, since the Treasury objected to dockets to pay Sandwich lump sums which were not calculated on a *per diem* or *per mensem* basis. At the end of the year Arlington wished to do something to settle allowances for foreign ministers on a more equitable basis. He ordered the Auditor of Receipts to certify the allowances given to all diplomats since the reign of Queen Elizabeth, and Downing was asked to collect a list of the highest and lowest salaries paid to ministers in every country.[6]

On the basis of these studies, the Lords of Trade made the following recommendations: allowances were always to be calculated at a specific rate, and they were to begin at the time the minister took formal leave of the King and terminate at his return to the royal presence. In 1667 the Lords of Trade and the Foreign Committee each made a suggested scale of payments for allowances, and came to agreement on a rate which was most like the plan proposed by the Lords of Trade. In 1669 Charles II and the

Foreign Committee standardized allotments for equipage, and raised the scale for salaries. Table VI shows the early plans and the final decision of the King, who sent a copy to the Treasury to remain as a rule for future reference. The regulations of 1669 also stipulated that if a minister remained in England above twenty days after leave-taking, he was not to be paid his ordinary allowance for that time.[7]

The post most drastically affected was The Hague. Since the initiation of the plan coincided with Temple's first mission to that place, he considered that the reduction was not part of a general effort at economy but a political move by Clifford, then one of the Lords of the Treasury, who was showing his disapproval of Temple's embassy. Whatever its implications, the plan of 1669 had the virtue of eliminating the extremes in diplomatic remuneration. No one again was to receive the high sums paid to ambassadors in France and Spain, nor the totally inadequate 20 shillings *per diem* paid to William Swann when he was at Hamburg. Swann had to petition the crown for an increase in salary in 1666 because he was forced to depend on his wife's friends in Germany for food.[8]

English ministers were paid less than their French colleagues, and better than the Venetians. At the time the government was taking diplomatic salaries into consideration, an agent in France submitted a chart of the wages paid to the diplomats of the French King.[9] This document shows that Comenges received 18,000 livres ($£9,000$) per annum when he was in England, about one and three quarters times as much as an English ambassador in France. In 1661 Venetian ambassadors in London received 300 gold ducats for equipage ($£50$), and 600 gold ducats per month ($£100$). An embassy secretary had 200 gold

TABLE VI

Remuneration of English Diplomats Abroad after 1668

Proposed by Lords of Trade 1667	£7 per diem	Proposed by Foreign Committee 1667	£10 per diem	Agreed by Lords of Trade and Foreign Committee	£10 per diem	Established by King 1669 — Equipage		Salary
FRANCE, SPAIN, EMPIRE								
Ambs. Extra. & Ambs. Ord.		Ambs. Extra.		Ambs. Extra.		Ambs. Ord.	£1,500	£100 per week
Envoys	4	Ambs. Ord.	7	Ambs. Ord.	7	Envoys	500	5 per diem
Residents	2.10	Envoys	5	Envoys	4	Residents	?	3
Ambassadors	5	Residents	3	Residents	2.10	Ambs. Ord.	1,000	10
Envoys	3	Ambassadors	7	Ambs. Extra.	7			
		Envoys	4	Ambs. Ord.	5			
OTHER COURTS								
Residents	2	Residents	2.10	Envoys	3	Envoys	200	4
				Residents	2			2.10
				Resident at Hague	2.10			

Compiled from B.M. Stowe MSS. 548; P.R.O. S.P. 9/166, ff. 71, 208; 84/183, f. 161.

ducats per month (£33).[10] Fauconberg had £1,500 for equipage and £10 per day as ambassador to Venice.[11]

Although the scheme of 1669 remained essentially unchanged during the next century,[12] in practise it was modified during the period before 1689. The rate for an ambassador to the Pope had not been designated. Under James II an ambassador extraordinary received £3,000 for equipage and £100 per week; an agent had £3 per day.[13] A tabulation of various entries in the Treasury Books shows that envoys to the Scandinavian countries regularly received £500 for equipage and £5 per day, adhering to the scheme for France, which was more than the amount to which they were entitled. Salaries for ministers in Germany were erratic, being sometimes more and sometimes less than the stipulated amount. In 1682 pay for a resident here was still being settled by individual petition.

Payment to embassy secretaries, omitted from the decisions of the government, had not fluctuated so radically from year to year. Ordinary entertainment was 40 shillings per day for everyone except Robinson in Sweden, who had only half as much in 1679 and 1680. Meredith received 20 shillings per day in 1677 from Temple, who was reimbursed in his accounts for extraordinary expenses, but the crown raised Meredith's salary to 40 shillings in 1678 when they began to pay him directly. Three secretaries received lump sums for their work. Wood got £100 for his services in Sweden; Werden's pay was £400 for assisting Sandwich at Madrid for a year, and £100 for a short journey as courier to the United Provinces; Blathwayt received £693 for three years employment at The Hague.[14] A survey of the allotments for equipage for the secretaries reveals no set pattern. Godolphin and Chudleigh had £200

when they went to Spain. The secretaries at Breda had
£100; at Cologne, nothing; at Nimeguen, £300. Chudleigh received £200 to prepare himself for employment
in France, and the other embassy secretaries at Paris had
nothing. £300 each was allowed for Litcott for Rome and
Meredith for the United Provinces, and £200 for Wyche
at Vienna.[15]

A few other members of the embassy staffs received
direct remuneration from the crown. A herald who accompanied Thomas Higgons when he went to present the
Order of the Garter to the Elector of Saxony received 30
shillings a day. Four of His Majesty's trumpeters and a
kettle drummer received a total of £100 to accompany
Arundel to Morocco.

All ambassadors, and some envoys, but no ministers of
lower rank, had additional financial help from the crown
in the form of plate from the Jewel House. This was to
help them furnish their embassies in style, without having
to spend their own funds. Ambassadors had to give a bond
or some form of surety for the plate, and were supposed to
return it intact at the conclusion of the mission.[16] If royal
permission was obtained, one minister could buy the plate
from his predecessor.[17] Warrants to deliver the plate usually specified only the number of ounces of white and gilt
objects. Downing's privy seal indicates that the plate was
valued at 6s. 4d. the ounce for white, and 9s. 6d. the ounce
for gilt, so that the pieces Downing received were worth
a total of £2,391 12s. 2½d.[18] Richmond's warrant, the
most specific, directed that he was to have "30 dishes of
white plate, 96 deep trencher plates, 1 cistern, 2 flagons, 3
salvers, 3 dozen spoons, 3 dozen forks, 3 dozen knives, 12
candlesticks, 1 chamber pot, 1 skillet & cover, 2 porringers
& covers, 4 rings for dishes to stand on, 1 kettle and ladle,

I warming pan, 3 pair of snuffers with chains and pans, 3 small chafing dishes, 12 saltcellars, 3 sugar casters, 6 basons & eures, 6 tumblers, 2 sweetmeat stands or frames, 1 oil crevit, 1 vinegar crevit, 1 mustard pot, 1 pepper bos, 4 intermesses or inside plates, 1 perfuming pan, 3 gilt basons, 1 large tea pot to make tea in, 1 large chocolate pot, 1 fountain to the silver kettle, both large, 1 large chafing dish: to the weight of 8,732 oz. of white plate in all to be made of such fashion as his Grace shall direct." [19] Other ambassadors received from 4,000 to almost 9,000 ounces of plate, for allotments were not standardized. Fanshawe received a cloth of state,[20] furniture, hangings, linen, and prayer books as gifts from the King. His wife added, "but there wanted a velvet bed, which he should have had by custom." [21]

A pay warrant for a diplomat indicated, in addition to his equipage and entertainment, that he was to be reimbursed at the discretion of a Secretary of State for his extraordinary expenses. Diplomats submitted their extraordinary bills quarterly. By the regulations of 1669, a minister had to deliver sworn testimony to the truth of his account, unless he was a peer, who had only to affirm and have his secretary or steward swear. No allowance was to be made for presents and entertainments at his reception, unless done by express order, except in the case of Sweden and Denmark. No charge was to be allowed for travelling home, unless these and other costs exceeded his ordinary allowance. He was to have no reimbursement for a secretary or other attendant, or for ordinary postage, unless so commissioned by the King.[22]

Extraordinaries included a heterogeneous group of items. Intelligence, letters sent by express, messenger service, gifts and entertainments for royal occasions, travels connected with embassy business, fees paid to the Exchequer for salaries, and interest on monies which were in arrears were the most common entries. Until 1680 only the last two items required the approval of the Treasury as well as the Secretary's office. Although return passage to England was not a valid claim, transportation home for the corpse of the Duke of Richmond, who died during his stay in Denmark, was allowed as "just and reasonable" by Secretary Coventry.[23]

More unusual items, which met with official approval, were ultramarine, seeds, and roses which Bevil Skelton purchased in France at the King's command, and Edward Wood's expenditures on apothecary bills for sick servants, and donations to poor Swedish scholars who presented him with some of their works.[24] Some ministers tried to collect, but failed, for personal clothing, lodgings en route to the assignment, security given for plate, repairs on the embassy dwelling, and ordinary postage.[25]

Since the system of extraordinary reimbursement was open to the abuse of padding the totals,[26] a time-honored tradition, the government made efforts to keep the claims within reasonable limits. Williamson inaugurated a plan in 1671 to limit the bills to £1,000 per year for ministers whose regular allowance came to less than that amount. After 1680 all extraordinaries had to be authorized by the Treasury before they could pass the Privy Seal, which made the Treasury at least more cognizant of, and perhaps more able to control, the outlay of government funds. In 1667 Sandwich received £6,000 towards his embassy in Spain out of the Navy funds, without the knowledge of the Treasury. Under James II an official scale limited extraordinaries from £200 per quarter for an envoy in France to £50 for a resident at Ratisbon. These regulations did not go into effect until 7 February 1687, and limited the bills of only three ministers during this period.[27]

The salary for the ambassador at Constantinople was usually 10,000 Rix dollars per annum, plus 2,000 Rix dollars gratuity, which means that the Turkey Company paid their ambassador about one half the ordinary entertainment that an ambassador to France received from the crown. In this post, too, payment varied. The equipage allotment was between £800 and £6,000. If an ambassador stayed longer than five years, he might receive an additional bonus worth £500.[28] Winchilsea obtained 1,200 dollars to cover the expenses of his return to England, but the company declared that this was not to be a precedent. He also had a free gift designated as "1 chest of moran glasses, 1 caso with 14 reames paper, 6 baskets with 6 cheeses, 2 barills of butter, 1 caso with a parmesan cheese." His terms were better than those of two of his successors. Chandos had only 8,000 dollars per annum, and neither he nor Harvey received the yearly gratuity. The King sometimes contributed furnishings for the Turkish embassy. Winchilsea received plate, Harvey a cloth of state, and Soame furniture, altar cloths, carpets, and linens from the Wardrobe. Winchilsea thought he should have received a bed, but Secretary Nicholas could find no precedent for it.[29] Winchilsea also complained that the King paid him no cash for his services in the Levant. He told his brother-in-law Southampton that the French ambassador received the same salary he did from the French Levant Company, and also £1,500 from the King, "which in twenty-three years time so enriched him that he departed with a treasure of £60,000 sterling." [30]

The costs of the crown for the Russian missions adhered to no scale. Carlisle received £5,000 for equipage, and a gift of a bed, damask canopy, chair of state, and a footstool. Wyche, envoy extraordinary, got £200 for equipage and £3 per day; Gordon, of the same rank, £400 and £4 per day.[31]

Diplomats also received gifts from the heads of state in the place of their assignment. The men expected presents appropriate to their rank, and were likely to cavil at gifts of inferior value. Jewelry, a portrait of the King set in diamonds, or objects in plate were the customary tokens in most countries. The United Provinces gave money.[32] The Master of the Ceremonies was in charge of presenting England's gifts to visiting foreign ministers, which ranged in value from £2,000 to an ambassador extraordinary from France to £107 to an attendant of the Russian ambassador. An envoy extraordinary was not supposed to receive a gift worth more than £500.[33]

The total cost of the foreign service is almost impossible to itemize. William A. Shaw's introductions to the *Calendars of Treasury Books* contain totals for most of the years from 1660 to 1688, which are calculated on the basis of entries for payment. These sums were lowest in the years immediately following the Restoration and after the accession of James II, and reached their height in the period between Easter and Michaelmas, 1676, when the total ran to £41,508 11s. 4d.[34] These figures are misleading because the Treasury Books contain only warrants for payment. Official records for the last quarter of the seventeenth century do not indicate whether the recipient of a tally ever received the monies to which he was entitled. We have a considerable amount of testimony that shows that diplomats had a great deal of trouble in collecting their salaries.

Almost every minister had some difficulty in collecting ordinary and extraordinary payment. If one received a promotion in grade while serving at a post, he did not automatically receive a corresponding increase in salary. He had to submit a written request to a Secretary of State, who referred the matter to the King, who indicated his pleasure in a formal document which went to the Treasury. This process meant that some time elapsed before the minister received his tally, or order for payment, for the new salary, and he then had to wait for his tally to fall due at the Treasury. Godolphin did not get official authorization for his payment as ambassador in Spain until a year and a half after he began to enjoy that character, at which time he was already owed £2,587 as envoy extraordinary, and did not even have the necessary funds to pay his couriers.[35]

The chronic arrears in diplomatic salaries is explained partly by the priority assigned to government expenditures. In France, when funds were settled at the beginning of each year, salaries for ambassadors had high priority, after the expenses of the King's household.[36] In England, an order of 1665 placed ambassadors low on the list, following allotments for the armed forces, royal households, overseas and home garrisons, buildings and works, and the wardrobe.[37] The current state of the Treasury affected all government salaries. In January 1671 salaries for ambassadors were excepted out of the Stop of the Exchequer, but payments to ambassadors abroad and presents to foreign ministers in the country were held to a total of £30,000, at which figure they remained until 1673. Danby ordered a temporary stop to all salaries and pensions in

1674, in order to pay off seamen's wages, and inaugurated another scheme of retrenchment in 1676 which reduced expenditures on ambassadors and presents to £40,000 per annum, from the £50,000 to which they had climbed in the two preceding years. When Danby left office in 1679, the Treasury was in worse condition than in 1673. Payment to diplomatic agents could no longer exceed £20,000, and this necessitated the withdrawal of ministers from several courts and a reduction in grade for several posts.[38]

The disparity between the amounts entered in the Treasury Books and the money actually received by the ministers may be guessed by comparing the pay warrants with information in the diplomatic correspondence. This method provides only a rough gauge, for a man did not always reveal how much money he received, and some undoubtedly painted the picture blacker than it was in an effort to obtain favorable action on their accounts. Temple's salary for his services at Brussels was supposedly paid six months in advance of his departure, but he said that by the end of his first year abroad it was six months in arrears. Berkeley, who was £4,000 out of pocket for his embassy in France by May 1674, did not receive his first money warrant until the end of 1675. Romney's arrears in 1680 came to £1,000 for extraordinaries and three months salary, yet these amounts had already passed the Treasury. Preston was at Paris for ten months in 1683 without receiving any pay, regular or extraordinary, although his bills were allowed by the Secretary and had been for some months before the Lords of the Treasury.[39] When Charles Bertie was Danby's secretary, he estimated that in 1679 payments to ambassadors were six or seven years in arrears. Salaries due in 1680 and 1681 had not yet been paid in 1685.[40]

Ministers managed to maintain themselves abroad in spite of these financial difficulties. A few secured some subsidy from the country of their assignment. Arlington was able to live well in Spain on the gifts he received from a Spanish courtier. Louis XIV paid Montagu 100,000 écus when the ambassador was in France, and subsidized Ignatius White, marquis d'Albeville, envoy of James II in the Netherlands.[41] Some kept their plate in lieu of unpaid salaries, or sold or pawned it to meet expenses while abroad. Very little actually found its way back to the Jewel House.[42] Diplomats had frequent recourse to two other methods to relieve financial distress. They borrowed money from men in London or merchants in the vicinity, and directed the Treasury to pay their salaries to their creditors.[43] The minister was then out of pocket for the interest on the loan, unless he could persuade the government to allow the amount in his extraordinary bills. Others sold their tallies for payment to investors. Tallies were negotiable items, which bore interest until paid, and one who was pressed for cash could sell them at a discount, depending on the length of time until they fell due. Lady Anne Fanshawe kept tallies for her husband's back salary for two years, until she was forced to sell them, getting £5,000 for tallies worth £5,900.[44]

Neither those who borrowed nor those who sold their tallies received the full amount for their services which the Treasury Books indicate. The various transactions involved in getting ready cash, and the inadequacy of public records for this period prevent an accurate analysis of the cost of the diplomatic service. We know that ministers of all ranks suffered from the financial distress that characterized the reigns of the later Stuarts. Against this dark picture must be balanced the organizational efforts in fiscal

policy which affected the corps. The government put
salaries on a fairer basis, commensurate with rank and
place of assignment, and made some progress in control-
ling and limiting the extraordinary bills.

VI

Protoco

_____

"An extraordinary courtesy is usually taken as a mere civility by him who receives it, and if omitted becomes an essential prejudice."

PIERO MOCENIGO, Venetian ambassador in England

An elaborate and stylized ritual surrounded the activities of the seventeenth century ambassador. From his arrival at his post, through the conduct of his mission and leave taking, a pattern of rigidly defined ceremony marked the ambassador for what he essentially was: the embodiment of the sovereign power that he represented. Each King wanted his foreign ministers to reflect his own glory, and he expected them to guard their movements carefully lest any shadow be cast upon his own majesty. Certain ceremonies formed an essential part of all missions. The public entry into the capital, the first formal audience with the King, a ritually correct exchange of visits with other diplomats in the city, and a formal audience *de congé* formed the basic framework upon which each court superimposed its own customs.

The purpose of the entry was to dazzle everyone who saw it. To insure that the entry would be properly splendid, and held at an auspicious time, an ambassador came into the city quietly, incognito, at his first arrival. He then set about getting settled in his house, seeing that his coaches and liveries were in condition, and, if necessary, hiring extra attendants on a short-term basis so that his suite would be a grand one. When residence, costumes, and equipage were all in readiness, he left the city for a point nearby. Then, accompanied by musicians, his working staff, and any of his fellow countrymen he could muster for the occasion, he re-entered the city in all his finery and took his place among the public dignitaries of the town.

An ambassador making his formal entry into London came up the Thames from Greenwich in the King's barge. A newly arrived ambassador first arranged the time and particulars of his entry with the Master of the Ceremonies, Sir Charles Cotterell. Cotterell chose the courtiers who were to accompany the ambassador at his reception and arranged for accommodations at Greenwich for the convenience of the entourage. He usually expected some material consideration for his efforts. "The Master of the Ceremonies, angling for himself and the Court officials, artfully contrived to show us the list of the presents left by the last ambassadors extraordinary of France and Spain, which, if true, are intolerably exorbitant," the Venetian ambassador reported in 1661.[1] Under ordinary circumstances, if the diplomat represented a crowned head or the Republic of Venice, he was accompanied from Greenwich by nine gentlemen of the Privy Council, with the Master of the Ceremonies and an earl as his special escort. If he represented a duke or a republic, he merited only a baron. When the barge reached the Tower, he received a salute of guns as he disembarked and entered the royal coach. The King's guards and several of the English nobility joined the diplomatic suite for a procession through the streets of the city to a special house in the yard of the Palace of Westminster where ambassadors were entertained.[2] The house belonged to Dame Rebecca Williams, who received £300 per annum for keeping it equipped with furniture, hangings, and linen, and ready for use at the King's command. Dame Williams made arrangements for members of the ambassador's suite who could not find accommodations in her house to stay in neighboring houses.[3] All ambassadors received three days entertainment at the expense of the King, except the ambassadors from Russia, whose expenses were defrayed, at great cost, for six months. Colbert, the French ambassador, chose a cash sum for provisions at his own residence, Leicester House, in lieu of three days entertainment with Dame Williams.[4]

The details of this general plan varied in special situations. When the Célèbre Ambassade arrived from France in 1665, Charles II despatched Cotterell to Dover to receive them with a special show of courtesy for his illustrious cousin. A judiciously placed bribe secured for Count Giovanni Luca Durazzo, the ambassador of the Duke of Genoa, the honor of an escort due a kingly representative.[5]

The official in charge of regulating ceremonies for diplomatic receptions in Paris was the Introductor of Ambassadors. The French court had two, each serving a half-year, with a coadjutor or lieutenant who was permanent. The official escort was the Maître d'Hôtel, whose primary responsibility was to stand at the diplomat's side during all the ceremonies with the staff of authority in his hand.[6] A letter of advice that Henry Savile wrote to Trumbull as he was about to undertake his mission to Paris describes the protocol in the French capital. "At your arrival at Paris the first step is to send to the Master of Ceremonies to let him know you are come upon such an occasion and to learn from him when you may see the secretary of state." The next step, Trumbull's mentor informed him, was to appoint a day for the entry and audience at the King's convenience, bearing in mind that the King's coachmen who would attend him that day expected a fee of 2 pistoles each. "Your countrymen that pray with you on Sunday will expect to dine with you, I mean the better sort . . . To end with the King himself, though he can be morose upon occasion, his reception of foreign Ministers is generally very affable, especially when the open countenance of the speaker draws the like from him; personal flattery (not too gross) takes wonderfully to him, whenever any favour is required of him." [7]

Once the ambassador had arranged the date of his entry, he was obliged to notify all foreign ministers in Paris two days ahead, and invite them to send their coaches to travel with his. The Introductor of Ambassadors informed the diplomat which persons of the court were also to be in his suite by special royal order. On the day of the entry a Marshal of France came in the royal coach to fetch the ambassador from his house, and the entire entourage departed to a spot two or three leagues outside the city. The ambassador chose the gate through which the procession came back to town. The Porte Saint-Denis or the Porte Saint-Antoine were the most popular routes, but there was

no absolute rule. Crowds of common people always followed the parade on foot. After entering the city the ambassador was conducted to the Hôtel des Ambassadeurs,
where he was treated for three and a half days at the
King's expense. While he lived there, the Introductor of
Ambassadors took every meal with him and the Maître
d'Hôtel dined once. The public audience always followed
on the day after the entry.[8]

In Spain the Introductor of Ambassadors and the Master
of the Ceremonies escorted the English diplomat on his
entry. The coaches of all foreign ministers and the members of the English colony in Madrid formed part of the
suite. The King provided ambassadors with royal coaches
and horses for the occasion and granted him free entertainment and the use of one royal coach for eight days. Sandwich received an additional three coaches from the Queen.
The Introductor, the Majordomo of the week, and the
Captain of the Guard all received fees for their services.
Customs in Portugal were much the same, but only three
days entertainment were offered.[9]

Venetian custom decreed that an ambassador making
his entry into the city withdrew five miles away to the
island of Santo Spirito, the site of an ancient convent of
friars, where he was attended by a cavalier of principal
quality and a retinue of senators. Ordinarily the ambassador received his escort in the church of the convent, but
Fauconberg contrived to have the meeting in the cloisters
lest his position as the representative of a Protestant prince
be compromised. Although Venice had no Introductor of
Ambassadors, Wicquefort considered the ceremonies to
be among the best regulated in Europe and Fauconberg's
entry as one of the most spectacular the Republic ever saw.
"Sixty Senators cloath'd in their Scarlet Robes, with as

many *Gondolas,* follow'd by above five hundred others, went and receiv'd him at the Convent of the Holy Ghost, and conducted him . . . to the Lodgings he had hir'd and furnish'd. . . . In the evening the Senate sent him all sorts of Refreshments." [10]

At Florence the Trattemitore Maggiore, as the Introductor was known, met ambassadors and travelled with the diplomatic suite to a point outside the city gate. Judges and officers of the town escorted the train, and the Grand Duke ordered all the cannon of the forts and garrisons to sound as the ambassador approached the city. As the parade passed through the gate a younger son of the ducal family made the formal greetings and accompanied the ambassador to the stairs at the foot of the palace, where the Grand Duke himself stood ready to receive the party. In former times the ambassador was entertained for his whole stay in Tuscany, but by 1670 efforts at economy reduced this courtesy to six days, during which time the royal coaches were lent to the ambassador for his own use. An ambassador or envoy, but no lower ranking minister, was entitled to spend three of these six days at the royal palace. Fauconberg marvelled at one feature of the Florentine ceremonies. "The Duke was not only so generous as to make me a present (which the other Courts had not done) but absolutely forbid the attendants receiving any gratuity, and was punctually obeyed that not the least officer in the house could be prevailed with to receive one farthing." [11]

The Dutch did not devote as much attention to the niceties of diplomatic protocol as the courts of southern Europe. "There is not any place where the business of Ceremonys is less regulated, than at The Hague; because there is not any one that makes it his business of Application." [12] The Greffier, a municipal officer, made the arrangements for the entry and audience, but the States General did not require or expect a grand show. When William Temple made his entry into The Hague in 1672, he left the town privately at eleven in the morning for Ryswick, travelling with his family and staff only. The Master of the Ceremonies of the States General joined them at Ryswick and treated them to dinner. Temple then travelled into town in his own coach, with his suite in a second coach following after. At a special point in the city devoted to the reception of ambassadors he was met and complimented by two deputies of the States General, one from Holland and one from Gelderland, who rode with him through the streets of The Hague. Temple received another supper the evening of his arrival [13] and two days entertainment at the expense of the States General.

Ceremonies at The Hague, which had few set rules, often differed from those accorded Temple. A diplomat might receive a ceremonial escort of seven provincial representatives, or no one but a clerk of Holland, and many received no entertainment at all.[14]

The ceremonies for the negotiations at Breda in 1667 were much more elaborate. The English ambassadors Holles and Coventry rode incognito out of the town of Breda to a summer house in the Prince of Orange's park. There they waited until M. Valkenhaen, the governor-general of the town, came to wait upon them. George Charnock, the marshal of the ambassadors, arranged the parade in the following order: first eight grooms on horseback followed by eight pages, all in the ambassadors' livery; then four of His Majesty's trumpeters and two gentlemen of the horse; next the knight marshal of the embassy bearing a staff and accompanied by his own footmen in ambassadorial livery. Holles rode next, in his own coach, "exceeding Rich and Royal," accompanied by Coventry, the governor of Breda, several Dutch noblemen, and Nicholas Morice, the secretary to the embassy. Fifty footmen in rich livery accompanied this coach, which was followed by other coaches belonging to the ambassadors carrying several persons of quality. Following these were the governors of all the other towns, nobility and gentry of Holland, three troops of horse, one led by the brother of Arlington's wife, and two thousand foot soldiers. During the whole procession the guns of the town were discharged to contribute to the joyful occasion. The States General allowed £1,800 sterling for the entertainment of Holles and Coventry during their stay in Breda.[15]

At Vienna an ambassador advised the Marshal of the Court when he wished to make his entry. On the appointed day, the ambassador rode out in his own coach to a village near the city to join the Marshal and some imperial ministers in two imperial coaches drawn by six horses. When they met, the Marshal stepped out and invited the ambassador into one of the imperial coaches and his gentlemen into the other. The procession returned to Vienna with the empty coaches of the ambassador bringing up the rear.[16]

The officials who supervised the public entry at Moscow were the Pristasse, high ranking courtiers who gave little thought to the comforts of their guests and who impressed the English as being rude and surly. Carlisle made his entry from Troitza, a town down the river from Moscow, which boasted a fine monastery (which the Russians did not permit him to see). On the date first set aside for the entry, the English assembled at nine in the morning on a cold day in February and waited until dusk for the Russian escort to arrive. Due to neglect by the court officials they did not start their procession until after nightfall, and finding it too dark to proceed in comfort, they postponed the ceremony until the next day when everything was managed properly. Trumpeters and drummers on horseback preceded Carlisle, who rose into the city with the Pristasse on sledges trimmed with bear skins. Carlisle's own sledge was drawn by two white horses, the color most esteemed by the Russians, and it was decorated with blue velvet and silver lace. The dresses of his pages, covered with silver and plumes for the occasion, cost £30 each. Carlisle's son, viscount Morpeth, rode in a glass coach, and his lady rode in her own carriage trimmed with crimson velvet. Two hundred sledges loaded with baggage followed the procession. Russian musicians and *boyars* met the entourage at the city limits and conducted the party to Carlisle's house. The Czar watched the entry secretly from a hiding place in the great wall.[17]

Ceremonies for the public entry into Stockholm did not differ markedly from those in Paris or Madrid. When Carlisle reached Sweden on his way home from Russia, he received a salute of cannon and an escort of principal senators. He rode into the city in one of the royal coaches to a house set apart for the use of ambassadors where he was entertained by the King for the customary three days.[18]

More exotic were the procedures for receiving ambassadors in Constantinople. Here Winchilsea was so impressed with Turkish protocol that he drew up a special report on the customs of the Turkish court. His entry began with a salute from sixty-one guns announcing the beginning of the diplomatic procession. Those participating were the officers of the court, the captain of the janizaries, and a

body of soldiers, English trumpeters, horsemen and merchants, the ambassador's own janizaries, a corps of dragomans, Winchilsea himself with pages, footmen and gentlemen, the ambassador's wife and ladies with four coaches
of their own, and the officers of the ship that carried Winchilsea to the Levant. The parade made a ceremonial stop
at Winchilsea's house at Pera and then went on to the tent
of the Grand Vizier. Here the retinue waited outside while
Winchilsea went in with two of his gentlemen to present
his credentials. Both parties sat during this ceremony; the
Vizier on cushions on the floor, and Winchilsea on a crimson velvet stool. When Winchilsea presented his letters,
the Grand Vizier deposited them in a bag of gold.[19]

Constantinople was the only court where the diplomat
presented his credentials at the entry. In other places this
ceremony was reserved for the first formal audience with
the sovereign. At this interview the proper official intro-
duced the ambassador to the King, and the ambassador
presented his papers, delivered a set speech of rather florid
compliments which had little to do with the purpose of
his mission, and withdrew in short order, leaving the business of his embassy to be initiated at a subsequent meeting.
Etiquette followed the Roman style, which decreed that a
sovereign should receive an ambassador sitting, with his
hat on.[20] After receiving obeisance from the ambassador,
the King stood, uncovered, and at a later point in the meeting replaced his hat, indicating to the ambassador that he
was to do so at the same time. Charles II, who held audiences in the Banquetting House, a section of Whitehall,[21]
tended to ignore these punctilios. "An enemy of formality,
& seldom keeping his hat on, or setting down in these
rooms, He receives them as they find Him, standing, his
hat in his hand, but yet without consequence, for if any

should take it as a respect due to them, or insist for it, they would find He only did it in the way of using his own liberty." [22] Visitors enjoyed the relaxed atmosphere. "He excels all other potentates in humanity and affability," the Venetian resident wrote as he described his audience, "He treated me personally very courteously." [23]

Louis XIV took these ceremonies much more seriously. He received visiting ambassadors in an audience room at the Louvre. When the ambassador entered, he saw the King sitting on an armchair surrounded by a low railing which separated him from the crowds of people constantly in attendance. At the approach of the ambassador and Introductor the crowd separated and the ambassador passed through to the inside of the balustrade on the arm of a Prince of the Blood, one of the few who were allowed to pass this barrier by right of birth. The King stood to remove his hat as he spoke to an ambassador, but uncovered from a sitting position for an envoy or a resident.[24] Louis XIV maintained the same air of formality when he received ambassadors for business. "The circumstances of an English minister in this Court are much different from those of a French one in England," Preston wrote, "for tho' we have access to the King at all times, and may discourse him upon different things, we cannot mention business to him without all the formality of an introducteur and of an audience." And yet he could be brisk. "This Kg doth not desire forrein Ministers sd be too familiar at Ct, but yt when they have busines they shd desire an Audience, then they must stay some time for it, till more be ready for one, & then the Kg will dispatch three or foure in the morning." [25]

The ceremonies in Moscow, held in the Byzantine splendor of the Russian court, were calculated to enhance the majesty of the Czar at the expense of the diplomat. Carlisle and his men had to remove their swords before they entered the throne room, and stand uncovered for the whole audience. Although the Czar rose to respond to Carlisle's speech, he did not uncover.[26]

The formal audiences in Spain and Sweden were much the same as in France.[27] The Elector of Brandenburg liked to hold his audiences at Potsdam, with less formality, after which the diplomat withdrew to Berlin to be entertained at the royal residence for one night.[28] At The Hague, the audience took place in the assembly room of the States General. Henry Sidney came in for his audience escorted by two deputies of the States. He took a great chair set for him opposite the President, who received his credentials and gave the speech of acceptance. When the ceremonies were over, the deputies withdrew to Sidney's house, where he entertained them for dinner.[29]

Whatever the form it took, the audience with the sovereign power marked the formal initiation of the mission. It had the characteristics of a symbolic rite, overriding the behavior of the participants. The Spanish Charles II, who inherited the crown in 1665, when he was four years old, had to endure the ordeal of receiving Sandwich and his numerous cavalcade. "His Majesty seeing so great a multitude, turned to his governess and said: this is too much, in my apartment, I do not want them . . . [he] seemed angry and wished to draw his sword, with a very charming gesture." [30] Louis XIV liked his whole family to participate in the ceremonies of welcoming ambassadors. Denzil Holles, entering into the spirit of the occasion, decided "to harange ye Dolphin, and did it till he cryed, yet at the last he embraced me." [31] The dauphin wept, no doubt, because he was then two years old.

Within the rigidly prescribed ceremonial forms, the representatives of different nations quarrelled, and at times fought, over minute observations of protocol which the seventeenth century regarded as indicators of international prestige. Disputes that seem incomprehensible unless they are understood in this light involved such questions as the order of precedence in procession and seating arrangements, whether a doorway should be opened part way or completely when a diplomat crossed the threshold, and whether a diplomat should extend his hand to the minister of another power in his own home or in a third place. Charles II did not attempt to be a pace-setter in matters of etiquette. Louis XIV assumed this role, for which, by power and personality, he was eminently suited.

The arch-rival of France for marks of honor in diplomatic protocol was Spain.[32] The most celebrated quarrel between the two occurred in London at the entry of Count Nils Nilssohn Brahe, the Swedish ambassador, in 1661, when the Spanish and French ambassadors and their men fought with muskets, swords, and sticks to secure a ranking place in the procession. The Spanish ambassador Batteville disabled all the French carriage horses and triumphed, to the delight of the crowds. "And indeed we do naturally love the Spanish, and hate the French," wrote Samuel Pepys.[33] Charles II ordered John Evelyn to draw up an account of the disturbance and sent a copy to Louis XIV, who forbade any of his ambassadors to yield to Spain at any time in the future. In London and Madrid orders went out that henceforth no coaches of foreign ministers were to take part in any processions except those in which they were immediately concerned, but Louis XIV flaunted the decree by ordering the French ambassador in Madrid to attend the entry of Richard Fanshawe in 1665.

The amount of attention that the interested parties paid to this skirmish in the streets provides a good gauge to national sensitivity in matters of protocol. Louis XIV made sure that Charles II understood clearly that he would yield to no other King. The English ambassador in Paris, St. Albans, sent home in his despatches an extract from Jean Bodin which set out in detail all the claims of France to precedence over Spain at the Council of Trent.[34]

Charles II, in fact, never attempted to dispute the French claims. England made some tentative attempts to secure a place above Spain, but the issue never came to blows. A publication of 1643 had reviewed some of the arguments made in 1600 by the diplomats of Queen Elizabeth against those of Philip III to establish England in a higher rank than Spain. The arguments were ingenious, if unlikely to be accepted by Catholic Europe: England had more Kings and royal Princes who were confessors and martyrs than Spain; the English Queen was inferior to none, acknowledging neither Pope nor Emperor; she was superior to her own clergy, and the King of Spain had no control over apostolic delegates; she was anointed and the King of Spain was not. Sir Leoline Jenkins, in 1668, made another attempt to justify England's superiority to Spain, on the rather tenuous basis that England had sat higher than Spain at the Council of Constance, occupying first place on the left, which was more honorable than the second place on the right, where the Spanish delegates sat.[35]

Another minor skirmish took place in 1668, the first year an English ambassador had been at The Hague for many years. The Privy Council was troubled lest Temple yield precedence to the Prince of Orange. An Order in Council avoided a prolonged dispute by permitting Temple to yield to William as a nephew of Charles II and a grandson of Charles I, but not as Prince of Orange.[36]

The only quarrel over protocol in which English diplomats withstood the desires of Louis XIV involved the order of the coaches at the entry into Paris. Although ready to accept the French monarch as the ranking King in Europe, the English would not agree to take second place after Princes of the Blood in ceremonial processions. Louis XIV decided to insist that Princes of the Blood precede all ambassadors in 1663 in order to humiliate the Spanish, who submitted, but Denzil Holles stalwartly refused. An exchange of letters with Clarendon resulted in the suggestion that Holles omit his entry and proceed directly to his audience. Louis XIV rejected this plan because it deprived him of an opportunity to exhibit his late advantage over Spain, entries being the principal occasions when he could flaunt this victory. "The King here means to incorporate the whole Maison Royale into one body, no other Prince or Potentate to come betweene but to give a precedency to the whole," Holles explained to Arlington. The quarrel lasted five months, both sides holding firm, until they reached a compromise whereby Holles had his entry at Saint-Germain, with the Princes of the Blood conveniently absent. "You will judge, perhaps, better yn I," he wrote to Arlington, "whether I made an Entry or no; it was something like it, & rather one than not, bec. I was treated to two meales, & all the Royall coaches fetched me . . . & yet not alltogether yt Sollemme Entry, yt wd have bene into Paris; but it was well enough, *super totam materiam*." [37]

Both parties considered the contest a draw,[38] and the issue came up again when Ralph Montagu began his mission in 1669. Montagu decided not to yield to the Princes

of the Blood because Holles had not. This time a conference with the French Queen brought a fresh solution.
Montagu made his entry bearing the arms of the English
Queen on his coach, since this made him appear as the
master of the horse of his own Queen and therefore entitled to precede the Princes of the Blood.[39] When it finally
took place, the entry was unequalled in magnificence.
Montagu had seventy-four pages and footmen leading
twelve horses, twenty-four gentlemen on horseback, eighteen English noblemen riding in four coaches each drawn
by eight horses, and another two chariots and six. Louis
XIV allowed Montagu to dispense with a public entry
when he came back to France as ambassador extraordinary
in 1676, but he was determined that this omission should
not become a pattern in the future. He instructed Barillon,
who went to England in 1677, that he had to make a public entry lest a ceremony of prime importance become ex-
tinct through lack of practise. Charles II had his revenge
by ordering Barillon to follow after the coach of the Duke
of York. "This message put the ambassador to his wits
end . . . till he understood his Majesty was firm in the
matter . . . and then he sat down and acquiesced in the
ceremony, which was performed accordingly."[40]

Visits, like entries and audiences, had their own rules.
Protocol required that a minister newly arrived in a city
inform all the other diplomats of his arrival. Then those
of equal or inferior rank paid him the first visit, which he
was expected to return in due course. If the newcomer was
outranked by other ministers already in residence, he had
to pay the first visit to them.[41] Other considerations embel-
lished this simple formula. The "courtesies of the hand
and the door" (extending the right hand to a visitor in
one's own house and accompanying him to the door) were

a point of contention until Charles II decided, by an Order in Council of August 1668, that English ambassadors were not to give the hand in their own houses to envoys of other princes, and that English envoys were not to expect this courtesy from other ambassadors. The King incorporated this point of protocol in instructions to ministers who began their missions after that date.[42] Ambassadors constantly gave the hand in their own houses to other ambassadors without hazard of diminution, but the restriction imposed upon ceremony between ministers of varying rank was enough to impair diplomatic friendships. England's ally, Sweden, had only an envoy at The Hague in 1668, and William Temple could not give him the courtesies he felt were appropriate to facilitate business. He protested the order because it obstructed the success of his mission, but the King held firm because it was French practise and he preferred to follow it.[43]

Diplomats who were mediators at a congress enjoyed a special status that entitled them to greater courtesies than those due their formal grade. At Cologne (1673) the Swedes were mediators between the French and English on one hand and the Dutch on the other. The instructions to the English delegation read: "It is fundamentally agreed between the . . . M. X^n King and us, That the first place shall be in all Occasions given to the Mediators, that is to say, the first Visits upon your Arrivall, even though you should happen to be the *first* upon the place, As also the upper Hand in the Place of the Conference, and in all Ord^{ry} Conversations."[44] At Nimeguen (1676) when the English were mediators in treaty negotiations between France and other belligerents, Williamson anticipated difficulties in getting France to give England the honor of the first visit, and the King and the Foreign Committee decided not to risk creating an incident by offending Louis XIV. The English delegates, Temple, Jenkins, and Berkeley, who had secured an agreement with the French to eliminate all entries, requested special instructions on how to conduct themselves at formal visits and other meetings. The King informed them that they were to "concert with the French" on questions of this kind.[45]

Mediators had the privilege of signing treaties in the most honorable place, the first line in the rank of names on the left. The parties to the treaty then signed two copies. One country signed on the left-hand side on one copy, and the second country signed on the left on the other copy. This process, called the *alternat,* was established between England and France in 1546.[46] An ambassador had to take care that he never signed below the signature of the opposite party. Sandwich committed this blunder in Spain in 1660, and the Privy Council ordered a new draft of the treaty so that Sandwich could sign it properly. These customs easily degenerated into spiteful practises. At the Treaty of Aix in 1668 the French ambassador Colbert scrawled his name across the top of the page so that the Spanish signature could not appear on the same line. "I was weary of so many comeings and goings with messages about these perplexing trifles," Temple said.[47]

Not the least "perplexing trifle" was the ceremonial use of language in diplomacy, involving the questions of language for diplomatic papers, the formal audience, and treaties. A generally accepted rule was that diplomats spoke their own language and used interpreters for ordinary business matters, for very few men, even in the comparatively professional corps of Louis XIV, were skilled enough to negotiate in Latin.[48] England used Latin for drawing up credentials and full powers, but gave instructions to diplomats in English. A copy of the instructions might be drawn up in Latin to be kept among the formal records in London.[49] When the English King corresponded with another head of state, he used Latin with everyone except Louis XIV, who received his letters in French. Charles II permitted ambassadors to address him in any tongue they wished, although he preferred them to use English, French, or Italian, which were the languages he understood. When he could, he answered them in the language they had used.[50]

Louis XIV allowed English diplomats to address him in their own language at formal audiences, if they secured permission to do so ahead of time. Holles chose this procedure, but he had to have one of his men deliver the speech in French when he had finished, and the King spoke French in his response. In Spain, too, a minister needed prior permission to use English at the first audience. The Spanish Queen refused to have an interpreter in her presence, so those diplomats who knew no Spanish omitted a formal call on the Queen. A few English ministers were able to deliver their formal oration in Latin. Carlingford did so at Vienna, and Higgons at Venice. The Dutch accepted French translations of orations delivered by foreign ministers, while the Danes and the Russians received a Latin text of formal speeches.[51] French was the language used to deliver memorials in Sweden, Denmark, and Holland. Southwell delivered his memorials to the Elector of Brandenburg in Latin, but with a French version, to avoid any errors in translation. French and Latin were both used in Russia as well.[52]

Latin was still the most common language for state treaties. Louis XIV declared war and concluded peace in his own tongue, but the rest of Europe clung to older patterns. English treaties concluded bilaterally with the United Provinces, Denmark, Sweden, Brandenburg, Spain, and the Hanse Towns were all in Latin, as was the Triple Alliance of 1667 with the United Provinces and Sweden, although Temple drafted the original version in French. The peace treaty of 1667 between England and the United Provinces was in Latin; between England and France, in French. The sale of Dunkirk (1662), the Treaty of Aix-la-Chapelle (1668), and all the treaties adhered to by Louis XIV at Nimeguen were, of course, in French. Louis XIV allowed the other countries represented at Nimeguen to use Latin for their negotiations, but not the vernacular, which he felt was presumptuous on their part.[53]

A description of diplomatic protocol at the end of the seventeenth century illustrates two general themes: the desire of each sovereign to insist on details of procedure which upheld his national honor, and at the same time the adoption of French forms as standard practise by the diplomats of other countries. Latin had fallen into desuetude as the language of diplomatic conversation, but remained the last vestige of an earlier day in formal documents. French ascendancy is most noticeable in the establishment of precedence and the adoption of French etiquette for entries, audiences, and visits. James II was more mindful of French etiquette than his brother had been. "When he sent over the Lord Churchill to the Court of France with the notice of his brother's death, he ordered him to observe exactly the ceremony and the state with which he was received, that he might treat him, who should be sent over with the compliment in return, in the same manner. And this he observed very punctually."[54]

# VII

Exterritoriality

"The necessity of Embassies makes the Security of Embassadors, by the universal consent of all the Nations of the Earth: and it is this general Consent that constitutes what is called the Law of Nations."
ABRAHAM DE WICQUEFORT, The Embassador and His Functions

Once an ambassador exchanged the safety and familiarity of his own court for the responsibilities of work in a foreign land, practical and legal problems arose from the role that he played in the country of his host. An ambassador might be considered an alien, albeit a friendly one, who was deprived of the protection enjoyed by natural subjects. He might be treated on an equal basis with these subjects, enjoying their privileges but at the same time subject to their King and to their courts. Finally, he might be considered a person apart, outside the criminal and civil laws of his host country, but bound to another code which circumscribed his behavior just as it protected him from the particular hazards of his employment.

Questions of diplomatic status extended to all members of the minister's household. Frequently the ambassador had legal subjects of the host King in his house and in his pay. To whom did these men owe their first allegiance, to their King or to their employer? The ambassador might claim privileges because of his exalted rank, but what of his secretary, his chaplain, or his cook? Beginning in the sixteenth century an increased amount of attention centered on the legal aspects of legations. The spreading institution of resident embassies, the greater complexity of international relations, and a revival of the study of Roman law all contributed to an interest in these legal problems.[1] As cases arose which called for decisions, a considerable amount of legal material developed which attempted to lay down general rules by which the diplomats and the princes they served could guide themselves. Each diplomat and sovereign felt these issues keenly, for on the solution of a case depended the safety of the one, and the national honor of the other.

The international lawyers who formulated the principles governing treatment of diplomatic agents dealt with two broad categories of cases: criminal matters, such as charges of conspiracy, murder, or theft; and civil matters, concerning primarily the question of liability for debts contracted for real and moveable property. The former category, which involved a greater danger to the state, and, potentially, a more severe punishment for the offender, received a greater share of their attention.

The first systematic codification of the law dealing with ambassadors arose from a situation that the English court faced in 1584. It became known that Bernardino de Mendoza, the Spanish ambassador in England, was plotting against the Queen, and the government asked the opinion of Alberico Gentili[2] on what action should be taken against the offender. Gentili explained his views in a lecture in 1584, and then incorporated his ideas in a book, *De legationibus libri tres,* which appeared the following year. Gentili decided that conspiracy by an ambassador did not justify more drastic punishment than dismissal. He argued that if Mendoza had been guilty of more than conspiracy, that is, if he had done overt harm to the sovereign, England would have been justified in putting him to death.[3] The government accepted Gentili's opinion and expelled Mendoza from the country.

In his treatise Gentili did not confine himself to the immediate question of Mendoza's fate. Expounding other aspects of diplomatic immunity, he took the position that an ambassador could not be punished for the crimes of his sovereign, nor could he be held liable for a crime that he committed before he undertook his embassy.[4] Gentili devoted much attention to the immunity of the ambassador's person. The ambassador's rights entitled him to safety even amidst his enemies, so that if war broke out between his sovereign and his host, he would not be treated as an enemy alien, but enjoy unrestricted liberty. The King bore the responsibility of seeing to it that none of his subjects harmed the ambassador. Should one injure a diplomatic agent, international law stipulated that the guilty party be surrendered to the sovereign of the injured ambassador. If the ambassador so desired, the sovereign of the offender might fix the penalty.[5]

Gentili's advisor in the Mendoza case, Jean Hotman,[6] wrote his own book on legal theory, *The Ambassadors,*[7] which he dedicated to William Herbert, earl of Pembroke. Like Gentili, Hotman recommended that the best course of action against an ambassador who offended against the state was appeal to the ambassador's master for his recall. Hotman, however, differed from his colleague in his legal reasoning. Where Gentili would allow the recall as a diplomatic privilege under the law of the nations, Hotman believed that an ambassador lost all his rights under the law of nations for treasonous attempts. Immunity from punishment was to be granted as a gracious act on the part of the sovereign, and on the basis of expediency: "For if besides the perill and inconvenience of a long voyage, to which they expose themselves, they should not be in safetie in the place whereunto they goe, there would never be any which would undertake the hazard thereof." [8] In this sense Hotman's definition of immunity is less broad than Gentili's.

The first international lawyer to advocate unqualified diplomatic immunity was Hugo Grotius.[9] In Book II of *De jure belli ac pacis* Grotius examined the questions of whether an ambassador could be punished for any crime, or only for an infraction of the law of nations, or for no crime. After studying numerous cases, Grotius learned that nations were not in agreement, and that conflicting precedents could be stated for each side of the problem. He ultimately formulated his own conclusion that the law of nations teaches that affairs of embassies are sacred and ambassadors therefore inviolable, so that diplomatic agents ought never to be brought to trial in the country where they work. Grotius felt that the advantage of security to ambassadors outweighed any advantage accruing from the right to punish them, and he framed his famous theory that "ambassadors were held to be outside the limits of the country to which they were accredited. For this reason they are not subject to the municipal law of the state wherein which they are living." [10] The legal fiction that

Grotius invented, that an ambassador is ever *quasi extra territorium,* is the basis of the modern concept that an ambassador's privileges derive legally from his diplomatic character.[11]

Although Grotius defined an ambassador as an inviolable person, he admitted that princes have certain rights to protect themselves and their subjects from excessive dangers to the state. These exceptions to the general diplomatic immunity included the right to detain and question an ambassador who was suspect and the right to refuse to admit a public minister who was undesirable. Private persons might use force against an ambassador in clear cases of self-defense, but no one might claim retaliation against an ambassador for the misdeeds of his sovereign.[12]

A contemporary of Grotius, Richard Zouche,[13] was one of Gentili's successors as Regius Professor of Civil Law at Oxford. Zouche's book, *Iuris et iudicii fecialis,* published in 1650, is considered the first attempt to formulate laws solely from precedents and earned its author the title of the first positivist among the international lawyers. Zouche came to many of the same conclusions as his Dutch colleague, advocating complete immunity for ambassadors in criminal proceedings.[14]

Two continental scholars, Samuel Pufendorf[15] and Samuel Rachel,[16] who published works on international law during this period, were alike in having diplomatic experience and holding professorships in international law in Germany. Neither of these men went so far as Grotius, or the English school as expounded by Zouche, in describing the extent of diplomatic immunities. Pufendorf placed all obligations between states under natural law (*ius naturale*) and denied that the law of nations (*ius gentium*) could provide any protection apart from what the natural law afforded: "Envoys, by the mere law of nature, are inviolable, provided that they play the part of envoys and not of spies, even among enemies, so long as they form no hostile designs against him to whom they have been sent."[17] The ambassador was free from the jurisdiction of the prince to whom he was sent only while he was conducting the business of his embassy. The prince could deny all other privileges provided he was willing to see his own envoys treated the same way.[18]

Rachel refuted Pufendorf's assertion that the inviolability of ambassadors derived from the law of nature. He explained that a primary injunction of the law of nature was to hurt no one, but an ambassador often came from an enemy power bearing a declaration of war. Rachel therefore attributed the inviolability of ambassadors to the deliberate choice of the law of nations. "If an Ambassador be only safe from unjust violence, there is nothing important or distinctive in the immunity. Now the functions of Ambassadors are not only useful but often of the highest necessity; and so nations seemed to have wished them to have a greater and distinctive immunity."[19]

The theorists also found it necessary to define their position on the liability of diplomatic agents in civil suits. In these cases Gentili placed the ambassador wholly under the jurisdiction of the national courts. A diplomat had to be bound by every contract he concluded during the course of his embassy, or no one would consent to make a contract with him and ultimately he would be barred from commerce. He had to give the owner a guarantee against possible injury to any property he rented. Any civil magistrate could force a minister of inferior rank to pay damages in a civil suit, but a royal judgment was necessary in cases involving ambassadors.[20] Hotman, too, believed that an ambassador had to obey local law in civil suits, although in no case might his moveable goods be attached.[21]

Grotius was the first to advocate complete immunity in civil as well as criminal suits. He disagreed with Gentili and Hotman that this freedom from financial obligations would prevent anyone from concluding a contract with an ambassador. Grotius maintained that a pledge of good faith ought to suffice in all contracts, and pointed out that kings were not subject to compulsion, and yet they had creditors. Grotius' departure from his predecessors in advocating immunity in civil suits reflected the changing nature of diplomatic missions. Medieval theory stipulated that an ambassador was immune from debts incurred before his embassy but liable for those incurred during the course of his mission. The development of resident embassies brought with it the constant problem of arrears in ambassadors' salaries, and this rule became unworkable in situations where ambassadors were forced to live for long periods of time in one place without a steady income.[22] Grotius therefore deduced from his concept of exterritoriality that a state could do no more to collect a debt from an ambassador than if it were seeking to collect payment from someone in another country.

The question of the extension of immunity to members of the diplomatic household brought a variety of opinions. Gentili, whose statement on this problem lacks clarity, preferred to make a distinction between those who assisted the ambassador in his duties and those who performed menial chores, but, he continued, if the goods of the household were immune from seizure, the people must be too. Hotman restricted the immunity of the ambassador's suite to those who were of the same nationality as the ambassador, and he limited the sanctuary provided by the ambassador's house to those who had never broken the law of the country where they resided.[23]

Grotius extended the full rights of the ambassador in every kind of case to all the members of his suite. A sovereign might request a diplomat to surrender one of his suite, but if he declined, the only recourse was to request the offender's recall. The asylum that the ambassador's house afforded depended on the concession of the prince who ruled the territory, for that right did not belong to the law of nations.[24]

Rachel's discussion of the immunity enjoyed by the diplomatic suite distinguished between the business staff and the domestics. The privileges of the ambassador's person extended only to those actually employed as instruments of the embassage: "According as their rank and degree vary, so will it be easier or harder for a violation of their immunity to occur."[25]

Zouche believed that the house of an ambassador provided a degree of protection to its inhabitants, but this privilege did not extend to sheltering those guilty of treason or heinous crimes.[26] He asserted these convictions again in 1654 when he served as one of the commissioners in the trial of Dom Pantaleo de Sá e Menses, brother of the Portuguese ambassador in England, who was convicted and executed for a murder committed in London. Sá was not an official member of the ambassador's suite and claimed his immunity on the grounds that he was the intended appointee of his King to fill the post in England after his brother's recall. The ambassador demanded that Sá be returned to him on the grounds that it was against

the law of nations for one of his family to be tried. The
opinion of the court was that since Sá had offended against
the law of nations he could not invoke the aid of this
law.[27] Chief Justice Sir Matthew Hale [28] later upheld the
decision, stating that no member of an ambassador's suite
could claim immunity from prosecution in the capital
offenses of murder, rape, and theft, in which cases they
had to be tried according to regular English procedure.[29]

The foregoing summary shows that the international
lawyers agreed solely in the basic premise that the person
of an ambassador was inviolable only when he was acting
in such a way that he could not possibly be giving any
offense under international law. The lawyers disagreed on
questions ranging from how to treat an ambassador who
in some way threatened national security, to how to insure that he meet his financial obligations before he returned home. The mass of theory provided conflicting
opinions on the degree to which the ambassador's immunity extended to activities unconnected with his mission and to the members of his staff.

Because legal advice was contradictory, practise tended
to follow expediency. Governments gave many decisions
in favor of immunity because they realized that they could
derive reciprocal benefits from good treatment of their
respective envoys. As Hale expressed it, "The business of
embassadors is rather managed according to the rules of
prudence, and mutual concerns and temperaments among
princes, where possibly a severe construction of an embassador's actions, and prosecutions of them by one prince
may at another time return to the like disadvantage of his
own agents and embassadors; and therefore they are rather
temperaments measured by political prudence and indul-

gence, than according to the strict rules of reason and justice." [30]

Adair has shown that the trend in international law was for case law, or the positivist view, to grow in relative importance to abstract theorizing.[31] The writings of Abraham de Wicquefort are an example of legal theory modified by events in the writer's own career. After serving as the resident of the Elector of Brandenburg-Prussia at Paris from 1626 to 1658, Wicquefort came to the Hague where he became concurrently secretary-interpreter for the States General and the resident of the Duke of Brunswick-Lüneburg-Celle. In 1676 Wicquefort's enemies accused him of communicating state secrets, which had been given to him to translate, to the English at the Congress of Nimeguen. The Dutch imprisoned him on the grounds that he was, even in his diplomatic capacity, still a Dutch national and in the paid service of the States. From his prison cell, Wicquefort wrote *Mémoires touchant les ambassadeurs et les ministres publics,* addressed to the congress, to prove that in his quality of resident he was exempt from the jurisdiction of the Dutch tribunals.[32] None of the delegates spoke up for Wicquefort, and he languished in prison until he escaped to Celle in 1679.

Wicquefort wrote again on the duties and privileges of ambassadors during the period of his asylum in Germany. His second treatise, *L'Ambassadeur et ses fonctions,*[33] modified some of his earlier views in favor of an even broader immunity for diplomatic agents. In *Mémoires touchant les ambassadeurs* he argued that an ambassador who transgressed against the law of the state ought to be expelled rather than imprisoned, but he urged this course of action as an exhibition of honor on the part of the prince and as a voluntary decision of practical wisdom. The later work advocated strongly that banishment was the only legitimate punishment.[34]

Turning to an examination of other legal disputes in which English interests were involved, it becomes apparent that in the latter part of the seventeenth century the inviolability of the ambassador's person was called into question only in situations of dual allegiance, that is, a conflict between loyalty to native country and loyalty to the head of state employing the ambassador. At the Congress of Cologne, the Emperor arrested his subject, Prince William of Fürstenberg, who was the agent of the Elector of Cologne. Fürstenberg was taken into custody because he was acting in the French interests, and his duties as an imperial vassal were considered to override his special status as a diplomatic agent. Although Wicquefort's case did not disturb the delegates at Nimeguen, the arrest of Fürstenberg created a temporary stir. Jenkins protested the matter as a violation of the law of nations, and the representatives of England, France, and Sweden threatened to dissolve the conference until Fürstenberg was released. Charles II took the position that the conference could proceed provided that Fürstenberg's acquittal be the first matter on the agenda. Ultimately the matter was dropped and the negotiations went on, although the prince did not regain his liberty until 1679.[35]

When the position of an ambassador was not complicated by dual allegiance, he was less vulnerable. England allowed immunity from arrest even in serious offenses. In 1677 Bernardo de Salinas, envoy from the Spanish Netherlands, and Manuel de Fonseca, the Spanish consul in London, intrigued to isolate England from France by deterring England from giving material aid to the French

King's armies. They approached members of Parliament
in an attempt to stir up dissension against Charles II's
francophile policy. At the same time they bribed Scottish
recruits bound for the Continent for information on English activity in raising troops in Scotland to fight for
France. Their actions came to the attention of Williamson
and John Maitland, duke of Lauderdale, who brought the
matter to the King and the Foreign Committee. Further
investigations proved that Salinas had written a letter
accusing the Privy Council of treason, and that he had
given out the story that the King had called some members of Parliament "a company of rogues." [36] The government charged the two men with sedition, libel, and
slander. Williamson ordered a study of treatment afforded
ambassadors who were guilty of interfering with the in-
ternal affairs of the country to which they were accredited,[37] and the government decided to expel the offenders.
With their dismissal went a demand to the King of Spain
that they be punished for their crimes.

Godolphin in Madrid took up the argument in a series
of memorials to the Spanish court. In the heated debate
that ensued both sides seized on the Mendoza case as a
precedent. "The wisest interpreters of the Lawes between
Nations . . . [pronounce] it most agreeable to equity that
a Prince should provide for his own safety by expelling
out of his domains whomsoever shall endeavour to raise
Sedition among his People & trouble the good order of his
Government," ran Godolphin's memorial to the Spanish
court. The rebuttal stated that a sovereign expelling an
ambassador had no right to insist on punishment. Invariably the sovereign of the evicted minister takes offense
and refuses to do what the first prince asks. Was not
Philip II so angry at the expulsion of Mendoza, the Span-

iards asked, that he threatened war and refused to admit the English ambassador to his presence? [38]

According to the international lawyers, a diplomat's status should protect him from all danger during hostilities between his own country and the place of his assignment. Evidence shows that the responsibility of the sovereign power to insure the safety of diplomatic persons within the realm during times of difficulty developed more slowly than ordinary diplomatic freedom from arrest. The court of Holland had, since 1647, prescribed the death penalty for anyone who attacked an ambassador's dwelling, but in 1665 Downing had to fortify his house at the Hague with earthworks and stones and post armed guards outside night and day. In 1667 Temple and his family chose to travel incognito from Brussels to Amsterdam, although he had a diplomatic passport that should have guaranteed his safety.[39]

Servants of the embassies were a constant source of trouble. Sensing themselves shielded from strict punishment for their offenses, they participated in numerous street brawls and other misdemeanors. Some authorities made attempts to lessen the opportunity for trouble to occur. A Spanish edict of 1665 forbade domestics to go about with the scabbards of their swords open. In Vienna, ambassadors could not walk in the city accompanied by armed servants. The delegates at Nimeguen agreed on a like prohibition, stipulating also that an affront by the servant of one ambassador against the servant of another was to be settled by private agreement between the interested parties. In Russia, servants could not possess arms or walk the streets late at night.[40]

In spite of these precautions, criminal offenses were frequent. Treatment of the embassy staff varied considerably

from country to country. In Madrid, some members of
Fanshawe's household suffered imprisonment for attacking an alcalde (justice of the peace).[41] In Russia, the Czar
threatened to send Carlisle and his retinue to Siberia for
refusing to accept a parting gift. A few years later, a capital offense went unpunished. One of John Hebdon's servants confessed in writing to the murder of the son of the
court interpreter. The Czar, who evidently felt this loss
less keenly than Carlisle's rejection of his generosity, wrote
personally to Charles II to say that he had decided to dis-
miss the culprit rather than put him to death.[42]

A few examples show that French justice dealt leniently
with members of the diplomatic suite, even when the
offender was himself a Frenchman. A native arrested for
smuggling established himself as a bona fide member of
Montagu's embassy and obtained his liberty. Employment
in an embassy could shield a man from punishment for an
offense committed before he joined the diplomatic suite.
A footman, guilty of robbing the Prince de Condé and
escaping with the money to England, returned to Paris
in Montagu's employ. He was taken into custody for his
earlier offense but released by order of the King when it
became known that he belonged to the diplomatic household.[43]

Anglo-Dutch enmity led to several instances of disputed
diplomatic status. In 1659 Downing engaged a Dutch advocate to serve resident English merchants in their legal
affairs. The lawyer soon suffered arrest for attacking a
man with a knife. Downing's protests were compromised
by two conditions. First, the advocate had made an agreement prior to accepting the commission that he would
make no claim for special prerogatives. Second, Downing's credentials came from the Protector, at whose death

Downing himself ceased to enjoy diplomatic status until he received official papers from the new government. Undaunted by these legal obstacles, Downing continued his argument until he received new credentials from the English Council of State. He spoke with such ardor that the Estate of Holland overrode the Court of Justice and ordered the prisoner released. Wicquefort thought the decision unjust: "Certainly Sas could not be considered a Publique Minister . . . for he had no letters of credit for the States . . . neither was he a Domestique, to which may also be added, that since Consuls are not recognized for Publique Ministers, Advocats, who are not in the least of a Publique function, are not to be admitted into the number of those which the Right of Nations comprehends under the name of *Legatus*."[44]

Downing was on firmer legal ground in his next encounter with the Dutch government. In the summer of 1665 the government of Holland ordered the arrest of his secretary, Nicholas Oudart,[45] as a retaliation against the arrest, in England, of the secretary to the Dutch ambassador Michiel van Gogh. Within a few weeks they had arrested another of Downing's secretaries and summoned a third employee to appear for questioning. The Dutch refused to release any of the English staff, and both sides used the affair as an excuse to terminate diplomatic relations on the eve of the Second Dutch War.[46]

The immunity of the diplomatic dwelling was not stipulated as a definite obligation under the law of nations, and countries varied in the degree to which they extended the privilege. England had no clearly defined policy.[47] Embassies to the United Provinces did not enjoy the right of asylum. A decree of the States General in 1663 established that "the houses or lodgings of residents in the Hague are by no means immune from search, whenever one seeks, lawfully and rightfully in behalf of the authorities or in the interests of justice, to arrest someone there." [48] Holland invoked this decree in action against Downing, although Downing's case rested on the argument that the Dutch had entered to take not a common criminal but one who was a member of the diplomatic suite and *ipso facto* immune from arrest anywhere. The Venetian Republic was as strict as the Dutch in forbidding diplomats to shelter outlaws in their dwellings. Dodington had to surrender a man wanted for smuggling, although he did not do so until the Venetian ambassador in London reported the offense to Arlington. [49]

Since the time of Philip II, embassies in Madrid had gained notoriety for sheltering criminals. Here the right to grant asylum was left to the discretion of the ambassador himself. Sandwich granted sanctuary to some Italian political refugees at the request of the Spanish minister, Ramiro Felipe de Guzmán, duke of Medina de las Torres. The authorities extended the immunity of the residence to the precinct of the dwelling, which allowed Fanshawe to rescue a man who lived within the barrier surrounding his house. [50]

Goodricke learned during his mission that while the Spanish were lenient, they would not tolerate flagrant abuse of this privilege. After the police arrested a woman in a public shop adjoining his house, he allowed two of his servants to rescue her. When officers came to the embassy to chastise him for the behavior of his servants, he shut them up in a room for offending his barrio, as the immunity of the dwelling was called. Goodricke then erected a gibbet before his door and announced publicly that he intended to hang the King of Spain's offenders. The King sent guards to pull down the gibbet and an alcalde to rescue the imprisoned officials. The Council of State, deciding that Goodricke's behavior warranted his expulsion, arrested him in his home and ordered him from the city. Both parties to the dispute were compromised. Goodricke, an envoy, had claimed the barrio, which was rarely invoked by any minister but an ambassador. Spain had failed to allow the usual courtesy of waiting until Goodricke was recalled through regular diplomatic channels. In order to reduce the chance for similar trouble to occur in the future, Spain restricted the right of asylum in 1684 to the threshold of the house itself.[51]

Just as the right of sanctuary varied from land to land, the privileges afforded the embassy chapels fluctuated with the political situation of the country in question. Wicquefort alone of the theorists discussed the *droit du chapel* of the embassy. Taking the careful position that the privileges of the chapel ought not to extend beyond the diplomatic household, he gave sovereigns the right to forbid their own subjects and all other foreigners within their borders to attend religious services at embassies.[52] Issues, when they arose, never disputed the right of a foreign minister to employ a chaplain of his own land and faith. They concerned the extension of chapel privileges to people not connected with the embassy, and the right to use a chaplain who was a subject of the host king.

In England, where hearing Mass was a legal offense, the government had to define its attitude toward the large number of recusants who made use of the embassy chapels to circumvent the penal code. The King in Council set forth the official position in a series of proclamations which made it clear that embassy chapels could not provide a haven for distressed Roman Catholics. In practise, however, during those periods that were marked by an absence of heated anti-Catholic sentiment, crowds of recusants attended the chapels without any interference. The Venetian chapel served the Catholics in London without hindrance from 1660 to 1663.[53] The French ambassador Comenges wrote that numerous people of quality attended Mass at his chapel and that on some Sundays in 1663 he had from sixty to eighty communicants.[54] Freedom to attend the embassy chapels was noted again in 1669, and a Venetian *relazione* of 1671 described the chapels of Venice, France, and Spain as exercising "in all freedom and drawing an admirable concourse." [55] This latitude toward the recusants did not survive the increased hostility toward Catholics in the period following the Second Dutch War. Then the government moved in two ways to insure that the English subjects' obligation to the secular authority could not be evaded by the exterritorial rights of the embassy chapels. First, to compel obedience to the standing prohibitions concerning attendance at embassy chapels, a new order stipulated that "fit persons be appointed to watch at the passages to the houses of ambassadors . . . at the time of the mass or other Romish service and without entering the said house or invading their freedom and privileges, observe what persons go thither, but on their return they are to apprehend them and bring them before the Board or bring the names of such as they cannot apprehend." [56]

Next, the government tackled the problem of native priests who served as chaplains in the embassies. Proclamations of 1663 and 1666 had ordered expulsion of all priests and Jesuits except those who were attending foreign ambassadors. Under these conditions, an English priest could still claim immunity from prosecution on the grounds that the exterritoriality of the chapel excluded him from laws affecting priests living in England, and that as an embassy chaplain, he was serving the diplomatic household only. A case that came to trial in 1674 might have settled these claims, but it was managed in such a way that the issues were blurred. The authorities arrested Alexander Burnet, a Scot, one of the chaplains of the Venetian embassy. Although the King was willing to release Burnet if he would leave the country immediately, anti-Catholic sentiment was so strong that the leading ministers decided it was unwise to offend the populace by cancelling the trial. Other ambassadors held their tongues lest their own chaplains be investigated. The Venetian ambassador himself decided not to claim Burnet as a member of his suite. His motives, as they appear in his letters, were somewhat confused. On the one hand he felt that England had already witnessed too many examples of gross violation of ambassadorial privilege, and on the other, that a claim of diplomatic immunity would not be accepted by the courts in any event.[57]

Burnet decided not to stake his defense on claims of diplomatic immunity, with the understanding that if he did not invoke his special status, the King would grant him his freedom. He stood trial, was condemned to death for treason, obtained the royal pardon, and made his way safely to Calais. The case points to the conclusion that Burnet was surer of his life by counting on the King's clemency than by gambling that his embassy employment would be accepted as a valid defense by the courts.[58]

The assumption that Burnet was wise not to plead that the embassy shielded him from the law is borne out by the action that the government took next. A letter went out to all foreign ministers in London forbidding them to employ English, Scottish, or Irish priests, and warning them that they must not allow sermons in English in their chapels.[59] During the hysteria of the Popish Plot ambassadors had to submit to the Secretaries of State the names and addresses of all their priests, and had to limit their number to four.[60]

The position of the Catholic chapel in England found its immediate counterpart in the English embassy chapel in Paris after Louis XIV revoked the Edict of Nantes in 1685. Immediately thereafter, the King informed Trumbull, through the Introductor of Ambassadors, that he would not permit French Protestants serving the embassy to enjoy the freedom from arrest due other employees in the household. Trumbull's chaplain could not venture out of the embassy without fear of arrest. James II reminded Trumbull that during the time of the Plot, English lawyers held that no minister could protect an embassy servant who was also a subject of the King from full rigors of the laws of England. The logic of the situation did not escape Louis XIV, who refused to heed any of Trumbull's protests.[61]

Limitations on the right of free speech did not arouse as much passion as the disputes over the embassy chapels. Restrictions on offensive statements were, apparently, accepted as a legitimate exercise of the sovereign authority without regard to diplomatic status. At Breda the Dutch arrested the chaplain of Holles for speaking prejudicially against the States General. They released him later so as not to hinder an amicable settlement of the peace, rather than on general principles of immunity. Fauconberg's secretary, Dodington, took offense at disparaging remarks about England made by a French official whom they met on their way to Venice. Dodington responded by calling the government of France tyrannical. Colbert soon learned of the matter and used his influence to have Dodington dismissed. The secretary's relative, Sir Richard Temple, persuaded Arlington to have Dodington reinstated, and the case was soon forgotten.[62]

Ambassadors in Russia suffered from general restrictions on communications. Strictly enforced regulations kept Carlisle from having an interview with anyone without official permission. When Wyche came to Moscow to negotiate for trading privileges in Russia in which Swedish interests were also concerned, the Czar forbade him to speak to the Swedes.[63]

Diplomatic immunity from civil jurisdiction took two forms: freedom from litigation and arrest for nonpayment of debt, and exemption from taxes and customs duties owed by others in the country. In this period only the United Provinces granted statutory immunity from arrest for debt to all members of the diplomatic household.[64] Although many ministers complained of going into debt while they were abroad, only those in Germany mentioned the possibility of arrest. Curtius came personally to London in 1662 to petition the King for money, declaring that he would not be safe from action by his creditors if he returned to Germany without giving them satisfaction. Wyche wrote from Hamburg that it was imperative for him to get funds immediately: "Unless the Lords Com^rs of the Treasury be pleased to . . . pay my Arrears due, I shall not be able to stir hence without being arrested and ruyned, which will be dishonourable to his Matie and destructive to mee his Minister." [65]

In Constantinople a diplomat was not immune from civil action in the courts. Finch became involved in a commercial dispute with the Pasha, who claimed that the ambassador was personally liable for the destruction of Turkish property by Englishmen in the area. Finch stood trial, and would have been imprisoned, had not the company saved him by recalling him to London.[66] The rights that English ambassadors did enjoy in the Levant were enumerated in a special treaty between the King and the Sultan, and stand as the only example of guaranteeing diplomatic privilege on this basis. The capitulations, drawn up originally by Rycaut for Winchilsea, and renewed in identical form for Finch in 1675, granted the house of the ambassador freedom from search and the employees of the embassy freedom from punishment for anything they said. The treaty also allowed the ambassador to keep wine in his house for the use of his own family, and exempted his servants, even if Turks, from the obligation to pay taxes.[67]

Various countries granted ambassadors exemption from paying customs duties as a privilege, but not as a definite obligation due their status. In England an Order in Council of 1668 established that all foreign ambassadors were to receive freedom from paying toll dues on imported wine, thus formalizing a privilege that most of them had been enjoying as "an extraordinary grace" since the beginning of the reign. Before 1668, however, ambassadors needed an express warrant from the King to bring in wines duty free, and they held the privilege tenuously. In 1662 Clarendon was able to deprive the Venetian resident of his free allowance as a favor to d'Estrades, who had taken offense at the Venetian for shielding a Spanish sympathizer in his embassy.[68] No statute or royal order defined the rule on duties due on other goods brought in by foreign ministers. The Acts which established and regulated the customs duties did not grant any specific exemptions,[69] but the rules were so complicated that one observer described them in 1670 as "both difficult in the discovery and doubtful in the interpretation." A well-established rule required ambassadors to pay a fee of 2s. 8d. per head on each servant that they brought into the country, but not until the tenure of Williamson was there any attempt to formulate a clear policy on the goods brought in by foreign ministers. Williamson ruled that an ambassador arriving for the first time could bring in goods duty free from any country, but after taking up residence in England he was not to be permitted to import forbidden French commodities, even if they were intended for his own use. English ambassadors returning from abroad were not allowed to bring in any prohibited goods, not even used clothing.[70]

By 1663 France did not extend the courtesy of exemption from customs duties to any entering diplomats, although she had granted it to the ambassadors from Cromwell to the French court. Holles was denied an allowance for duty-free wine, and his claim for the courtesy on the grounds that England granted it to the French ambassador in England brought no result. Louis XIV decided that he gained more for himself by denying what was, in fact, a privilege and not a right. He gave Charles II his consent to withdraw the privilege from French ambassadors in London, but French policy did not alter the English tradition of granting the exemption to French ambassadors arriving after Holles' complaint.[71] Montagu resented this inequity and had his secretary write to Williamson to request that ambassador Colbert be denied the privileges of the customs. "What they alledge on this side is that it would bee a president for other Ambrs of the Princes who would demand the like, & that in England ye custome is to give it to all foreigne Ministers, but these arguments are *mal fondée* when it was ever given to ye English

Ambrs before Lord Holles's time." Arguments for deciding the question on a reciprocal basis did not sway Louis XIV, who continued to exact all fees from entering diplomats, even on used household goods. Trumbull had to pay duty on his tapestry hangings because the customs on tapestries had been ceded, by a special grant, to a private individual.[72]

France was consistent in levying import duties on all ambassador's goods, but the United Provinces, resentful of the Navigation Acts, singled out the English for payments not required from other ministers. Ambassadors from Spain and Sweden brought in their wines and beer duty free, but Downing had to pay excise on his spirits, a burden that he bore bitterly for he paid the rate levied on the meanest subjects in Holland rather than the comparatively light fee paid by the nobles of the province. Nor was this his only point of contention: "Whereas by the eighteenth Article of the Treaty of Breda it is expressly stipulated and provided that all the Subjects & inhabitants of either side exercising their trade in each others Countrys & dominions shall not be obliged to pay hereafter any more customes imposts or other dutyes than according to that proposition which other nations trading in the said places do pay: It cannot but seeme very strange & is directly against the good meaning of the said Articles, that the Amb^r of the King his Master should be worse treated & pay more imposts & dutyes in this Country than other Ambassadors, yea than the Inferior ministers of other Princes."[73]

The cases discussed indicate that nations divided the privileges afforded to resident foreign ministers into two broad groups: those to which they were entitled by the general consensus of the law of nations, and those which were granted as an extraordinary courtesy and could be withdrawn at the sovereign's pleasure. In the former category were immunity from arrest in criminal cases and the freedom to maintain a chapel. The right of sanctuary of the dwelling, freedom of speech, and immunity from jurisdiction in civil affairs belong in the second group. Moreover, even in those areas recognized as exterritorial rights, the degree to which the diplomats could enjoy these rights reflected the political tensions of the moment. The outbreak of war or a change in government policy towards religious minorities affected the status of the diplomatic suite, in spite of the best opinions of the international lawyers. On the other hand, practise sometimes gave immunity to criminal offenders beyond what the theorists recommended, when these cases were considered too unimportant to risk an international incident in periods of good will. In the second group the diplomats themselves used their best efforts to have privileges accorded on a reciprocal and equitable basis, but in areas where the sovereign reserved the right to decide these matters they did so in their own best interest rather than by rules of impartiality.

 VIII

Writings

The diplomatic memoir, skillfully executed, has much to offer the reader, combining as it does the general interest of a travel book and the special knowledge gained from participation in state affairs. Happily, Sir William Temple, first among the ambassadors for his skills as a negotiator, was also a man of literary skill, whose diplomatic experiences in the Netherlands inspired two of his many writings. Temple was the only Restoration diplomat of first rank to publish, but several others applied themselves to the task of enriching their countrymen's knowledge of other lands. Temple had the use of an earlier work on the United Provinces by Dr. William Aglionby, who joined

Temple's staff as secretary in 1678.[1] Of all the members of the corps, the most prolific was Sir Paul Rycaut, who spent several years in the Levant as secretary to Winchilsea and consul at Smyrna before his promotion to resident at Hamburg in 1689. Other works on Turkey came from the pen of ambassador Harvey's chaplain, Thomas Smith, a scholar of Oriental lore, who accepted the post in the embassy as a means of furthering his own studies.[2] Sir George Etherege was in Constantinople with Smith as Rycaut's successor in the post of English secretary, and later became minister at Ratisbon. He was able to combine his diplomatic activity with a literary career, for he is remembered for some popular dramatic works produced between 1664 and 1676, and wrote two minor works on Turkey and Germany, the former unpublished.

The compatibility of authorship and embassy service is also illustrated in the works of other men. Guy Miège, Carlisle's secretary in Russia, Sweden, and Denmark, wrote a memoir of the triple mission, and later, an independent description of Denmark, as well as miscellaneous writings on geography and French and English grammar. The Reverend John Robinson's service as chaplain and resident in Sweden from 1678 to 1687 provided the material for his account of that nation which appeared in 1694. A complete catalogue of publishing diplomats must include the names of Thomas Higgons, who served in Venice and wrote of the republic's war over Candia, and Sir Bernard Gascoigne, who described conditions in the Empire at the time of his assignment. The energetic Rycaut and Smith, together with Wyche, Southwell, Talbot, Curtius, and Dodington, found time to furnish the Royal Society with the fruits of scientific investigations conducted while they were abroad.

A literary form that was already popular by the seventeenth century was the "Relation" or "Present State" of a given nation. The prototype of these books was the Venetian *relazione,* which characteristically included some recent history, a sketch of the contemporary government and leading personalities, national characteristics, resources, industries, and defenses. The "Present State" was usually impersonal, in that it omitted reference to the diplomat's conduct of his mission, but it was a good vehicle for political propaganda as well as simple description. Its flexibility permitted the author to emphasize what he found admirable or blameworthy, and he could easily make clear his own views on the best English policy towards that nation.

The first example of a book of this kind by a Restoration diplomat was Rycaut's *Present State of the Ottoman Empire.* The earliest edition of this work is usually given as 1668,[3] but it first appeared, in two separate editions, before the Great Fire of London (September, 1666). Pepys first mentioned the book in October 1666, when he called it "a new booke, set out by one Rycault . . . of the policy and customs of the Turks, which is, it seems, much cried up." The following March he began to bargain for it with a bookseller at the Temple: "It is strange how 'Rycaut's Discourse of Turky': which before the fire I was asked but 8s. for, there being all but twenty-two or thereabouts burned, I did now offer 20s., and he demands 50s., and I think I shall give it to him, though it be only as a monument of the fire."[4] Pepys finally paid 55s. in April 1667 for the better edition. "Whereas it was sold plain before the late fire for 8s., and bound and coloured as this is for 20s.; for I have bought it finely bound and truly coloured, all the figures, of which there was but six books done so, whereof the King and Duke of York, and Duke of Monmouth, and Lord Arlington, had four. The fifth was sold, and I have bought the sixth." [5] The copy that Pepys purchased, dated 1667, and bearing an inscription on the flyleaf that reflects what he said in the *Diary,* is now in the Pepys Library, and is probably the oldest extant edition of the work.[6]

Rycaut was essentially an open-minded observer. He told Arlington, to whom he dedicated the book, "This [account] . . . may be termed barbarous, as all things are, which are differenced from us by diversity of Manners and Custom, and are not dressed in the mode and fashion of our times and Countries; for we contract prejudice from ignorance and want of familiarity." [7] An easy impartiality characterizes the whole. Rycaut did not admire the absolutism and severity of the Sultan's rule, but he thought that it was necessary to keep a naturally mutinous people, dispersed in a large empire, bound together in a forceful state. He attributed much of the success of the government to the painstaking education of young slaves, whom the Turks abducted from Christian families and brought up in the Seraglio. Here a strict regimen of academic studies and athletic exercises prepared them to assume the principal offices of state. Rycaut knew, however, that the traditional strength of the empire was being undermined by corrupt military discipline, sloth, and inordinate ambition in the army officers.

An extensive discussion of the Mohammedan religion is remarkable primarily for its condemnation of the Turks for failing to keep their early promise of freedom for all religions. Rycaut was to emphasize the necessity of religious tolerance among his own people in his next book, *The Present State of the Greek and Armenian Churches,*

Anno Christie, 1678,[8] written at the King's command after
he returned from Smyrna. He pleaded for the rejection of
sectarian fanaticism and for a reunion of all Christian peoples in one faith. "How can we expect or hope for the
conversion of Turks or Heathens, when they shall be
affrighted at the Church Gate, by some Opposites . . .
and meet almost as many Anathemas as when they remain
Infidels?"

Rycaut later returned to his first subject in *The History
of the Turkish Empire from the Year 1623 to the Year
1677,*[9] which he undertook as a continuation of *The Generall Historie of the Turkes from the First Beginning of
That Nation,* by Richard Knolles.[10] The *History* is tedi-
ous and repetitious, and is noteworthy only as an illustration of Rycaut's industry. He explained that his book was
the product of eighteen years' labor in Turkey,[11] and that
he was attempting to emulate the French and Italian ministers, very few of whom left their posts without carrying
with them memoirs, journals, or historical observations of
their times. England had been defective in this regard, he
thought, and except for the writings of Knolles one could
scarcely find five sheets of paper written by his countrymen on Turkish history.

Of all his works,[12] Rycaut's *Present State* drew most contemporary notice. Sir Dudley North, a treasurer of the
Turkey Company, thought the book superficial and, in
some cases, erroneous. He drew up a list of specific mis-
statements, which, together with several papers of his own
on Turkish curiosities, was unfortunately lost.[13] Lady
Mary Wortley Montagu, who lived in Turkey from 1716
to 1718 while her husband was ambassador there, thought
that Rycaut erred in describing the *muterin,* a Moslem
sect, as atheists rather than deists.[14] More favorable com-

ments came from Jean Louis Dusson, marquis de Bonnac, French ambassador at the Porte from 1716 to 1724, who studied it in its French translation before he left for his assignment. Bonnac lamented the absence of any work by a French author giving the information that a European ambassador to Constantinople needed.[15]

In England, too, the *Present State* enjoyed considerable popularity, going through six editions by 1686. No doubt its rich collection of anecdotes about people at the Turkish court contributed to its success. One of these, a story of a cook who rose to be Grand Vizier, was used by the writers of *Cato's Letters* to teach that the common people are basically worthy.[16] More character sketches of Sultan Mohamed IV, the Grand Vizier Ahmed Kiuprili, and lesser officials can be found in Winchilsea's "Memorandums Touching the Turkish Empire" (1669) [17] and in a short unpublished relation of the Sultan's household written by Etherege to Williamson in 1670.[18]

Curiously, Thomas Smith made no mention of Rycaut's writings in his *Remarks upon the Manners, Religion, and Government of the Turks Together with a Survey of the Seven Churches of Asia and a Brief Description of Constantinople*.[19] Smith was less sympathetic than Rycaut, and quicker to condemn. He castigated the Turks for their contempt of learning, described their religion as gross and brutish, and derided the education of the young slaves, in which Rycaut had found much merit, because it hardened the pupils against all impressions of pity and good nature.[20] Higgons, too, in *The History of Issuf Bassa, Captain General of the Ottoman Army at the Invasion of Candia*,[21] emphasized the ferocity and purposeless cruelty of the Turkish regime. Higgons, however, was not able to conceal a degree of grudging admiration for Issuf Bassa, born of a poor family in Dalmatia and educated in the Seraglio, who rose by intelligence and initiative to become the leader of the Turkish forces against the Venetians.[22] The second section of Smith's account is similar in tone to Rycaut's *Present State of the Greek and Armenian Churches,* in that both expressed a desire for a rapprochement between the churches of East and West. Smith pointed to the pitiful condition of the Greek churches in Ottoman lands as a lesson to all Christians that security lies not in military might but in mutual agreement and the virtues of the religious life.

A comparison of Turkish and Russian absolutism strikes a note of overt antagonism to Russia in Guy Miège's *Relation of Three Embassies from His Sacred Majestie Charles II to the Great Duke of Muscovie, the King of Sweden, and the King of Denmark,* published in 1669. The book differs from the classic "Present State" in that the greater part is a narrative of the English embassy itself. The hostility that Miège felt towards the country of the Czar was, no doubt, kindled by Carlisle's failure to achieve the political ends of his mission, the absence of comforts for the travellers, and the rude treatment all received from Russian officialdom. "Civility and Complacence among them is so rare," Miège complained, "Tis no wonder if they be very Sparing of it before Strangers." He made it clear, however, that the tyranny of the Czar was his principal target. He believed that monarchy was the most advantageous form of government, but that the despotic absolutism of Alexis I was no better than the rule of the Grand Seigneur of Turkey. The people submitted weakly to the caprices of their rulers, who maintained discipline by forbidding their subjects to travel out of the country lest they learn the sweetness of liberty; by marrying no foreign princesses; and by keeping their people ignorant of other languages and cultures. "And indeed Experience doth teach us this truth, that Seditions and Revolutions have not been anywhere so frequent as in Commonwealths, where Learning was commonly in great esteem, and even where it triumphed most."[23]

On the return leg of their journey the company paid brief visits to Stockholm and Copenhagen. Miège was impressed with the civility and courtesy of the Danes, rather like the Germans', in his opinion, only more solid and of better invention. After the formal audience he met King Frederick III's young brother, Prince George, who struck him as a handsome youth of great hopes.[24] The Prince's fortunes ultimately caused Miège to write again. In 1683 George's marriage to England's Princess Anne caused some agitation in England, for many attributed the alliance to the designs of Louis XIV and feared that George might become a Catholic.[25] Miège then used the notes he took during his travels with Carlisle to produce *The Present State of Denmark*.[26] He declared his purpose was to honor the union by encouraging amity between the two kingdoms.[27]

In *The Present State of Denmark* Miège showed signs of being a political turncoat, for he was able to describe an absolute state in flattering terms when the occasion demanded. Intent on pointing out the community of interests between the English and the Danes, he stressed their racial brotherhood and the similarity of the liturgy in the Lutheran and Anglican churches. He mentioned that Christianity was firmly established in Denmark during the reign of Pope Adrian IV, an Englishman. On the revolution of 1660, by which the Danes exchanged a limited, elective monarchy for an absolute, hereditary one, he had no disparaging remarks. Rather, he took pains to show that the city of Copenhagen retained its privilege to vote in all deliberations concerning the public good, and that the freeholding peasants were exempt from oppressive contributions. A laconic statement on royal power admitted simply that the King "imposes Taxes upon his Subjects as occasion requires." [28]

An entirely different emphasis is found in *An Account of Denmark as It Was in the Year 1692,* published anonymously by Robert Molesworth, later viscount Molesworth, in 1694, shortly after his service as envoy extraordinary in Copenhagen was terminated by a quarrel with the Danish court. Molesworth described the loss of ancient Danish liberties as an object lesson to the English. "The Commons have since experienced that the little Finger of an Absolute Prince can be heavier than the Loins of many Nobles." [29]

Molesworth's *Account* immediately became the center of political dispute. Its attendant popularity caused the publisher to bring out Robinson's *Account of Sueden* in the same year, which he did without the consent of the author, currently employed as resident at Stockholm.[30] Robinson was able to discuss the Swedish government dispassionately. He had, as a churchman, an interest in Swedish religious life, for which he had qualified praise: The clergy were but moderately learned, but the people were devout and loyal to Church and King. He noted that a free education was available to every Swedish child, but "Such as are not design'd for Studies, do very seldom go, nor waste their Time in other needless Improvements." Robinson's most damaging remarks concerned Swedish foreign policy, for he declared that although Sweden had all the land she could easily defend, she was likely to seize more territory in the near future.[31]

Interest in foreign policy during the period focussed on the relations between England and the United Provinces. Two books on the Netherlands appeared before and after the Third Dutch War. During these years popular feeling towards England's traditional enemy changed from one of commercial hostility directed against a rival sea power to one of sympathy for another Protestant nation ranged against French aggression. Aglionby's *Present State of the United Provinces of the Low Countries*[32] is an early illustration of the metamorphosis in attitude.

Aglionby admired the Dutch constitution. Its principal virtues, to him, were an equitable distribution of financial obligations, which required the rich province of Holland to provide more support for the state than the poorer districts, and a nice balance of political power, which gave equal rights in deliberation and authority to all the members of the confederation. He was optimistic about the future of the United Provinces. If one considered the reasons for the founding of the state, it seemed unlikely that it would ever be dissolved, for they had come together to preserve their liberties, prized by all mankind but particularly by the peoples of the North.[33] Since neighboring states had nothing to fear from Dutch independence, why should others molest the Provinces? Moreover, the government established in 1579 had changed only the sovereignty of the state, and had not altered the ancient laws and customs of the people. This prevented the formation of a disaffected element in the state, often present when governments underwent radical changes.

Aglionby found many virtues in the Dutch people. He thought no other country had produced so many learned men. "It is not only the Professors, but even the citizens that are curious in Libraries." [34] In painting they were the masters of the world. One could travel freely through the whole country without fear of being robbed, and all peoples worshipped in peace.

A work of greater political interest is William Temple's "Observations upon the United Provinces of the Netherlands," completed in 1672 and first published in February or March of the next year. [35] Temple knew Aglionby's book, and may have used it as a general model for his "Observations," but the two accounts differ in arrangement and factual detail. Temple said that his immediate inspiration was the account of the travels of the Grand Duke of Tuscany, Cosimo III, in England, which Temple read in manuscript form in 1669. [36] Temple credited the Dutch with two virtues which contributed to the success of their government: a good business sense, and simplicity and modesty in the manner of living of their magistrates. "No great riches are seen to enter by public payments into private purses . . . but all public monies are applied to the safety, greatness, or honour of the State, and the Magistrates themselves bear an equal share in all the burdens they impose." [37]

Temple was interested in the influence of geography and climate upon economic factors and national characteristics. The country's position on the coast and its access to the Rhine and the Meuse made the people turn naturally to trade, while the moist cold air, Temple believed, was responsible for Dutch cleanliness and the neatness of their houses. Aglionby had earlier remarked that their homes were so immaculate strangers made a scruple of spitting in them. Temple admired the industry of the people, yet thought long disuse of arms and parsimony in eating meat had sapped their native courage.[38]

Writing after Parliament had forced Charles II to withdraw the Declaration of Indulgence, Temple did not hesitate to argue for liberty of conscience. Since all religions agreed in teaching moral virtues, and had as their aim the future happiness of mankind, was it not foolish, he asked, to destroy peace and order for the propagation of one creed? He would have conditions as they were in Holland: "Men live together, like citizens of the world, associated by the common ties of humanity, and by the bonds of peace, under the impartial protection of impartial laws. . . . The power of religion among them, where it is, lies in every man's heart." [39] In conclusion Temple offered his analysis of the reasons for the military disasters that befell the Dutch in 1672. The chief causes were the diversion of the genius of the nation to trade rather than war, a false sense of security dating from the Treaty of Münster, and, especially, the disloyalty of the burgomasters of Holland to the Prince of Orange.

Homer E. Woodbridge argues convincingly that Temple's purpose in writing the "Observations" was to propagandize for a resumption of friendly relations between England and the United Provinces.[40] The same intent, veiled by ostensible impartiality, characterizes Temple's "A Survey of the Constitutions and Interests of the Empire, Sweden, Denmark, Spain, Holland, France, and Flanders; with Their Relations to England in the Year 1671, and Then Given to One of His Majesty's Principal Secretaries of State, upon the ending of My Embassie at the Hague." [41] Here Temple laid before Trevor three alternatives in English foreign policy: to preserve the Triple Alliance; to encourage France to invade Holland with the assurance of English neutrality; or to join with France against the Dutch. Temple pointed out the dangers of each course, without making a positive suggestion, but succeeded in conveying the thought that the maintenance of the Alliance would bring the greatest gain with the least risk.

About the same time that Temple published his "Observations," Bernard Gascoigne sent to the King from Vienna "A Description of Germany," [42] a short essay limited to the political institutions of the Empire. Gascoigne criticized the imperial government for its lack of sovereign authority, and the system of taxation because it enriched powerful persons at public expense. The most interesting passages are those in which he described, evidently as an eye witness, the seating plan at the Imperial Diet, and the rules of procedure for speaking and voting.

The same impatience with the imperial structure can be found in *The Present State of Germany,* published anonymously in London in 1690. This author analysed the causes of the inadequacies of the German constitution, "An irregular Body, and like some mis-shapen Monster, if it be measured by the Common Rules of Politics and Civil Prudence." He concluded that the laziness of the Emperors, the ambitions of the secular princes, and the turbulence of the German clergy were to blame. The "Person of Quality" who composed *The Present State of Germany* mentioned that he had spent some years in Ratisbon.[43] Possibly he was George Etherege, who was resident there from 1685 to 1689. Etherege's only acknowledged piece from Germany was a pamphlet, *An Account of the Re-*

joycing at the Diet,[44] which describes the celebrations at the birth of the English prince in 1688.

Because of the interest that the Royal Society took in scientific intelligence from other lands, the diplomats produced a variety of short works on technology, geography, and other disciplines. Apparently the Society regularly furnished departing ministers with a formal questionnaire to stimulate research while they were abroad. Thus, for example, the records of the Society indicate for 5 December 1666: "It being intimated, that . . . Mr. Rycaut was to go to Turkey, and offered his service to the Society in inquiring into philosophical matters, it was ordered, that the Secretaries should get ready, both a copy of the general inquiries of all countries, and of such particular ones, as were proper for Turkey." Rycaut limited his reply, submitted in 1668, to topics other than those covered in his book: an investigation of the causes of the high incidence of plague in the Levant, a clinical report on the Turkish habit of taking opium, and information on vegetation, winds, and tides in the area.[45]

Sir John Finch, a Fellow of the Society and a physician, prepared a report of like nature, "Remarques in Turkey (1675–1681)," [46] which contains observations on animal life and farming in Egypt, and information on the endemic diseases of the eye in that part of the world. Finch never published these notes, nor did he present them at a meeting.

The Society heard about Turkey again when Thomas Smith presented "Historical Observations Relating to Constantinople," [47] condensed from his book. Later the Society published Smith's "A Journal of a Voyage from England to Constantinople, Made in the Year 1668," [48] a log of temperatures, winds, and ocean conditions on the trip.

More practical information came from the Iberian peninsula. Sandwich sent a letter to the Society describing a new plough, invented by an Italian, which had been used to great benefit in Spain and the Indies.[49] Working with his secretary, Godolphin, he produced a translation of a work by Álvaro Alonso Barba, *The First Book of the Art of Metals*.[50] Peter Wyche was an active servant of the Society's interests. At their request he engaged as correspondents an English Jesuit who was professor of mathematics at Lisbon, and an "ingenious merchant" who offered to make astronomical observations if the Society would provide him with a quadrant. He furnished the Fellows with a Portuguese manuscript on the River Nile and the Red Sea, originally procured by Robert Southwell from a man in Lisbon who had spent some time in Ethiopia. The Society granted Wyche a license to print a translation of the manuscript, which he published in 1669 as *A Short Relation of the River Nile,* dedicated to Arlington because it was the secretary's duty to obtain intelligence from the South.[51]

Wyche presented an original report to the Society after he returned from Russia in 1670. His "Observations on Muscovy" are concerned with the effect of the Russian climate on agriculture, animal husbandry, and certain metals. He noted some experiments that had been done on frozen calves and sheep, and that human blood could be frozen successfully.[52]

Short scientific notices from other diplomats can be listed briefly. Robert Southwell completed the arrangements begun by Wyche by depositing an astronomical quadrant with some mathematicians at Lisbon. Later he contributed a Portuguese manuscript on medicine, which the Society ordered to be translated into Latin and English.[53] Gilbert Talbot obtained some data on minerals from a scientist in Sweden, published as "A Description of Swedish Stone, Which Affords Sulphur, Vitriol, Allum, and Minium." [54] Talbot offered information on how the minerals could be extracted from the rock, with the suggestion that a similar stone in England yielded the same products, except for minium. Wilhelm Curtius supplied the Society with a sample of mastic, or gum resin, which he found in Franconia. Curtius believed that the substance was produced from the secretions of fir trees by colonies of ants.[55] John Dodington wrote "An Account of the Aponensian Baths near Padua," [56] which explained the primitive procedures used by the natives to extract salt flakes from the hot mineral springs.

The writings of the diplomats are of unequal value from the point of view of literary worth and scholarship. Among them, only Temple's and Rycaut's writings enjoyed much popularity in England and on the Continent. The wide public these men received shows that they were able to infuse their collection of data with a message that was meaningful to their readers. Both authors were making positive appeals for tolerance. Rycaut wanted men to overlook the despotism of the Sultan's regime and focus attention on what was admirable in Turkish territories: a successful administration of an unwieldy empire, a fine system of education for future state officials, and a learned body of jurists and religious teachers. Temple expressed what was rapidly becoming a popular wave of sympathy for the United Provinces. He accomplished this by pointing out the Dutch virtues of representative government, simple living habits, and toleration for Protestants. Miège, who tried to convince the English of the benefits Denmark enjoyed under an absolute regime, never attained the popularity of Molesworth, who later denounced their tyranny.

The polemical intent of the various books was apparently independent of any official encouragement. None but Rycaut's account of the Eastern Churches was written at the specific request of the crown, although Miège's book on Denmark must have had the royal blessing. The most political of the writings, Temple's "Observations," appeared at a time when its sentiments ran counter to the King's pro-French tendencies in foreign policy. The absence of any original works from France and Spain, countries which received a relatively high number of English diplomats, is in contrast to the several writings on the nations of the East and Russia, which taken together account for almost half the total. Perhaps these books catered to a taste for the exotic; more probably they were welcomed as a means of supplying information about those countries where the ordinary diplomatic channels of intelligence were lacking.

Conclusions

The accession of Charles II wrought no immediate changes in English foreign policy, nor did it affect, in any appreciable way, the structure of the diplomatic corps. Outwardly, to be sure, the corps had changed. The distribution of diplomatic posts in the years following 1660 went to the faithful in the King's cause, or to their sons, while most of the appointees of the Protector were retired from the service. But not even the changes in personnel were complete. Downing remained in Holland because the King could find no one better to serve him in that post, and with the passing of time Charles II showed that he was not adverse to using old Cromwellians who were capable and could claim experience in diplomatic affairs. In 1689 William III was to follow a similar policy, electing to employ in his corps a few men who had proved their worth and reliability by service under his predecessor.

The capitals which saw the representatives of Charles II and James II were the same ones, with minor differences, to which Cromwell's diplomats had travelled. Brandenburg-Prussia and other minor German courts did not receive English diplomats during the Protectorate. England sent occasional representatives to these places from 1660 to 1688, but the Restoration did not increase the number of permanent overseas embassies. Cromwell had maintained a resident in Switzerland, but that state did not receive another English minister until 1689.

One result of the Revolution of 1689 was to increase the number of diplomatic posts and to upgrade the status of others of long standing, although this transformation was not realized until after Louis XIV gave official recognition to the new English government at Ryswick in 1697.[1] The expansion of the corps did not affect the embassies at Copenhagen, Berlin, Stockholm, Paris, The Hague, and Constantinople.

In one sphere of diplomatic activities, the obtaining of foreign intelligence, the Restoration seems to have marked a regression. Secretary of State John Thurloe earned a reputation for keeping his government well informed through efficient intelligence operations both at home and abroad. In 1668 a parliamentary investigation of the responsibility for a naval disaster in the Second Dutch War led Colonel John Birch to contrast the faulty information available to England at that time with conditions under Cromwell, who "carried the secrets of all the Princes of Europe at his girdle."[2] Secretary Morice defended himself with the claim that the Protector had allowed greater sums for buying information than the royal Secretaries received.[3]

The diplomatic correspondence from 1660 to 1688 shows that the ministers, as well as the secretaries, suffered from inadequate funds allotted for gathering news. Nowhere was this more apparent than in the embassy at Constantinople, where the Turkey Company and the crown declined to assume financial responsibility for purchasing political news. Handwritten newsletters sent abroad from Whitehall were supposed to keep the ministers informed of developments at home and in other courts, but complaints from every quarter showed that the system never operated perfectly. Ministers usually had to buy intelligence with their own funds, and await reimbursement from the Treasury, which limited the amount they were able to supply. In the eighteenth century the allowances to the Secretaries for secret service increased, and substantial sums were available to ministers for espionage, but D. B. Horn doubts that the quality of foreign intelligence was high, particularly after the collapse of Jacobitism, when the Secretaries began to neglect this sphere of their activities.[4]

The Restoration was an important period in the history of the English diplomatic service in two fields: the establishment of fixed salaries, and an increase in the professionalism of the members of the embassy staffs. In the years immediately following the accession of Charles II the government had not yet decided upon a standard pay scale for its ministers. Most salaries were determined on an individual basis, with precedents established by the late King as a general guide. After 1668 remuneration was settled by grade and place, bringing to an end the extravagantly high amounts formerly paid to ambassadors in Spain, and the inordinately low wages allotted to ministers in Germany. Nor at the beginning of the century did countries have a standard scheme for paying their diplomats,[5] and the efforts to regularize financial procedure under Charles II can be regarded as a positive attempt to ameliorate the lot of the English ministers of the second order, who made up a majority of the corps.

The economic position of the ministers of middle rank does not seem to have altered appreciably. Salaries had been growing steadily higher during the last hundred years,[6] but, with the passing of time, expenses had increased proportionately, and certainly salaries were no more promptly paid. The pay scales in force under Charles II and James II remained essentially the same in the ensuing century, without increases to offset a general rise in the cost of living; the salary paid to the ambassador to Constantinople declined after 1689. Not until the reign of George III did the government begin to award pensions to men who had a long record of active service in the corps.[7]

Under the later Stuarts the accepted method of rewarding a diplomat for service overseas was political preferment at home. Terms of service were usually short, since men accepted posts more with the hopes of spearing a political plum than with the idea of devoting themselves to a career in the corps. The method worked fairly well for those who had connections at court, and a high number of leading statesmen had a record of embassy service during their youths.

A greater degree of professionalism characterized the embassy staffs. Two significant developments distinguished the period. On important missions—delegations charged with negotiating peace, marriage alliances, and treaties—the crown appointed and paid an official secretary, who assisted in the duties of correspondence, gathering intelligence, and keeping the embassy files. Generally the secretaries had more embassy experience than the ambassadors, for they were selected from the men who had spent some years as private clerks serving individual ministers. The career of Thomas Chudleigh, official secretary to five legations between 1672 and 1679, is the best example of the emerging civil servant on the embassy staff. Another pattern is visible in those embassies where the government did not provide the head of mission with secretarial help. In these instances, notably in France, Holland, and Turkey, successive ministers engaged the private staff of their predecessors, thus assuring a continuity of trained men at the post. These practises bear comparison to those of the turn of the century, when a state-appointed secretary accompanied only special missions headed by more than one full ambassador, and the rest of the clerical staff travelled to and from the place of the assignment as part of the minister's personal household, in the same manner as his personal servants.[8]

The appointment of secretaries as *chargés d'affaires* during the intervals between the departure and arrival of successive diplomats was not yet general practise, but occurred occasionally at Paris, Rome, Venice, and the Hague. An official secretary did not become a regular member of every mission until late in the eighteenth century, when the government adopted the custom of naming certain staff members ministers plenipotentiary, to make sure that a qualified official would always be on hand to discharge business whenever the head of mission was absent from his post.[9]

Certain procedures affecting the English diplomatic corps reflected the political realities of the European scene. The ascendancy of Louis XIV changed traditional patterns of diplomatic etiquette, involving a hard-fought dispute with Spain for precedence and a gradual adoption of French forms for entries, audiences, and visits by the diplomats of other sovereigns. Charles II, whose attitude toward the punctilios of diplomatic protocol tended to be casual, nevertheless resisted his cousin's attempts to place the French Princes of the Blood in a more honorable place at state occasions than the English ambassador in Paris. The general pattern, however, was to accept the dictates of Louis XIV, and James II was scrupulous in observing the newer forms of etiquette.

Hostilities between nations had the effect of lessening diplomatic immunity, although legal scholars of all countries agreed that this should not be so. Some diplomats endured personal insecurity in hostile countries; others suffered restrictions in the employment of native co-religionists, a disability shared by Roman Catholic ambassadors in England at the time of the Popish Plot and the English ambassador in France after 1685. Some disputes about privilege were contrived as an excuse to terminate diplomatic relations: Downing was not above employing these tactics in 1665.

When a minister returned from his assignment, the King expected him to present an informative report on the latest conditions in the country he had visited. In the majority of cases the diplomat discharged this obligation by rendering an oral summary to the Foreign Committee. In certain cases, however, the men used their notes to produce "Relations" of their travels. These books, modelled on the Venetian *relazione,* have a polemical interest apart from the factual information they contain. Rycaut asked for a more tolerant attitude toward Turkish institutions and the Christian churches of the East. Smith, writing on the same topics, limited his sympathy to the Greek churches, while condemning Turkish political and religious practises. Aglionby and Temple argued for friendlier relations with Holland, England's traditional enemy, and Miège, in the face of popular hostility to the marriage of Princess Anne and Prince George of Denmark, pleaded for a closer friendship with the Danish crown.

While practise lagged behind theory in the selection of ambassadors and in their legal protection abroad, the late seventeenth century was a period when men thought seriously about the status of the diplomatic corps of their nations. A close look at the English corps at the time of the Restoration shows a system that worked imperfectly. It also shows that improvements in the machinery of diplomacy occurred, albeit slowly and at an uneven pace.

Appendix I:
Illustrative Documents

I. DIPLOMATIC PAPERS

[Few complete sets of official papers for the diplomats of the late seventeenth century are extant. The following are the documents which Sir Robert Southwell took with him in 1680 on his mission to Frederick William, Elector of Brandenburg-Prussia. (P.R.O. S.P. 105/49.)]

Credentials

Carolus Secundus Dei Gratia magnae Britanniae Franciae et Hiberniae Rex, fidei defensor &. Serenissimo Principi Frederico Wilhelmo marchioni Brandenburgensi, Sacri Romani Imperii Archicamerario et Principi Electori Magdeburgi, Prussiae, Suliae, Cliviae, Monitum, Stetini, Pomeraniae, Cassubiorum, Vandalorumqu^e nec non in Silesia Crosniae et Carnoviae Duci, Burgravio Norinbergensi, Principi Halberstadii, mindae et caminae, Comiti marcae et Ravensbergi, D^{no} in Ravenstein Lunenburgh et Butan, fratri Cognato et Affini et Amico nostro charissimo Salutem. Ser^{me} Princeps frater, Cognate Affinis et Amice Charissime quandoquidem ad Celsitudinem vestram Electoratem mittendum duximus Nobilem nobis dilectum et fidelem Robertum Southwell Equitem Auratum tamquam ablegatum nostrum Extraordinarium ut Ipsi quaedam quae ad communem utriusq^e nostri et populorum nostrorum Salutem conservandam adeoq^e ad Universalem Europe quitem praesenti rerum state multum conducere poterint, proponat. Cel^{nem} V^{ram} Electoralem Integram adhibere fidem, ni vis omnibus qua homine nostro expositurus sit, et praesentim ubi Cel^{nem} vestram Electoralem de sincera nostra versus ipsam amicitia (quam strictioribus adhuc nexibus adaugere cupimus) et propensissimo nostro animo ad omnia quae Celsitudinis vestrae Electoralis commodo promovere ullo modo possint certiorem fecerit. Quod superest Celsitudinem Vestram Electoratem summa Numinis tutela ex anima committimus. Dabantur in Palatio nostra de Whitehall 27 Die Februarii Anno D^{ni} 1679/ 80 Regnique nostri 32.

Celsitudinis Vestrae

Bonus frater et Consanguineus

Carolus R.

Pass

Charles R.

Charles the Second by the grace of God King of England Scotland France and Ireland Defender of the Faith &. To all our Admiralls Vice Admiralls Captains Commanders Governors, Majors Sheriffs Justices of the Peace Constables Customers Comptrollers Searchers and all others whom it may concern Greeting. These are to will and Require you to furnish and suffer the bearer our Truly and Well beloved Sr Robert Southwell Kn^t whom wee have appointed our Envoy Extraordinary to the Elector of Brandenburg with Charles Edmund Pooly, and Francis Rogers, Gent. and with seven Servants and with his Eqipage Goods and Necessaryes freely and without any molestation to Embark in any Port of this our Kingdome, and thence to pass into Holland and so to return again. Given at Whitehall the 20th day of Feb. 1679/80 in the 32nd Year of our Reigne.

By his Maties Command

Sunderland

Instructions

Instructions for our Trusty and Wellbeloved Sir Robert Southwell Knt whom wee have appointed our Envoy Extraordinary to the Elector of Brandenburg. Given at our Court at Whitehall the 28th day of Feb. 1679/80 in the Two and Thirtieth year of our Reign.

Charles R.

Taking into our Consideration the present state of the affairs of Christendom and particularly what has just lately at the Hague in the Matter of the Alliance proposed by

France to the States General, and being also desirous to
constitute what may lye in us to the preservation of the
Peace and Quiet of Europe Wee did some weeks ago write
to the King of Denmark and Elector of Brandenburg to
desire them not to engage themselves in any Alliances till
such time as common measures might be taken by us
joyntly with them for the natural safetye and Defense. In
order whereunto wee have Instructed the Lord Bodmyn
(who goes to reside on our part at the Court of Denmark)
to propose to that King, the Entering into a Defensive
Alliance with us; and intending to make the same pro-
posal of the Elector of Brandenburg Wee have thought fit
out of the good opinion and Experience wee have of your
prudence and Discretion to make choice of and nominate
you to go to the said Elector in quality of our Envoy
Extraordinary.

2. You shall accordingly upon receipt of these our Dis-
patches forthwith pass to the Hague and there address
yourself to our most Dear Nephew the Prince of Orange
and communicate to him these our Instructions together
with the Project wee have ordered to be put into your
hands of a Treaty with the said Elector upon which you
shall in our Name desire his opinion; and if you find any
Material Objection made by him as to any part of it, you
shall forthwith represent the same to us, and stay in Holland till you have received our Directions upon the same
if the Prince be likewise of that mind. You shall likewise
impart so much of this matter to the Pensioner as our said
most Dear Nephew shall advise. If you find no cause to
expect any further orders from us upon what the Prince
shall say unto you you shall proceed with what convenient
speed may be to the Place where you shall hear the said

Elector of Brandenburg to be, and being arrived there you shall ask an audience and in it acquaint him what the great Value wee have for his Person and Friendship hath induced us in pursuance of what wee lately did write to him, to send you to propose the Entering with him into a Defensive Alliance and a Treaty of Friendship, adding that you are empowered by us to negotiate and conclude the same you desire his Highness would appoint you Commisioners sufficiently authorized to treat with.

3. In case it should happen that the Elector should insist to have a like Article as was in the Treaty of 1661 inserted in this (that this Treaty being only Defensive shall in no way derogate from these Agreements and Treatys whereby either of the Parts stand already engaged to others, whether the Emperor or the Kings of States) you shall represent to him that the like Article would in effect take of the Force of the whole Treaty but that if his Highness be content it should be explained and restrained to any Obligations he has entered into with the Emperor and the Empire, as a Prince thereof, Wee will agree to it in which case the Article must be worded accordingly and not left at large as it was in the old Treaty.

4. You are not only to entertain a good Correspondance with the Minister from the States General whom you shall find in the Elector's Court but likewise to communicate with him from time to time about this Affair; the Dutch Ambassador here having assured us, his Masters will give their said Minister orders to do the same to you and also Powers to conclude a like Defensive Treaty between them and the Elector as is now proposed by us in case there be not one already subsisting, which the Prince of Orange

will at your Passage by the Hague be best able to instruct and inform you in.

5. Whereas wee did by order in Council bearing Date the 26th of August 1668 direct our Ambassadors not to give the Hand in their own house to Envoyes in pursuance of what is practised by the Ambassadors of other Princes, and do not therefore think it reasonable our Envoyes should be treated Differently from the Treatment wee have ordered our Ambassadors to give to the Envoyes of other Princes You are to govern yourself accordingly and are not to insist to have the Hand from any Ambassador who may happen to be in that Court during your stay there in his own house.

6. You shall protect and Countenance on all occasions our Subjects trading to any of the Dominions of the Elector or who may have any suites or pretensions depending there procuring for them good and speedy Justice and all the favour you are able. Yet for our Honour and your own you must not engage yourself in every Complaint which may raise Clamour without a Justifiable cause of legall Proofs but only such as may deserve the Interposition of our Name for our Subjects Rights.

7. You shall make it of Care to inform yourself of all Matters and affaires relating to that Princes Gouvernement and his Principall Ministers, so as to be able at your return to give a perfect account in writing thereof.

8. You shall from time to time observe and follow such further Directions and Instructions as you shall receive from one of our Principall Secretaryes of State with whom

you shall likewise constantly Correspond, and by his hand give us frequent account of all Occurences which may be of Consequence, and may Concern our Interest and Affairs.

C.R.

Full Powers

Carolus Secundus Dei Gratia Magnae Britanniae Franciae et Hiberniae Rex. Fidei Defensor &. Omnibus et singulis ad quos praesentes litterae pervenerint Salutem. Cum nihil nobis Antiquius sit quae ut amicitiam eam, qua Nobis cum serenissimo Principe Domino Frederico Wilhelmo Marchione Brandenburgense Sacri Romani Imperii Archi-camerario et Principe Electore & est. Fratre Cognato affine et amico nostro charissimo intercedit, integre semper colamus, cunq^e in finem Nobilem nobis dilectum et fidelum Robertum Southwell Equitem Auratum, ad dictum Principem Electorem ablegandum duximus, ut de tractatu Amicitiae et archioris foederis ad communem utriusque Nostri subditorumq^e invicem nostrorum, Salutem conservandam contra quamcunq^e vim et injuriam quae nobis hinc inde inferri contigerit, cum ipso agat et conveniat. Sciatis quod nos fide Industria et in rebus Transigendis Experientia praefati Roberti Southwell ablegati Nostri Extraordinarii plurimum confisi, eundem constituimus fecimus et ordinavimus et per praesentes manu nostra signatas, constituimus, facimus et ordinamus Nostrum verum verbum et Indubitatum Commissarium et Procuratorem. Dantes eidem et concedentes omnem et omnimodam facultatem Potestatem Authoritatemq^e nec non mandatum Generale Pariter ac Speciale pro nobis et nostro nomine cum praedicto Serenissimo Principe Electore ejusve Commissariis et Procuratoribus sufficientem ad hoc potestatem habentibus super omnia et Singula quae ad ejusmodi Tractatum Amicitiae archioris foederis ad Communem utriusq^e nostri Subditorumq^e invicem nostrorum Salutem conservandam contra quamcunq^e vim et Injuriam quae nobis hinc inde inferri contigerit, in eundem pertinebunt, conveniendi, Tractandi, consuetendi, et concludendi; Quaeq^e ita conclusa erunt et conventa nobis nomine Subsignandi mutoq^e extradendi recipricendiq^e reliquaq^e omnia facti necessarie Praestandi perficiendiq^e tam amplis modo et forma, ac Nosmet ipsi si interessimus facere et praestare possemus. Spondentes, et in verbo Regis promittentes, Nos quamq^e a dicto nostro Commissario vi Praesentium concludi contigerit, rata ea omnia grata et accepta omni meliori modo habituros, neq^e passuros unquam, ut in toto vel in parte a quopiam violentur aut contraveniantur. In quorum omnium majorem fidem et Robur Magnum nostrum Angliae Sigillum apponi Iussimus. Quae Dabantur in Palatio nostro de Whitehall 27 Die Februarii anno domino 1679/80 Regnique nostri Tricesimo Secundo.

Carolus R.

II. REPRESENTATIVE CIPHERS

Numbers assigned for proper names
(B.M. Add. MSS. 23,898, f. 1).
e.g.   9 = England
24 = Whitehall
44 = Duke of Monmouth
53 = Protestants

Cryptograms with number substitutions
(Add. MSS. 23,898, f. 8).

A	B	C	D	E
21	24	26	28	30
22	25	27	29	13
23				32

Numbers assigned to combinations of letters
(B.M. Add. MSS. 32,253, f. 62).

e.g.   62 = Ta   93 = ca
       63 = Ts   94 = ce
       65 = ti   95 = co

Diagram cipher (B.M. Add. MSS. 23,898, f. 12).

ABC	DEF	GHI
3	7	2
KLM	NOP	QRS
5	9	4
TUW	XYZ	000
6	8	1

A number with no mark—1st letter of the square.

A number with an asterisk (*) above—2nd letter of the square.

A number with an asterisk after, or any other sign over—3rd letter of the square.

The insertion of the figure 1 serves to further the disguise.

III. HOUSEHOLD AND EXPENSES OF THE DUKE OF RICHMOND ON HIS EMBASSY TO DENMARK IN 1672

"A List of the Servants Belonging to his Grace the Duke of Richmond and Lenox" *(B.M. Add. MSS. 21,951, f. 9).*

		Yearly support £
Mr. Boneman Secretary		50
Mr. Witham Gen. Horse[mn]		50
Roger Payne Steward		50
Mr. Wiggfield		20
Mr. Littleton Gent. washer		20
Mr. Dirkson Chirurgeon		30
Ambrose barber		12
taylor		20
Mr. Hoard Clerke		12
Rich. Rade Caterer		20
Dickenson Cook		30
Tho. Cozens Butler		10
Richard Groome of the Chamber		08
Mr. Waldron		
Mr. Tinny	Pages	no salary
the little boy		
2 coachmen		16
2 postilions		10

Tho. Thotford		07
Kitt Johnson		07
Ed. Alcock	Groomes	07
Arthur		07
Matt		07

2 helpers to coach and stable & other stable   no salary

Tom Witherby		06
Phill. Shorte		06
Tom	Footmen	06
Hobbe		06
M. Williamson		06

Women in waiting

Margaret Cutiles Gentlewoman	20
Me Jones	06
Me Harvey	06
Mimi Housemaid	04
Mary Laundrymaid	05
Washmaid	04
Nan Cookmaid	04
Scullery maid	03

"Linen taken from Cobham the 17 of December 1671
to be carryd for Denmark"
(B.M. Add. MSS. 21,951, f. 10).

 1 pairs of fine Holland for my m^{trss} bed
 6 pairs of indifferent fine Holland sheets
 6 pairs of coarse Holland sheets
 6 pairs of coarse canvas sheets
14 coarse tabel clothes for ye stewerds tabell

8 Damask tabell Clothes
3 dozen and seaven damask napkins
1 Damask towell
24 draper tabel Clothes
10 dozen of draper napkins

———————

6 tabel Clothes of draper
4 dozen wanting 4 of draper napkins
4 flaxen tabel Clothes
3 paire of fine holland sheets
3 pillowers

"Chaple Plate" (B.M. Add. MSS. 21,951, f. 16).
2 Large candlesticks Guilt
2 Large Flaggons
2 Large Chalices
1 Large Guilt Bason

———————

4 Silver fruit Dishes
3 Paire of Silver Candlesticks
2 Silver Chafing dishes

———————

1 Travelling Casc wth Ewers
2 Sugar boxes   1 Oyle box   1 Vinegar pot   1 paper box
4 pair of Candlesticks
1 great Guilt pot
1 Tin pott to boyle things in for me
1 Silver box for ye Jewelrie

"Quantities From Y^e Wardrobe"
(B.M. Add. MSS. 21,951, f. 35).

One singing boy

Cloth 2 yds
Sattin 2 yds
Taffeta
Silver Lace 25 yds
Silver Lace 13 yds
Brest buttons 3 doz.

One trumpeter

Cloth 7 yds for cloth Breeches & stockings
Crimson velvet 6 yds
Blew serge 11 yds
Blew velvet for cloake cape
Silver Lace 8 doz.
Sky silk lace 4 doz.
Buttons and loopes for a coate 5 doz.
Buttons and loopes for a Cloak 3 doz.
Silver Brest buttons 8 doz.
3 shamoy skins

One Yeoman

6 yds of scarlet cloth
3 yds of bla. velvet
3 yds of bla. padway serge

"Extraordinary accounts of the Duke of Richmond in Copenhagen compiled after his death by John Taylor, steward" (Longleat, MSS. of the Marquis of Bath, Coventry Papers, XXVI, ff. 149–51).

	£	s.	d.
House rent and stable rent	16	00	00
For fireing and washinge	3	10	00
For Dyet of forty servants	20	00	00
	39	10	00

This being the weekly expense it
amounts in nine months to   1424   00   00
The horses being dock'd it spoyled
the sale of them there. The servants we could get no transport for.

IV. THE STAFF IN CONSTANTINOPLE

*"Anno 1677—An Account of what payd to his Excellency
Sir John Finch Lord Ambassador his entertainment the
Secretary Minister & Druggermen their Salarys for the
present year, viz." (P.R.O. S.P. 105/176, f. 12).*

1676/7

7 March	Due to his Excellency his first quarter weighty dollars	2000
7 June	Due in the like manner the second quarter weighty dollars	2000
	drawn from Smyrna in Lyon dollars 7½%	350
7 Sept.	Due in the like manner for the third quarter weighty dollars	2000
	drawn from Smyrna in Lyon dollars 8½%	370
7 Dec.	Due in like manner for the fourth quarter weighty dollars	2000
	drawn from Smyrna in Lyon dollars 8½%	370

His Excellency's gratuity not being payd
before hand as is his entertainment but at
the end of the yeare falls not due untill
the 7th March so cant be placed in this
Account but in the next.

	[weighty dollars]
To Mr. Thomas Coke Secretary for one yeare	600
To Mr. Edward Browne Minister	400
To Sig. Giorgio Draperiis for one yeare [dragoman]	600
To ditto for his gratuity of vest and Culpae	57
To Sig. Antonio Perone for one yeare [dragoman]	400
To ditto his vest, &tc.	40
To Sig. Demetrasco Timone for one yeare [dragoman]	200
To ditto his vest &tc.	20
To Sig. Draco Yerachi for one yeare [dragoman]	200
For his vest	20
To Petracchi formerly acknowledged by Sig. Giorgio for his sonne upon whose merit he was entertained, but being disavowed by him & of no use nor hopes was discharged att the 9th month of the yeare	75
To Demetrasco Yerachi for one yeare	50
To Andrea Dance for one yeare [giovanni di lingua]	50
	50
To Giovanni Rochere for one yeare	50
To Old Zambac the Jew for one yeare	500
To Dudley North Treasurer	600
	12002

V. FINANCIAL PAPERS

"Herein are the Disbursements made by me Theobald,
Earl of Carlingford, Extraordinary Envoye to his Imp^{ll}
Ma^{ty} & severall of the German Princes"
(P.R.O. S.P. 80/12, f. 147).

From Bruxelles to the Duke of Newburg, the
Elector of Collon, the Bishop of Munster, ye D. of
Brunswick, ye D. of Brandenburg, the Duke of
Hesse Cassell, ye Elect. of Metz and from thence
to Vienna. Eleven hundred pounds.   £1100

At Vienna where I arrived about ye end of December 65 untill ye later end of April 66 in Equipage
and all one thousand three hundred pounds.   1300

I parted Vienna by his Maties Orders about the
end of Aprill aforesaid and came to Prague, where
having received new orders to return again to
Vienna, I arrived there about ye beginning of May
& stayed till the 6th of November following. W^{ch}
cost me One thousand eight hundred pounds.   1800

My journey from Vienna to London came to
Eight hundred & eighty pounds   0880
                                                   ─────
                                                   £5080

To which disbursements I have re'd as followeth

Re'd of Sir John Shaw's brother at Antwerp
(a hundred pound being stopt for exchange)
Nine hundred pounds   £0900

Re'd of Mr. Loving by bill of exchange
Eight hundred pounds   0800

Rec'd of Sir Will. Temple by bill of exchange
Eight hundred pounds   0800

And I am to receive of Alderman Blackwell
One hundred pound   0100

                                    ─────
                                    £2600
W^{ch} being deducted out of ye above   £5080
                                    ─────

                        Remaines   £2480

[The Treasury issued a money warrant to Carlingford for
£2,480 in July 1667. He also received twenty tuns of wine
as royal bounty (*C.T.B.* II, 169, 170, 565).]

"To the King's Most Excellent Majesty
The Humble Petition of Edmund Poley Gent"
(B.M. Add. MSS. 37,987, f. 135).
                        December 1682
sheweth
      That y^r Majesties humble Petitioner since his having had
ye honour to be employed by y^r Maj^{ty} abroad, hath by y^r
Maj^{tys} especiall grace and Favour received for his Ordinary
Allowance 40s. per diem; But that he hath lately at Frank-
furt been obliged to a greater expense to make himselfe
more usefull to y^r Maj^{tys} service than such an Allowance
will beare; And that having now received y^r Maj^{tys} orders
to remove to Ratisbonne where the Emperor is certainly
expected in February next, y^r Petitioner will consequently

be forced to be att a much greater expense that his present Allowance will enable him to undergoe. That y^r Petitioner doth humbly hope that y^r Maj^{ty} will be graciously pleased to consider how hard it is to give y^r Maj^{ty} a true intelligence in this Conjuncture of Affaires, and ye necessary expence required to doe it upon this occasion; as also that your Maj^{tys} late Resident at Hamburg had 3 pound per diem for his ordinary expence, and that y^r Maj^{tys} present Resident att Brussells hath ye same Allowance. In consideration of which and wth an humble Profession of y^r Petitioners hearty zeale for y^r Maj^{tys} Service

> Your Petitioner doth humbly Pray that y^r Ma^{ty} would be graciously pleased to increase his ordinary Allowance to 3 pound per diem, that y^r Pet^r may therefore be enabled to serve y^r Ma^{ty} wth more ease and success, than he can doe wth ye addition of soe very little a fortune as he hath of his owne; and your Maj^{tys} Petitioner shall ever Pray, etc.

[Poley's petition was accepted by the King in 1683 (B.M. Add. MSS. 37,987, f. 299).]

Bills for Extraordinary Expenses

"Account of my extraordinary Expenses at my Entry to Paris and first publick audience at Versailles"
(P.R.O. S.P. 78/139, f. 192) .

Payed to the officers of his most most Xan ma^{tie}s house who treatted me at dinner at Versailles and to the kings grooms, dauphins, & Monsieur's Coaches and footmen and those of the princes of the blood who accompanyed me at my publick entry into Paris and after at my audience at Versailles as also to the Kings, Queens dauphins Monsieurs and Madames Guards of Swisses who made Guarde at my respective audiences, according to a list given by the Masters of the Ceremony, as fees or Gratuitys pretended due to them the summe of which particulars amounted in all to £117

Given in plate to the Master of the Ceremonies and a small present to the Master of Monsieurs Ceremonies to the Vallew of 45

Given to two persons who are obliged to wryte to me from Mr Turennes Camp and the other from the prince of Condes to each 100 crowns in all 200 crowns which in English Mony ammounts to 50

Given to Mr de Pompones first Com^{rs} by way of present 125 and to every other gentlemen belonging to him 15 in all 40

_____
£252

For fitting a large room for a chappell and furnishing it with a pulpitt and other Necessarys £ 47

For one expresse 20
_____
£ 67

The totall of both pages is £319

Will Lockhart

1674
France

[A Money warrant was issued to William Lockhart on 18 September 1674 for £319 (*C.T.B.* IV, 583).]

"The Extraordinarys of Sr Peter Wyche his Maties Resident with the Hanse Townes resideing at Hamburg for the whole Yeare 1679 Beginning on Lady Day 1679 and ending March ye 24th in the same yeare"
(B.M. Add. MSS. 37,982).

Passage for my own letters, to and fro, and of all those that came from, or were sent to his Maties Ministers, in Denmark and Sweden.	£118	10	00
Four journies to the King of Denmark while hee was neare Hamburg, two of wch were by his Maties command, and the others to discharge my duty in protecting ye English Company	35	00	00
Intelligence	40	00	00
For the Discompt of a Tally for £639-15s.-6d. levyd August 19th 1679 wch was not payable before the 19th of September	115	4	8
	£326	1	2

Sir Peter Wyche having formerly made oath that he wished just and true in whatsoever Bills of Extraordinary charges he shall send during his employm^t at Resident at Hamburgh, does allow ye first Articles of ye within written bill and submitt ye two last viz. the discompt of a Tally and Fees for receiving money in ye Excheq. to ye Right hon^{ble} ye Lords Com^{rs} of ye Treasury.

L. Jenkins

July 12th, 1680.

[Wyche received his money warrant for several back bills of extraordinaries in September 1682. This bill is not mentioned separately. The total came to £968-8s.-2d. (B.M. Add. MSS. 37,982).]

A Royal Order Establishing a Salary
(B.M. Add. MSS. 34,332, ff. 49–50).

Charles R.

Whereas about the Feast of St. Michael, in the Three and Thirtieth year of our Reigne, Wee appointed Our Right and Trusty, and Right Welbeloved Cousin Robert Earl of Sunderland to goe in the Quality of Our Ambassador Extraordinary to the Crown of Spaine; and at the same time having named Our Trusty and Welbeloved Sir William Godolphin Knt (who had then for some yeares resided in the Court of Spaine, as our Envoy Extraordinary) to be joyned with him in the charge of the said Embassy, under the character of our Ambassador in Ordinary, Wee then thought fitt for the lessening of the charge of the said Embassy to allow noe more than Tenn pounds by the Day to him the said Sir Wm. Godolphin for his ordinary Allowance and Entertainment, to commence from the said Feast of St. Michael inclusive in the Yeare 1671, as by Our Letters of Privy Seal bearing date the 11th day of November in the said Yeare, may appear yet with intention nevertheless, that if the said Sir William Godolphin should after the expiration of the said joynt Embassy remain there under the said Character of Ambassador in Ordinary, We would from that time make good unto him an allowance and Entertainment of one hundred pounds by the Weeke, being the Allowance usually made and Established for Ambassadors in the Courts of France and Spaine, for the better support of Our honour and Dignity. And whereas since Our Revocation of the said Earl of Sunderland, from the said Court of Spaine, (from whence he departed the 20th of May in the yeare 1672)—the said Sir Wm. Godolphin hath by Our especiall appointment resided there, as Our Ambassador in Ordinary, and sustained that Character with entire Satisfaction to us, and that just regard to Our Honour, that must have required an allowance equall with any of his Predecessors in the said Court, Wee have accordingly thought fitt, for his compleat reimbursement for the time past, and his sufficient Support in the future, hereby to signify our Will and Pleasure; and our Will and Pleasure is, That you prepare a Bill for our Royal Signature to pass our Privy Seale, warranting and authorizing the Treasurer and under Treasurer of our Excequer now, and for the time being of such our Treasure is, or shall be remaining, within the Receipt of our Excequer, to pay or cause to be paid unto him the said Sir William Godolphin Knt. Our Ambassador in Ordinary in the Court of Spaine or his Assignes the Summe of Thirty Pounds Sterling by the Week to commence from the said 20th day of May in the Yeare 1672 (being the day of Departure of the said Earle of Sunderland from the said Court) inclusive, to the 29th day of September past exclusive, over and above the said Ordinary Allowance of Ten Pounds per diem directed to be paid unto him, by our said Letter of Privy Seale, bearing date the 11th day of November 1671. And further to pay unto him or his Assignes from the said 29th day of September past inclusive (from which time Wee will that our said former Letters of Privy Seale bearing date the said 11th day of November 1671 cease and Determine, and be to all future Intent and purposes wholy void and frustrate) the Summe of one hundred pounds Sterling by the Weeke, for his

Ordinary Entertainment and allowance in the said Court
from three months to three months, as the same shall
from time to time grow due, and the same continue untill
the day of his returne into Our Presence inclusively, as
likewise such other summes of mony, for Intelligence, Ex-
presses, Ordinary Postage of Letters, and other Extraordinary Expenses, as by Bills under his hand, being first sub-
scribed and allowed, by one of Our Principall Secretaryes
of State for the time being shall appeare to be due unto
him, And for soe doing this shall be your Warrant. Given
at Our Court at Whitehall, the 12th day of December
1673.

By his Maties Command

To the Clerke of our   Arlington
Signet attending

Appendix II:
Personnel

[A name in italics indicates a member of an embassy staff
with experience in more than one embassy, either as secretary to several ministers or promotion to the corps after
service on staff. A name followed by * indicates official
secretary paid by the crown. The absence of names of staff
members does not necessarily mean the diplomat had no
secretary or chaplain. Many wrote their own letters, or
signed reports written by a secretary without indicating
the secretary's name.]

PLENIPOTENTIARIES AT CONGRESSES

Breda (1667)
  Henry Coventry
  Denzil Holles
       Secretaries: Nicholas Morice *
                    William Griffith
                       (secretary to Coventry)
       Marshal: Sir George Charnock
       Chaplain: Mr. Packington

Cologne (1673)
  Robert Spencer, earl of Sunderland [a]
  Sir Leoline Jenkins
  Sir Joseph Williamson
       Secretaries: *Thomas Chudleigh* *
                    René Petit

Nimeguen (1675-1679)
  John Berkeley, baron Berkeley of Stratton
  Sir William Temple
  Sir Leoline Jenkins
  Laurence Hyde (later earl of Rochester)
       Secretaries: *Thomas Chudleigh* *
                    Trevor Massam
                       (secretary to Hyde)
       Chaplains: Dr. Henry Maurice
                       (chaplain to Jenkins)
                    Dr. Richard Lucas
                       (chaplain to Jenkins)
                    William Levett
                       (chaplain to Hyde)

[a] Sunderland was accredited, but never arrived, due to illness.

ACCREDITED DIPLOMATS

(listed chronologically under states, in alphabetical order)

Denmark
  Sir Gilbert Talbot (1664–1666)
        Secretary: *Du Moulin*
  Charles Howard, earl of Carlisle (1664)
  Sir Thomas Clifford (1665)
        Secretary: *Du Moulin*
  Arthur Capel, earl of Essex (1670)
        Secretary: *William Loving*
  Charles Bertie (1671–1672)
        Secretaries: *Charles Fanshawe*
                          Thomas Ross
                          John Werden
  Sir John Paull (1672–1679)
  Charles Stuart, duke of Richmond and Lenox (1672)
        Secretaries: *Thomas Henshaw* *
                          William Blathwayt
  Thomas Henshaw (1673–1674)
  Sir Peter Wyche (1679)
  Robert Robartes, viscount Bodmin (1680–1681)
  John Churchill (later duke of Marlborough) (1683)
  Bevil Skelton (1684)
  Sir Gabriel Sylvius (1685–1689)

France
  Henry Jermyn, earl of St. Albans, (1660–1661; 1667–
    1669)
  William Crofts, baron Crofts of Saxham (1660)
  Sir Samuel Tuke (1661)

Ralph Montagu, duke of Montagu (1662; 1669–1672; 1676–1678)
  Secretaries: *René Petit* *
                Du Moulin
                Francis Vernon
  French Secretary: Falaison
  Chaplains: Nathaniel Cole
                Thomas Plomer (Blomer)
  Intelligencer: *William Perwich*
Sir John Trevor (1663; 1668)
Sir George Carteret (1663)
Denzil Holles, baron Holles of Ifield (1663–1665)
  Secretaries: Mr. Chaffin
                René Petit
  French Secretary: M. Quesnel
  Chaplains: Richard Russell
                Richard Pettys
                Henry Compton
Charles Berkeley, viscount Fitzhardinge (1664)
William Perwich (1669–1677)
Henry Arundell, baron Arundell of Wardour (1669)
Walter Montagu (1669)
Sir Leoline Jenkins (1669)
  Secretary: *Francis Vernon*
Sidney Godolphin (1669; 1670; 1672)
  Secretary: *Mr. Tempest*
Charles Sackville, baron of Buckhurst (later duke of Dorset) (1670)
George Villiers, duke of Buckingham (1670; 1672)
Henry Bennet, earl of Arlington (1672)
George Savile, marquis of Halifax (1672) [b]

[b] Buckingham, Arlington, and Halifax were on a joint embassy in 1672.

Secretaries: *Sir Joseph Williamson* *
        Ellis Leighton
        (secretary to Buckingham)
        James Vernon
        (secretary to Halifax)

Chaplain: Thomas Sprat
        (chaplain to Buckingham)

Henry Sidney (later earl of Romney) (1672)

James Scott, duke of Monmouth and Buccleuch (1672)
  Chaplain: James Gardiner

Sir William Lockhart (1672–1675)
  Secretary: *René Petit*
  Chaplain: *John Hersent*

Henry Savile (1672; 1679–1682)
  Intelligencer: Mr. *Fen*
  French Secretary: *M. Godet*

Robert Spencer, earl of Sunderland (1672–1673; 1678–1679)
  Secretaries: *Thomas Chudleigh* *
        James Vernon
  Chaplain: Constantine Jessup

Bevil Skelton (1674; 1686–1688)

John Berkeley, baron Berkeley of Stratton (1675–1676)
  Secretary: *Ellis Leighton*

John Brisbane (1676–1679)

Louis Duras, earl of Feversham (1677)
  Chaplain: Alexander Davison

Richard Graham, viscount Preston (1682–1685)
  Secretary: Mr. *Tempest*
  French Secretary: M. *Godet*
  Intelligencer: Mr. *Fen*
  Chaplains: Mr. Wake
        Mr. Wiggan

James Douglas, duke of Hamilton (1683–1685)
John Churchill, later duke of Marlborough (1685)
Sir William Trumbull (1685–1686)
    Secretary: *Jacques Dayrolle*
    French Secretary: M. *Godet*
    Chaplain: William Hayley
Henry Waldgrave, baron Waldgrave (1688–1689)
    Chaplain: Father Peters

German States:

Brandenburg-Prussia
  Theobald Taaffe, earl of Carlingford (1665)
  Sir Walter Vane (1665–1666)
  Sir Gabriel Sylvius (1669)
  Sir William Lockhart (1672)
  Sir Robert Southwell (1680)
  Edmund Poley (1680–1682)

Brunswick-Lüneburg-Calenburg (Hanover)
  Sir Gabriel Sylvius (1669; 1680–1681)
  Bevil Skelton (1681–1685)

Brunswick-Lüneburg-Celle
  Theobald Taaffe, earl of Carlingford (1665)
  Sir Gabriel Sylvius (1669; 1680–1681)
  Bevil Skelton (1681–1684)

Brunswick-Lüneburg-Wolfenbüttel
  Sir Gabriel Sylvius (1681)
  Bevil Skelton (1682–1685)

Cologne
  Charles Bertie (1680–1681)
  Johann Hogius (1686)

Frankfort-on-Main
  Wilhelm Curtius (1665–1673)

Hanse Towns–Bremen, Hamburg, Lübeck
  Joseph Averye (1660–1663)
  Sir William Swann (1663–1678)
      Chaplain: Dr. Elborrow
  Sir Peter Wyche (1678–1681; 1685–1689)
  Bevil Skelton (1682–1685)
      Chaplain: Mr. Walthen

Hesse-Cassel
  Theobald Taaffe, earl of Carlingford (1685)
  Sir William Lockhart (1672)
  Sir Gabriel Sylvius (1680)
  Charles Bertie (1680–1681)
  William Legge (1680–1681)
  Bevil Skelton (1681)

Mainz
  Sir Wilhelm Curtius (1654–1661)
  Theobald Taaffe, earl of Carlingford (1665)
  Charles Bertie (1680–1681)

Münster
  Sir William Temple (1665)
  Sir Gabriel Sylvius (1680)

Palatinate
  Roger Betridge (1664)
  Sir Wilhelm Curtius (1666)
  William Keene (1670)
  Charles Bertie (1681)

Saxony
  Sir Thomas Higgons (1669)
  Sir William Swann (1678)
  Sir Robert Southwell (1680)
  Bevil Skelton (1682)

Germany: The Emperor
  Theobald Taaffe, earl of Carlingford (1666)
      Secretary-
          Intelligencers: Father Nicholas Donellan
                            Abbot Scarlatti
      Secretary: *William Loving*
  Sir Bernard Gascoigne (1672–1673)
  Henry Mordaunt, earl of Peterborough (1673)
      Secretaries: *Sir Peter Wyche* *
                        John Dodington
  Bevil Skelton (1676–1680)
      Secretary: *René Petit*
  Charles Middleton, earl of Middleton (1680)
  Edmund Poley (1682–1685)
  Sir George Etherege (1685–1689)
      Secretary: *Hugo Hughes* [c]
  Nicholas Taaffe, earl of Carlingford (1688–1689)

  [c] Representative of William III at the Imperial Diet, 1689–1694.

Modena
   Henry Mordaunt, earl of Peterborough (1673)
      Secretary: *Sir Peter Wyche* *

Morocco
   Thomas Warren (1665–1666)
   Henry Howard, earl of Arundel (later duke of Nor-
   folk) (1669)
      Secretary: *Thomas Warren* *
   Sir James Leslie (1680–1682)

Papacy
   Philip Howard (1686)
   Roger Palmer, earl of Castlemaine (1686–1687)
      Secretary: *John Litcott* *
   John Litcott (1687–1688)
   Thomas Howard (1688)
   Lord Ward (1688)

Poland
   Laurence Hyde (later earl of Rochester) (1676)
      Chaplain and Latin Secretary: Robert South

Portugal
   Edward Montagu, earl of Sandwich (1661–1662; 1666)
   Sir Richard Fanshawe (1661–1666)
      Secretary: *John Price*
      Chaplains: Thomas Marsden
                          Henry Bagshaw
   Sir Robert Southwell (1666–1669)
      Secretary: *Francis Parry*
   Sir Peter Wyche (1668)
      Secretary: *Francis Parry*

Francis Parry (1670–1680)

Charles Fanshawe (1681–1684)

Henri de Massue, marquis de Ruvigny (later earl of Galway) (1682)

Charles Granville, viscount Granville of Lansdowne (1685)

Charles Scarburgh (1686–1689)

Russia

Charles Howard, earl of Carlisle (1684)

    Secretaries: Andrew Marvell

    Chaplain: Guy Miège

                    Brian Turner

Leontij Marselius (1664)

Thomas Brejn (1664–1666)

Sir John Hebdon (1667–1668)

John Hebdon, junior (1676–1677)

Sir Patrick Gordon (1687)

Savoy

Thomas Belasyse, earl Fauconberg (1670)

    Secretary: Mr. Russell

Bernard Granville (1675)

Sir William Soame (1678)

Spain

Henry Bennet (later earl of Arlington) (1657–1661)

Sir Richard Fanshawe (1664–1666)

    Secretary: *John Price*

    Chaplain: Henry Bagshaw

Sir Robert Southwell (1666)

Edward Montagu, earl of Sandwich (1666–1668)

    Secretaries: *William Godolphin* *

John Werden *
Under-secretaries: Richard Gerald
                  Joseph Chalmers
    Chaplain: Mr. Moore
Robert Spencer, earl of Sunderland (1672)
    Secretary: *Thomas Chudleigh* *
Sir William Godolphin (1669–1680)
Sir Henry Goodricke (1680–1682)
Peter Levett (1682–1685)
Charles Granville, viscount Granville of Lansdowne
    (1685–1688)

Spanish Netherlands
    Sir Henry De Vic (1649–1661)
    Sir Charles Cotterell (1665)
    Sir William Temple (1665–1668)
        Secretary: *Thomas Downton*
    Sir John Chicheley (1670)
    Sir Robert Southwell (1671–1672)
    Thomas Porter (1675)
    Sir Richard Bulstrode (1676–1689)
    Sidney Godolphin (Pater earl of Godolphin) (1678)
    John Brisbane (1678)
    John Churchill (later duke of Marlborough) (1678)
    Louis Duras, earl of Feversham (1678)
    William Legge (1680)
    Thomas Howard (1682)
    James Porter (1686)

Sweden
    Charles Howard, earl of Carlisle (1664; 1669)
        Secretaries: *Francis Vernon*
                         Sir Edward Wood
    Henry Coventry (1664–1666; 1671)

Secretaries:　　*Thomas Ross* *
　　　　　　　　Henry Thynne
　　　　　　　　William Griffith
　　　　　　　　Charles Fanshawe

Sir Thomas Clifford (later baron Clifford of Chudleigh) (1665)

Thomas Thynne (later viscount Weymouth) (1667–1669)

John Werden (1670–1672)
　　　Secretary:　　*William Blathwayt*

Sir Edward Wood (1672–1679)
　　　Secretary and chaplain: *John Robinson* *

Philip Warwick (1680–1683)
　　　Secretary and chaplain: *John Robinson* *

John Robinson (1684–1685)

Edmund Poley (1687–1689)

Turkey

Sir Thomas Bendyshe (1647–1661)
　　　Dragomans:　　Giorgio Draperis
　　　　　　　　　　Antonio Foscolo
　　　Chaplain:　　Benjamin Denham

Heneage Finch, earl of Winchilsea (1661–1667)
　　　English secretary: *Sir Paul Rycaut*
　　　Chaplains:　　Benjamin Denham
　　　　　　　　　　Henry Denton
　　　Dragomans:　　Giorgio Draperis
　　　　　　　　　　Antonio Perone

Sir Daniel Harvey (1668–1672)
　　　English secretary: *Sir George Etherege* [d]

[d] Etherege was at one time connected with an embassy to The Hague before he came to Turkey. The date of this employment is uncertain (Edmund Gosse, "George Etherege," *Seventeenth Century Studies* [London, 1958], p. 254).

Private secretary: Mr. Newman
Chaplains: Thomas Smith
                    John Covel
Dragomans: Giorgio Draperis
                    Antonio Perone
Sir John Finch (1673-1681)
    English
        secretaries: William Carpenter
                        Thomas Coke
    Chaplains: John Covel
                        Mr. Brown
                        Mr. Hickman
    Dragomans: Perote
                        Antonio Perone
James Brydges, baron Chandos (1681-1687)
    English secretary: *Thomas Coke*
    Chaplains: Mr. Hickman
                        Mr. John Hughes
    Dragomans: Giorgio Draperis
                        Antonio Perone
Sir William Trumbull (1687-1691)
    English secretary: *Thomas Coke*
    Private secretary: *Jacques Dayrolle*
    Chaplain: William Hayley

Tuscany
  Joseph Kent (1659-1664)
  Sir John Finch (1665-1671)
      Chaplain: *Mr. Denham*
  James Hamilton (1670)
  Thomas Plott (1678-1679)
  Sir Thomas Bereham (1679-1681; 1682-1685; 1689)

United Provinces

Sir George Downing (1658–1665; 1671–1672)
       Secretaries: Charles Gringand
                        Nicholas Oudart
                        Mr. Manley
                        James Vernon
                        William Blathwayt *
                        Thomas Williamson
                        John Ellis
Sir William Temple (1668–1671; 1674–1676; 1678–1679)
       Secretaries: *William Blathwayt* *
                        Thomas Downton
                        John Werden
                        Roger Meredith *
                        William Aglionby [e]
Sir Gabriel Sylvius (1676) [f]
Sidney Godolphin (later earl of Godolphin) (1678) [f]
Henry Sidney (later earl of Romney) (1679–1681)
Thomas Plott (1681–1682)
Thomas Chudleigh (1682–1685; 1688)
Bevil Skelton (1685–1686)
Ignatius White, marquis d'Albeville (1686–1689)

Venice

Thomas Belasyse, earl Fauconberg (1670)
       Secretaries: *John Dodington* *
                        H. Yerbury
       Chaplain: Mr. Durham
John Dodington (1670–1672)
Sir Thomas Higgons (1674–1679)

---

[e] Secretary at The Hague, 1689; later agent in Spain, envoy in Savoy, Sardinia, and Switzerland.
[f] Accredited to the Prince of Orange.

Appendix III:
George Etherege's Description of Turkey Written to Williamson, 3 May 1670[*]

Sr:

Were yo^u acquainted with this place you would not condemn mee much for not giving you before this time any account of ye affaires of Turky. During ye Warr of Candia, the News wee had from thence was sent us from Smyrna, where you hold a correspondence wth Consul Ricaut, so that advices wch I should have given you would have bin stale and insignificant; besides ye remotenes of ye Court (which has bin ever since our arrivall in Thessaly and Macedon) has made this citty as barren of intelli-

*P.R.O. S.P. 97/19, f. 150.

gence as a Village: here seldome happens any thing worthy remarke and when there does it is so uncertainly reported to us by our Druggermen who are our only Intelligencers, that experience makes us very incredulous; what Wee heare one day, is comonly contradicted ye next, and should I give you a dayly account of things according to yor desire, my busines would bee almost every other Letter to disabuse you in what I had writt to you before.

My Lord is lately return'd from Salonica, where hee has had audience. Hee arriv'd there some days before ye Court and had notice given him that hee should expect ye Grand Signor's coming from Larissa. The Grand Sig^r. arriv'd upon Thursday 25th Nov: in ye evening, came incognito to visit his Hassachi or Sultana, and ye next morning went out againe to make a publique entry. His traine consisted of Footemen & Pages, Faulconers and Huntsmen, who were in all about two thousand: hee was attended by no men of note but ye Mufti, ye Kaimakam of ye Port, and his favorite comonly called Culogli. His footmen were all clothed in cloth of gold & silver, and his Pages who are his Guard were clad in coates of Male with Olive coloured sattin Vests over them, all, Young men pick'd out for their strength & beauty. Severall Doggs were lead cover'd with Vests of cloth of gold & silver. Doubtless this Entry wanted much of magnificence hee appeares in when hee enters Adrianople or Constantinople, yet it made a very handsome showe, and was a very splendid hunting equipage, for such it was accounted. The Munday following My Lord visited ye Chimacam, and ye next day had audience of ye Grand Signor, who treated him with extraordinary markes of respect & civility. The Grand Signor is about thirty yeares of age, of a middle stature, leane & long visag'd, hee has lately let ye haire grow on his chin,

his complexion is a darke browne, his aspect is not dis-
agreeable, however hee is generally accounted very ugly.
Hee is a Bigot in his Religion and a most extravagant
lover of hunting, the fatigue hee undergoes in it is almost
incredible, great numbers of poore people are summon'd
in to attend him and many of them perish in ye field
through hunger & cold; This has chiefly got him ye hatred
of his subjects. In all other recreations hee is moderate,
hee is very constant to his Hasachi and not given to that
unnatural vice with wch hee has bin slander'd. The Sultana is a Candiot, and though women here are not so
polite & refined as in Christendome, yet shee wants not
her little arts to secure her Sultan's affection, shee can dis-
semble fondnes & jealousy and can swoone at pleasure.
The Grand Sig.^r has had two children by her, a son & a
daughter, the Son is called Sultan Mustapha, hee is about
six yeares old and desig'd by his father to be circumciz'd
when hee comes to Constantinople to make ye allaigresse
ye greater. The Daughter is not much more than a year
old, and is already marryed to the favorite Culoghi, a man
of seven & twenty yeares, well featured, modest & wise,
hee avoids busines and by that meanes makes himself less
lyable to ye envy of ye Ministers of State. His equipage is
not much inferior to his Masters, his footmen and pages
weare ye same Livery. Hee is allowed six hundred thousand Dollers a yeare besides all necessaries for his retinue,
and yet this vast income is not able to keepe him out of
debt, but whether that bee an effect of his generosity or
prudence is uncertaine, for there is nothing here more
dangerous than to be rich. The Grand Signors Privy
Councell consisted here but of five persons, ye favorite, y^e
Chimacam of the Port, ye Mufti, Vani Effendi a famous
Arab preacher and one of ye Pashas of ye Bench; most of

the great men being with ye Vizier who is imploy'd in
Candia in fortefying & setling the affaires of that Kingdome. Hee is to come to Court in the spring as it is reported, and then ye Grand Signor intends to begin his
journey hither. The Chimacam's name is Mustapha Pasha,
hee was formerly Capt Pasha or Admirall of ye Gallies
and has married ye Vizier's Sister, yet this allyance keeps
them not from secret emulations & hatreds, and it is
thought ye Chimacam will dispute ye Grand Sig.^rs favour
with him at his returne. The Vizier they say exceeds not
ye age of two & thirty yeares, hee is of middle stature and
has a good Mine, hee is prudent & just not to bee cor-
rupted by money the generall vice of this country, nor
inclin'd to cruelty as his father was. The Chimacam is
about ye age of forty five, well spoken, subtill, corrupt & a
great dissembler, hee flatters ye Grand Signor in his in-
clinations, and ever accompanies him in his hunting, a
toyle which nothing but excessive ambition & interest
could make him undergoe. All conclude ye Vizier will
commence another Warr, but who will fall under y^e
sphere [?] of it is unknowne. The Chimacam of this place
Ibrahim Pasha has a particular respect for my Lord, and
is exceeding courteous & obliging whensoever hee treats
with him about any busines; hee is a man of great resolution, wisdome and honesty, hee is neere sixty yeares old
but very vigorous of his age, hee was bred a souldier and
by his courage & other merits has rais'd himselfe to this
eminent degree. Hee was Kiabeigh or Lieutenant of the
Janizaries at ye battel of Rab, where hee was shot through
ye shoulder, and upon ye death of his Captaine was there
made Aga, hee serv'd in that charge at Candia till hee was
this yeare sent hither to bee Chimacam in the stead of
Useph Pasha a timorous doting old man who was remov'd

for multiplying ye danger of giving a dreadfull account to ye Court of some little stirrs that happened here some months since upon a report that ye Grand Sig.^{r} had sent to cutt off his brothers Sultan Soliman: Sultan Achmet; 'tis thought these princes will bee in great danger when ye Grand Sig.^{r} arrives here. My business was at ye beginning to excuse my not writing to you, & now I ought to begg yo^{ur} pardon for having writt soe much, but I hope you will let mee know you have forgiven mee ye impertinencies of this Letter, and that will incourage mee to give you notice of whatsoever I shall bee inform'd of here worthy yo^{ur} knowledge. I am

S^r

Yo^{ur} very humble Servant
Geo. Etherege

Abbreviations

B.M.	British Museum
Add. MSS.	Additional Manuscripts
Harl. MSS.	Harleian Manuscripts
C.J.	*Journals of the House of Commons*
Cont.	Edward Hyde, earl of Clarendon, *The Life of Edward Earl of Clarendon . . . in Which Is Included, A Continuation of His History of the Grand Rebellion*
C.S.P.D.	*Calendar of State Papers, Domestic Series*
C.S.P.V.	*Calendar of State Papers and Manuscripts Relating to English Affairs Existing in the Archives and Collections of Venice, and in Other Libraries of Northern Italy*
C.T.B.	*Calendar of Treasury Books*
D.N.B.	*Dictionary of National Biography*
E.H.R.	*English Historical Review*
Grey's *Debates*	Anchitell Grey, *Debates of the House of Commons, from the Year 1667 to the Year 1694*
H.M.C.	Historical Manuscripts Commission
HM. Stowe MSS.	Huntingdon Library, Uncatalogued Stowe Manuscripts: Temple Correspondence
P.R.O.	Public Record Office
C.O.	Board of Trade: Minutes
E.	Privy Seal Books
L.C.	Records of the Lord Chamberlain's Office
S.P.	State Papers Foreign
Trans. R.H.S.	*Transactions of the Royal Historical Society*

Notes

I. THE STRUCTURE OF
THE DIPLOMATIC CORPS

[1] Louis Batiffol, "Charge d'ambassadeurs du 17ᵉ siècle," *Revue d'Histoire Diplomatique*, XXV (1911), 339–55.

[2] James Howell, *A Discourse Concerning the Precedency of Kings, Wherein the Reasons and Arguments of the Three Greatest Monarks of Christendom, Who Claim a Several Right Thereunto, Are Faithfully Collected and Render'd, Whereunto Is Also Adjoyn'd a . . . Treatise of Ambassadors, etc.* (London, 1664), pp. 179–81; Abraham de Wicquefort, *The Embassador and His Functions*, trans. John Digby (London, 1716), pp. 36–39.

[3] Thomas Brown, ed., *Miscellanea Aulica: Or, A Collection of State-Treatises, Never before Published* (London, 1702), p. 101.

[4] Sir Ernest Satow, *A Guide to Diplomatic Practise*, 2 vols. (London, 1917), I, 232–34.

5 Tables I and II, compiled from *Repertorium der diplomatischen Vertreter aller Länder seit dem westfälischen Frieden* (1648), ed. L. Bittner and L. Gross (Berlin, 1936), *C.S.P.D.* 1660 ff., and *C.T.B.* 1660 ff. refute the statement by Thomas Babington Macaulay, *The History of England from the Accession of James II,* 5 vols. (Philadelphia, 1856), I, 239, that under Charles II "the only diplomatic agent who had the title of Ambassador resided at Constantinople, and was partly supported by the Turkey Company. Even at the court of Versailles England had only an Envoy; and she had not even an Envoy at the Spanish, Swedish, and Danish courts."

6 *The Bulstrode Papers: The Collection of Autograph Letters and Historical Documents Formed by Alfred Morrison,* 2 vols. (London, 1897), I, 78; H.M.C. *Finch MSS.* I, 493.

7 Edward Montagu, earl of Sandwich, *Hispania Illustrata . . . in Letters from . . . the Earl of Sandwich, the Earl of Sunderland, and Sir William Godolphin during Their Embassies in Spain* (London, 1703), p. 52.

8 *C.S.P.V.* XXXVII, 115.

9 *C.S.P.V.* XXXVII, 332; XXXVIII, 250.

10 The assignment of this relatively inferior grade to a country where English interests were strong arose from a quarrel during the reign of Charles I. Queen Elizabeth sent the earl of Leicester as ambassador to the Hague in 1585. One of the responsibilities of his mission was to command the Dutch forces, and for this reason the Dutch allowed him a seat in their Council of State. The English ambassador retained this seat until 1626, when the States felt the procedure was no longer justified. They informed Charles I that the recently accredited ambassador was to have all the honors due his rank except a seat in the Council. The English took offense and responded by sending a minister of the second order (J. Heringa, *De Eer en Hoogheid van de Staat* [Groningen, 1961], p. 315; Wicquefort, *The Embassador,* p. 9).

11 Thomas Peregrine Courtenay, *Memoirs of the Life, Works, and Correspondence of Sir William Temple, Bart.,* 2 vols. (London, 1836), I, 219.

12 *Recueil des instructions données aux ambassadeurs et ministres de France depuis les traités de Westphalie jusqu'à la Révolution Française . . . Angleterre,* ed. J. J. Jusserand, 2 vols. (Paris, 1929), II, 192–93.

13 Henry Bennet, earl of Arlington, *The Right Honourable the Earl of Arlington's Letters to Sir William Temple, Bart.,* 2 vols. (London, 1701), II, 329.

14 Courtenay, *Temple,* I, 415.

15 H.M.C. *Various Collections* II, "Wombwell MSS.," p. 149.

16 In 1679, at the end of the tenure of Thomas Osborne, the Treasury was put into commission for the second time in the reign. Arthur Capel, earl of Essex, and Laurence Hyde served as Treasury Lords in 1679.

17 Henry Bennet and Henry Coventry, et al., *Letters from the Secretaries of State, and Other Persons, in the Reign of King Charles the Second, to Francis Parry, esq., English Envoy in Portugal* (London, 1817), p. 53; Sir Henry Savile, *Letters to and from Henry Savile, esq., Envoy at Paris,* ed. William Durrant Cooper, Camden Society, series I, vol. 71 (London, 1858), p. 104.

18 Andrew Browning, *Thomas Osborne, Earl of Danby and Duke of Leeds, 1632–1712,* 3 vols. (Glasgow, 1951), II, 513. Temple to Danby, 11 February 1678.

19 B.M. Add. MSS. 37,986, f. 60; Add. MSS. 35,101 *passim.*

20 In 1663 Richard Bellings undertook a mission to the Pope on behalf of the Queen, but he came in a private character. Even this unofficial visit was so resented it became one of the charges directed against Clarendon in 1663 (*C.S.P.D.* 1663–1664, p. 199; *Cont.* II, 25). The visit of Sir Clement Cotterell to the papal court in 1676 at the election of Clement X was also unofficial.

21 Turkey and Russia were among the last states to receive regular diplomatic representation from England (O. Krauske, *Die Entwickelung der ständigten Diplomatie vom 15. Jahrhundert bis zu den Beschlüssen von 1815-18, in staats-und socialwissenschaftliche Forschungen,* ed. Gustav Schmoller [Leipzig, 1885], III, 143-44, 147-48).

22 *C.S.P.D.* 1660–1661, p. 270.

23 *C.S.P.V.* XXXII, 212.

24 *C.S.P.D.* 1664–1665, pp. 230, 285; 1667, p. 65; Jacob M. Price, "The Tobacco Adventure to Russia," *Transactions of the American Philosophical Society,* n.s. LI:1 (1961), 20–21.

25 *C.S.P.D.* 1676–1677, pp. 299, 332; P.R.O. S.P. 91/3, ff. 206, 266, 268; *C.T.B.* VII, part 2, 1095, 1101.

26 Sir Patrick Gordon, *Passages from the Diary of General Patrick Gordon of Auchleuchreis, A.D. 1635–A.D. 1699* (Aberdeen, 1859), p. 55. Gordon referred to Brejn as Bryan.

27 Jusserand, *Instructions,* I, 259.

28 Florence May Greir Higham (Evans), *The Principal Secretary of State: A Survey of the Office from 1558 to 1680* (London, 1923), pp. 131-35; Mark A. Thomson, *The Secretaries of State, 1681–1782* (Oxford, 1932), pp. 3 ff.; Violet Barbour, *Henry Bennet, Earl of Arlington* (Washington, 1914), p. 58.

29 References to instructions being framed at the Foreign Committee are in P.R.O. S.P. 105/49 (Southwell to Sunderland, 31 April 1680);

C.S.P.D. 1678, p. 224; H.M.C. *Ormonde MSS.* n.s. IV, 580; Abel Boyer, *Memoires of the Life and Negotiations of Sir William Temple . . . 1665 to . . . 1681* (London, 1714), p. 199. In certain cases folio numbers are missing. These documents are identified by correspondents and date following the number of the manuscript collection.

[30] *C.S.P.D.* 1667–1668, pp. 503–04; Longleat, MSS. of the Marquis of Bath, Coventry Papers, II, ff. 52–53.

[31] P.R.O. C.O. 391/1, ff. 159, 206, 212, 269.

[32] A. C. Wood, "The English Embassy at Constantinople, 1660–1762," *E.H.R.,* XL (1925), 533–61; P.R.O. S.P. 91/3, f. 212 (Instructions from the Muscovy Company to Hebdon); S.P. 105/155 (Minutes of the Levant Company).

[33] Howell, *Discourse,* p. 208.

[34] E.g., P.R.O. S.P. 78/117, f. 115; 78/126, f. 42. Other instructions to ministers to France omitted mention of a chaplain, and I have not found a chaplain named in instructions to ministers to other countries.

[35] E.g., Instructions to Sir Leoline Jenkins, printed in William Wynne, *The Life of Sir Leoline Jenkins,* 2 vols. (London, 1724), I, 351–52.

[36] B.M. Stowe MSS. 191, f. 18.

[37] See discussion of protocol, *infra,* for regular directions on diplomatic etiquette. A special paragraph on protocol concerning the specific nature of the mission was included when necessary, e.g., instructions to Peterborough (P.R.O. S.P. 104/88, f. 29): "Now although it be unusual to send Extraordinary Amb[rs] to a single Prince in Italy of that Sphere, yet We have condescended unto it to honour Our most Deare Brothers choice of this Princess for his wife, but that on the other side Our owne dignity may not suffer thereby, you must be carefull at your appearance in that Court to stipulate & adjust the manner of your reception there, to the full extent of such Ceremonies, as have been given to the Amb[rs] of France and Spain."

[38] P.R.O. S.P. 80/13, ff. 262–64.

[39] P.R.O. S.P. 84/182, ff. 90 ff.

[40] Southwell to Ormonde 5 March 1677, H.M.C. *Ormonde MSS.* n.s. IV, 412. Danby despatched Godolphin to get the opinion of the Prince of Orange on the peace terms at Nimeguen, but kept the Secretaries of State in the mistaken belief that Godolphin was going to adjust the matter of Ostend between England and Spain (Browning, *Danby,* I, 271–72, II, 335).

[41] The foregoing is a description of the credentials that William Temple carried to Christian Bernhard, bishop of Münster, in 1665 which are in B.M. Add. MSS. 9803.

[42] B.M. Stowe MSS. 195, f. 1: Instructions to Bernard Grenville going to the Republic of Genoa.

[43] P.R.O. S.P. 98/11 *passim* shows the delays Fauconberg met in Tuscany because his papers were addressed to the Grand Duke Cosimo II, who died in 1670. All foreign ministers in London on the eve of the Restoration needed new letters to give to Charles II (*C.S.P.V.* XXXII, 113, 143, 164–65).

[44] Georg Friedrich von Martens, *Summary of the Law of Nations,* trans. William Cobbett (Philadelphia, 1795), pp. 216–17.

[45] *C.S.P.D.* 1673–1675, pp. 314–15.

[46] H.M.C. *Fourth Report,* part 1, "Bath MSS.," p. 245.

[47] Rijksarchief Staaten Generaal: Engeland 6928, f. 26. Chudleigh was made Commissioner of the Customs at his return.

[48] Anchitell Grey, *Debates of the House of Commons, from the Year 1667 to the Year 1694,* 10 vols. (London, 1763), V, 248. Montagu, ambassador at Paris, made the same suggestion. If the King withdrew his delegates from Nimeguen and secured London as the place of the congress, he would save the cost of keeping ambassadors abroad and would gain income from other foreign ministers living in London (Browning, *Danby,* II, 263).

[49] Grey's *Debates,* VI, 189; *C.J.* IX, 539; H.M.C. *Ormonde MSS.* n.s. IV, 471, 577; Narcissus Luttrell, *A Brief Historical Relation of State Affairs from September 1678 to April 1714,* 6 vols. (Oxford, 1857), I, 38; Gilbert Burnet, *History of My Own Time,* ed. Osmund Airy, 2 vols. (Oxford, 1897, 1900), II, 40. Other Catholic ministers who served Charles II were Arlington, Tuke, Walter Montagu, Arundel, Arundell of Wardour, and Bulstrode. Chudleigh and Peterborough avowed Catholicism after they had served abroad. Feversham may have been a crypto-Catholic; he took the precaution of taking an Anglican chaplain to France (*C.S.P.D.* 1677–1678, p. 95). Only Bulstrode and Feversham were abroad at the time of the Plot, and both continued on their missions during the investigations with no trouble from Parliament. James Porter, envoy of James II to the Spanish Netherlands in 1686, was named ambassador to Spain in 1679. Saville said that the nomination was withdrawn "by reason of some politic reflections out of England, as I am told by some Catholics here in Paris, who are scandalized at the change" (Henry Sidney, earl of Romney, *Diary of the Times of Charles the Second,* ed. R. W. Blencowe, 2 vols. [London, 1843], I, 135, 141).

[50] Grey's *Debates,* II, 190.

[51] Mark A. Thomson, *A Constitutional History of England, 1642–1801* (London, 1938), pp. 104–14. Instances of clashes between the King and Parliament over the management of policy are discussed in detail by E. R. Turner, "Parliament and Foreign Affairs, 1603–1760," *E.H.R.,* XXXIV (1919), 172–97; Grey's *Debates,* II, 348.

II. DUTIES AND RESPONSIBILITIES

1 *A Discourse Concerning the Precedency of Kings, Wherein the Reasons and Arguments of the Three Greatest Monarks of Christendom, Who Claim a Several Right Thereunto, Are Faithfully Collected and Render'd, Whereunto Is Also Adjoyn'd a . . . Treatise of Ambassadors, etc.* (London, 1664), p. 196.

2 Thomas Peregrine Courtenay, *Memoirs of the Life, Works, and Correspondence of Sir William Temple, Bart.* 2 vols. (London, 1836), I, 218.

3 F. R. Harris, *The Life of Edward Montagu, K.G. First Earl of Sandwich (1625–1672),* 2 vols. (London, 1912), I, 198; II, 45–46.

4 H.M.C. *Fourth Report,* "De La Warr MSS.," p. 279.

5 Christopher Lindenov, *The First Triple Alliance: The Letters of Christopher Lindenov, Danish Envoy to London, 1668–1672,* ed., trans., and introd. Waldemar Westergaard (New Haven, 1947), p. 182.

6 John Beresford, *The Godfather of Downing Street: Sir George Downing, 1623–1684* (Boston, 1925), pp. 247–49.

7 Narcissus Luttrell, *A Brief Historical Relation of State Affairs from September 1678 to April 1714,* 6 vols. (Oxford, 1857), I, 462; *Recueil des instructions donneés aux ambassadeurs et ministres de France depuis les traités de Westphalie jusqu'à la Révolution Française . . . Angleterre,* ed. and introd. J. J. Jusserand, 2 vols. (Oxford, 1929), II, 403–04.

8 H.M.C. *Ormonde MSS.* n.s. IV, 441, 443; *C.S.P.D.* 1678, p. 287.

9 Anchitell Grey, *Debates of the House of Commons, from the Year 1667 to the Year 1694,* 10 vols. (London, 1763), VI, 341.

10 Andrew Browning, *Thomas Osborne, Earl of Danby and Duke of Leeds, 1632–1712,* 3 vols. (Glasgow, 1951), I, 284–313; Grey's *Debates,* VI, 337–48; *C.J.* IX, 559–60.

11 Peter Fraser, *The Intelligence of the Secretaries of State and Their Monopoly of Licensed News, 1660–1668* (New York, 1956), pp. 28 ff.; John Evelyn, *Diary,* ed. E. S. De Beer, 6 vols. (Oxford, 1955), I, 127–28.

12 *The Bulstrode Papers: The Collection of Autograph Letters and Historical Documents Formed by Alfred Morrison,* 2 vols. (London, 1897), vol. I; W. D. Christie, ed., *Letters Addressed from London to Sir Joseph Williamson While Plenipotentiary at the Congress of Cologne, in the Years 1673 and 1674,* 2 vols. (London, 1874).

13 Printed in Fraser, *Intelligence,* pp. 153–55.

14 Printed in Christie, *Williamson,* II, 161–65.

[15] B.M. Add. MSS. 37,983, f. 5. See also *C.S.P.D.* 1671–1672, indicating weekly schedule of letters to an embassy secretary.

[16] Edward Montagu, earl of Sandwich, *Hispania Illustrata . . . in Letters from . . . the Earl of Sandwich, the Earl of Sunderland, and Sir William Godolphin during Their Embassies in Spain* (London, 1703), pp. 117–18.

[17] P.R.O. S.P. 78/117, f. 230.

[18] P.R.O. S.P. 78/121 (to Williamson, 14 October 1665).

[19] Sir Henry Savile, *Letters to and from Henry Savile, esq., Envoy at Paris,* ed. William Durrant Cooper, Camden Society, series I, vol. 71 (London, 1858), p. 104. Simon Arnauld, marquis de Pompone, was French minister for foreign affairs.

[20] P.R.O. S.P. 82/15, f. 14; Longleat, MSS. of the Marquis of Bath, Coventry Papers, XXV, f. 2; Cyril Hughes Hartmann, *Clifford of the Cabal* (London, 1937), p. 92; H.M.C. *Montagu Bertie MSS.,* p. 199.

[21] Violet Barbour, "Consular Service in the Reign of Charles II," *American Historical Review,* XXXIII (1927–28); Fraser, *Intelligence,* pp. 67–71; David Baynes Horn, *The British Diplomatic Service, 1689–1789* (Oxford, 1961), p. 217. Left to his own resources, the resident in Denmark wrote in 1672, "This place affords so little news that I cannot finde matter anoff for a letter" (Longleat, MSS. of the Marquis of Bath, Coventry Papers, XXVI, f. 63).

[22] P.R.O. S.P. 78/127, f. 239.

[23] H.M.C. *Seventh Report,* part 1, "Graham MSS.," p. 208; Thomas Plott and Thomas Chudleigh, *The Despatches of Thomas Plott (1681–1682) and Thomas Chudleigh (1682–1685), English Envoys at The Hague,* ed. Frederick Arnold Middlebush (The Hague, 1926), p. 1.

[24] P.R.O. S.P. 78/122, ff. 146, 226; 78/143, f. 77; 104/19 (3 June 1679).

[25] P.R.O. S.P. 78/143, f. 143.

[26] B.M. Add. MSS. 37,985, f. 54; Add. MSS. 35,101, f. 179; H.M.C. *Various Collections* II, "Wombwell MSS.," p. 144.

[27] Samuel Pepys, *Diary,* ed. Henry B. Wheatley, 9 vols. (London, 1910), VII, 177.

[28] *C.S.P.V.* XXXIV, 52.

[29] Letters from Preston's spies, many undated and unsigned, are in H.M.C. *Seventh Report,* part 1, "Graham MSS.," pp. 392–404.

[30] *C.S.P.D.* 1660–1670, *Addenda,* p. 666.

[31] *Moneys Received and Paid for Secret Services of Charles II and James II from 30th March, 1679, to 25th December, 1688,* ed. John Yonge Akerman (London, 1851), pp. 6, 150, 163, 195, 207; James Walker, "The Secret Service under Charles II and James II," *Trans. R.H.S.,* 4th series, XV (1932), 211–42; *C.S.P.D.* 1663–1664, p. 501; H.M.C. *Seventh Report,* part 1, "Graham MSS.," p. 393. This discussion has

been confined to spies who worked with the diplomatic corps. The government also employed spies in Holland during the war years when diplomatic relations were severed (Fraser, *Intelligence,* pp. 75, 96–113).

32 H.M.C. *Finch MSS.* I, 111, 112, 120–21, 132, 181, 250, 447; *Downshire MMS.* I, part 1, 302.

33 Longleat, MSS. of the Marquis of Bath, Coventry Papers, LX, f. 16.

34 B.M. Stowe MSS. 219, f. 150.

35 P.R.O. S.P. 98/7, *passim.*

36 P.R.O. S.P. 98/5; 80/11, ff. 38, 51, 54, 55, 63; 80/12.

37 Walker, *Trans. R.H.S.,* XV, 219.

38 P.R.O. S.P. 82/11–15; Longleat, MSS. of the Marquis of Bath, Thynne Papers, XXX.

39 P.R.O. S.P. 78/126, ff. 241, 267, 292.

40 P.R.O. S.P. 78/118, ff. 187, 219; 78/119, f. 232; 78/122, f. 114; Baschet Transcripts, 3/113, 3/115; B.M. Add. MSS. 23,894, f. 20; P.R.O. S.P. 78/144, f. 156.

41 P.R.O. S.P. 78/148, f. 551; Henry Bennet, earl of Arlington, *The Right Honourable the Earl of Arlington's Letters to Sir William Temple, Bart.,* 2 vols. (London, 1701), I, 87; P.R.O. S.P. 78/127, f. 169; Montagu, *Hispania Illustrata,* pp. 1, 89; P.R.O. S.P. 98/5 (Finch to Arlington 5 September 1666); *C.S.P.D.* 1667–1678, pp. 259–60; Longleat, MSS. of Marquis of Bath, Coventry Papers, XXV, f. 179.

42 Howard Robinson, *The British Post Office: A History* (Princeton, 1948), pp. 54–55; J. J. Jusserand, *A French Ambassador at the Court of Charles II, Le Comte de Comenges, from His Unpublished Correspondence* (New York, 1892), pp. 50, 232.

43 E.g., Instructions to Holles (B.M. Stowe MSS. 191, f. 4) "You shall keep frequent, & att least weekly Correspondance with Our principall Secr^y of State, to whom ye despatch of the French Business is more especially committed, and be very careful how you wryte, in or out of Cypher any thing of more then Ordinary secrecy, takeing for granted, that there is littel faire dealing in the conveyance of l^rs there, for wch reason you must also be very carefull of disposeing of anything that shall through yor hands be transmitted from us into Italy & Spaine."

44 A. Bryant, *Samuel Pepys: The Man in the Making* (New York, 1933), pp. 78–79.

45 B.M. Add. MSS. 23,898, ff. 8–9.

46 Jusserand, *Instructions,* II, 28. When Ruvigny realized his mail was being read, he advised his government, "au pis aller, on connaîtra ici, que je ne suis pas mal averti et que je ne suis pas le dupe de M. Arlinton."

[47] Sir Richard Fanshawe et al., *Original Letters and Negotiations of Sir Richard Fanshawe, the Earl of Sandwich, the Earl of Sunderland and Sir William Godolphin, Wherein Divers Matters between the Three Crowns of England, Spain and Portugal from 1663 to 1678 Are Set in a Clearer Light Than Is Anywhere Else Extant*, 2 vols. (London, 1724), I, 32; Bennet, *Letters to Temple*, I, 281; Longleat, MSS. of the Marquis of Bath, Coventry Papers, XXVII, f. 38; LX, f. 370; B.M. Add. MSS. 37,986, f. 150; P.R.O. S.P. 78/117, f. 136; Courtenay, *Temple*, I, 192.

[48] Jusserand, *Instructions*, II, 97–98. The courier was Sir Elisha Leighton (d. 1685), later a member of Berkeley's embassy to France in 1675. Leighton, an unscrupulous conniver for money, sold information to Ruvigny (II, 47, and note).

[49] *C.S.P.V.* XXXV, 148.

[50] Fraser, *Intelligence*, pp. 76–77.

[51] B.M. Add. MSS. 16,272, f. 18; P.R.O. S.P. 78/127, f. 137; H.M.C. *Finch MSS.* I, 230; B.M. Harl MSS. 7010, ff. 233, 473.

[52] P.R.O. S.P. 104/18 *passim;* H.M.C. *Fourth Report*, part 1, "Bath MSS.," pp. 244–45.

[53] Mark A. Thomson, *The Secretaries of State, 1681–1782* (Oxford, 1932), pp. 97–100; Browning, *Danby*, II, 479, 492. Temple, Montagu, Sunderland, Brisbane, Jenkins, and Hyde maintained a regular correspondence with the Treasurer (II, 257–619).

[54] H.M.C. *Seventh Report*, part 1, "Graham MSS.," p. 326; Fanshawe, *Original Letters*, I, 243.

[55] E.g., B.M. Stowe MSS. 191, f. 38 (instructions to Higgons; Venice); P.R.O. S.P. 78/126, ff. 40 ff. (instructions to Montagu, France).

[56] P.R.O. S.P. 91/3, f. 212 (instructions to Hebdon).

[57] Fanshawe, *Original Letters*, I, 21.

[58] P.R.O. S.P. 9/166, f. 417.

[59] *C.S.P.V.* I, xliii; Heinrich Kretschmayr, *Geschichte von Venedig*, 3 vols. (Gotha, 1920), II, 99. A Venetian *relazione* of England under Charles II is in *C.S.P.V.* XXXVIII, 54–73.

[60] Jusserand, *Instructions*, II, 168–69, 197.

[61] *C.S.P.V.* XXXIV, 99; *C.S.P.D.* 1667–1668, p. 470; 1671–1672, p. 123; H.M.C. *Ormonde MSS.* n.s. IV, 381.

[62] *Diary*, VIII, 137.

[63] B.M. Add. MSS. 34,331, f. 98.

[64] *C.S.P.D.* 1672–1673, p. 403; *C.S.P.D.* 1683, p. 152; *Bulstrode Papers*, I, 50, 51.

[65] "Viscount Fauconberg's Report to the King, upon His Mission to Italy" is printed in H.M.C. *Various Collections* II, "Wombwell MSS.," pp. 205–26, and in identical form in *Archaeologia*, XXXVII:1 (1857),

158–88, under the title "Relation of the Lord Fauconberg's Embassy to the States of Italy in the Year 1669, Addressed to King Charles II." References here are to H.M.C.

66 H.M.C. *Various Collections* II, "Wombwell MSS.," p. 205.

67 *Ibid.,* 206, 209, 212, 219.

68 H.M.C. *Various Collections* II, "Wombwell MSS.," p. 217.

III. PERSONNEL

1 Young men who came to London in the train of Venetian ambassadors of this period in order to qualify for future embassies are mentioned in *C.S.P.V.* XXXII, 308; XXXIII, 90; XXXV, 281.

2 Cited by J. J. Jusserand, *The School for Ambassadors and Other Essays* (New York, 1925), p. 45. The quotation is from *The Spectator* (no. 305), 19 February 1712.

3 Garrett Mattingly, *Renaissance Diplomacy* (London, 1955), pp. 211–22.

4 *The Application of Certain Histories Concerning Ambassadours and Their Functions* (London, 1651), pp. 13–18.

5 *The Ambassadors* (London, 1603), pp. 14–20.

6 *De legationibus libri tres,* trans. Gordon J. Laing, introd. Ernest Nys (New York, 1924), pp. 136–72.

7 Sir George Etherege, *Letterbook,* ed. and introd. Sybil Rosenfeld (London, 1928), p. 377.

8 Abraham de Wicquefort, *The Embassador and His Functions,* trans. John Digby (London, 1716), p. 50.

9 *Ibid.,* pp. 47–94.

10 Wicquefort's discussion of great ambassadors who were living when he wrote his book includes nine French, eight Dutch, four Germans, three Swedes, two Spaniards, and two Italians. His list of outstanding ministers of the sixteenth century had no English. Here again the French carried off the honors with nine men to their credit. Of the others Venice had four, Spain and the United Provinces two, and the Papacy and Savoy one each (pp. 416–30).

11 *Réflexions sur les mémoirs pour les Ambassadeurs, et response au ministre prisonnier avec d'examples curieux et d'importantes recherches* (Ville-Franche, 1677), pp. 72–73: "En France on n'étoit si animé contre les Etats Généraux que contre sa personne. . . . C'est le plus glorieux trait de son Eloge."

12 Sir William Temple, *Letters . . . Containing an Account of the Most Important Transactions . . . in Christendom from 1665 to 1672,* 2 vols. (London, 1700), I, 119.

[13] Alfred Francis Pribram, *Franz Paul Freiherr von Lisola, 1613–1674, und die Politik seiner Zeit* (Leipzig, 1894), pp. 692–94.

[14] Excluding admirals who carried messages of state to Tunis, Algiers, and Tripoli and were not part of the regular diplomatic corps.

[15] David Carnegie Agnew, *Protestant Exiles in England* (Edinburgh, 1866), pp. 91–97.

[16] J. Hora Siccama, "Sir Gabriel de Sylvius, 1660–1696," *Revue d'Histoire Diplomatique*, XIV:4 (1900), 598–630.

[17] John Evelyn, *Diary*, ed. E. S. De Beer, 6 vols. (Oxford, 1955), III, 36, and note.

[18] Edmund Ludlow, *Memoirs, 1625–1672*, ed. C. H. Firth, 2 vols. (Oxford, 1894), I, 205.

[19] He may possibly have been related to Lewis Ferdinand Marsigli, born in Bologna, soldier, philosopher, and F.R.S., who was the author of several scientific tracts published in the eighteenth century, described by Robert Watt, *Bibliotheca Britannica or a General Index to British and Foreign Literature in Two Parts*, 4 vols. (Edinburgh, 1824), Part I.

[20] Evelyn, *Diary*, IV, 178, and note.

[21] William Wynne, *The Life of Sir Leoline Jenkins*, 2 vols. (London, 1724), I, xviii–xix.

[22] John Venn and James A. Venn, *Alumni Cantabrigensis*, Part I, *From the Earliest Times to 1751*, 4 vols. (Cambridge, 1922); Anthony Wood, *Athenae Oxonienses*, 2 vols., 2nd ed. (London, 1721).

[23] Throughout Europe, clergy were becoming increasingly rare in important diplomatic positions. Louis XIV employed very few, and those grudgingly. A few in the French corps were *noblesse de robe*. The majority in important positions were *noblesse d'épee*, with prior military experience (Camille G. Picavet, "Carrière diplomatique en France sous Louis XIV," *Revue d'Histoire Economique et Sociale*, XI [1923], 383–408).

[24] *The Bulstrode Papers: The Collection of Autograph Letters and Historical Documents Formed by Alfred Morrison*, 2 vols. (London, 1897), I, 93.

[25] *C.S.P.V.* XXXIV, 3.

[26] George Edward Cokayne, *The Complete Peerage of England, Scotland, Ireland, Great Britain and the United Kingdom*, 12 vols. (London, 1910–1959).

[27] F. R. Harris, *The Life of Edward Montagu, K.G., First Earl of Sandwich (1625–1672)*, 2 vols. (London, 1912), II, 67; Thomas Peregrine Courtenay, *Memoirs of the Life, Works, and Correspondence of Sir William Temple, Bart.*, 2 vols. (London, 1836), I, 47; B.M. Add. MSS. 37,984, f. 321.

²⁸ B.M. Add. MSS. 37,982, f. 206.

²⁹ *C.S.P.D.* 1660, p. 296; P.R.O. S.P. 81/56, ff. 39–40.

³⁰ Evelyn, *Diary*, II, 72, and note; III, 332, and note.

³¹ Samuel Pepys, *Diary*, ed. Henry B. Wheatley, 9 vols. (London, 1910), III, 150; Sir Patrick Gordon, *Passages from the Diary of General Patrick Gordon of Auchleuchreis, A.D. 1635–A.D. 1699* (Aberdeen, 1859), pp. 79 ff. Hebdon also accompanied Carlisle to Russia (Guy Miège, *A Relation of Three Embassies from His Sacred Majestie Charles II to the Great Duke of Muscovie, the King of Sweden, and the King of Denmark* [London, 1669], pp. 180–81).

³² Cited by John Beresford in *The Godfather of Downing Street: Sir George Downing, 1623–1684* (Boston, 1925), p. 179. Downing taught junior students at college in 1643.

³³ Galardi, *Réflexions*, pp. 92–3; Beresford, *Downing*, p. 141; *Cont.* II, 49–51; *C.S.P.V.* XXXVI, 113.

³⁴ *Diary*, IV, 28; *C.S.P.V.* XXXVIII, 38, 249, 418–19.

³⁵ *Bulstrode Papers*, I, 301, 302, 306.

³⁶ *C.S.P.V.* XXXIII, 167; XXXV, 30; XXXVI, 66, 69, 93–94, 116–17, 239, 287; Temple, *Letters*, II, 120–21.

³⁷ *Cont.* II, 398.

³⁸ *Parliaments of England, 1213–1702*, Part I and Index (London, 1878); J. R. Jones, "Court Dependents in 1664," *Bulletin of the Institute of Historical Research*, XXXIV:89 (May, 1961), 81–91; Andrew Browning, *Thomas Osborne, Earl of Danby and Duke of Leeds, 1632–1712*, 3 vols. (Glasgow, 1951), III, 34 ff. Cotterell, Montagu, Talbot, Rochester, Downing, Sidney Godolphin, Thynne, and Henry Savile were members of a committee to consider the reception of foreign ambassadors in England in 1678. All of them had, by that date, already served on embassies (*C.J.* IX, 544). Thomas Higgons, absent as envoy to Venice from 1674 to 1679, also appears on this committee, due to a clerical oversight. Article in *D.N.B.* erroneously names Higgons envoy to Vienna 1673 to 1676. See *C.T.B.* III, 1355; IV, 3, 343, 428; V, 231; VIII, 874–76, 895, 899; *C.S.P.V.* XXXVIII, 10, 130, and *passim*.

³⁹ Sir John Reresby, *Memoirs*, ed. and introd. Andrew Browning (Glasgow, 1936), pp. 88–89.

⁴⁰ Anchitell Grey, *Debates of the House of Commons, from the Year 1667 to the Year 1694*, 10 vols. (London, 1763), VII, 228–29, 231, 233–236; *C.J.* IX, 619; *C.S.P.D.* 1679–1680, pp. 596, 618; 1680, p. 16.

⁴¹ Harris, *Sandwich*, II, 43.

⁴² *C.S.P.V.* XXXV, 239; XXXVIII, 441.

⁴³ Henry Sidney, earl of Romney, *Diary of the Times of Charles the Second*, ed. R. W. Blencowe, 2 vols. (London, 1843), I, 1; B.M. Add. MSS. 37,983, f. 100; *C.S.P.D.* 1680–1681, p. 305; Thomas Plott

and Thomas Chudleigh, *The Despatches of Thomas Plott (1681–1682) and Thomas Chudleigh (1682–1685), English Envoys at The Hague*, ed. Frederick Arnold Middlebush (The Hague, 1926), pp. 5–6, 14, 19, 118.

44 Christopher Lindenov, *The First Triple Alliance: The Letters of Christopher Lindenov, Danish Envoy to London, 1668–1672*, ed. trans., and introd. Waldemar Westergaard (New Haven, 1947), pp. 71, 258, and notes; *Cont.* II, 72; H. C. Foxcroft, *The Life and Letters of Sir George Savile, Bart., First Marquis of Halifax*, 2 vols. (London, 1898), I, 71.

45 Ruvigny to Louis XIV, *C.S.P.V.* XXXVIII, 441, note.

46 *Recueil des instructions donneés aux ambassadeurs et ministres de France depuis les traités de Westphalie jusqu'à la Révolution Française . . . Angleterre*, ed. J. J. Jusserand, 2 vols. (Paris, 1929), I, 233; II, 305, *C.S.P.V.* XXXIV, 55; Reresby, *Memoirs*, p. 37.

47 Sir Richard Bulstrode, *Memoirs and Reflections upon the Reign and Government of King Charles the Ist and K. Charles the IInd.* (London, 1721), pp. 240–42.

48 *Cont.* II, 398–99; Temple, *Letters*, I, 404; P.R.O. S.P. 98/12, f. 269; Browning, *Danby*, I, 223; William Perwich, *The Despatches of William Perwich, English Agent in Paris, 1669–1677*, ed. M. Beryl Curran (London, 1903), p. 27; Cyril Hughes Hartmann, *Clifford of the Cabal* (London, 1937), pp. 83, 94; *C.S.P.D.* 1664–1665, p. 544; J. P. Kenyon, *Robert Spencer, Earl of Sunderland, 1641–1702* (London, 1958), p. 11.

49 B.M. Add. MSS. 37,986, ff. 198, 308; *C.S.P.D.* 1680–1681, p. 55; Etherege, *Letterbook*, p. 15; Henry Bennet and Henry Coventry, et al., *Letters from the Secretaries of State, and Other Persons, in the Reign of King Charles the Second, to Francis Parry, esq., English Envoy in Portugal* (London, 1817), p. 71; P.R.O. S.P. 78/139, f. 76; *C.S.P.D.* 1676–1677, p. 380; 1679–1680, p. 618; 1680–1681, p. 53.

50 Browning, *Danby*, I, 35; II, 540. In 1678 Danby had already offered the Paris embassy to Reresby, who did not accept it (Reresby, *Memoirs*, p. 173).

51 P.R.O. S.P. 98/12, f. 269; Temple, *Letters*, I, 404; Browning, *Danby*, I, 223; Hartmann, *Clifford*, pp. 83, 94; *C.S.P.D.* 1664–1665, p. 544; Perwich, *Despatches*, p. 27; Kenyon, *Sunderland*, p. 11.

52 H.M.C. *Finch MSS.* I, 81; *C.S.P.V.* XXXII, 168, 170; *C.S.P.D.* 1660, pp. 65, 136; *Bulstrode Papers*, I, 12–13; P.R.O. S.P. 105/62, ff. 30, 31; B.M. Stowe MSS. 219, f. 246.

53 *C.S.P.D.* 1667–1668, p. 258.

54 H.M.C. *Finch MSS.* II, 75–76; *Ormonde MSS.* n.s. V, 311; *Twelfth Report, Appendix*, part VII, "Le Fleming MSS.," p. 167; Narcissus

Luttrell, *A Brief Historical Relation of State Affairs from September 1678 to April 1714*, 6 vols. (Oxford, 1857), I, 42; George Abbott, *Under the Turk in Constantinople* (London, 1920), p. 313.

55 H.M.C. *Downshire MSS.* I, part 1, 208, 209, 213; B.M. Add. MSS. 34,799, f. 2; P.R.O. Stowe MSS. 220, ff. 12–13.

56 Pribram, *Lisola*, p. 277: "Carlingford . . . ist gar lieber Cavalier . . . aber scheint doch nit gar zu pfeilfindig zu sein."

57 P.R.O. S.P. 80/11, f. 75.

58 *Diary*, VII, 291.

59 *C.S.P.V.* XXXV, 20; XXXVIII, 248. Godolphin's "remarkable talents" in negotiating in Spain may be inferred from *Memoirs of the Duke of Ripperda: First Embassador from the States-General to His Most Catholic Majesty*, 2nd ed. (London, 1740), p. 373: "All Civility, all Complaisance, passes with the Spaniards for want of Courage. . . . To quicken Spaniards whenever they raise one Difficulty, you must start two. Sharp usage, and a quick Resentment of Injuries, are with them indubitable Marks of a Man of Honour."

60 M. Lane, "The Diplomatic Service under William III," *Trans. R.H.S.*, 4th series X (1927), 87–109; David Baynes Horn, *British Diplomatic Representatives, 1689–1789* (London, 1932).

61 Kenyon, *Sunderland*, pp. 18–19.

62 David Baynes Horn, "The Diplomatic Experience of Secretaries of State, 1660–1852," *History*, n.s. XLI (1956), pp. 88–99.

IV. THE EMBASSY HOUSEHOLD

1 Garrett Mattingly, *Renaissance Diplomacy* (London, 1955), pp. 240–41. The Italians had already developed a system of officially accredited secretaries, paid by the state, by 1600.

2 See Appendix II: all official secretaries designated by *.

3 See Appendix II, where secretaries who served on several missions are indicated.

4 Article in *D.N.B.* on Chudleigh is inaccurate. It lists his employment as embassy secretary in Sweden and at Nimeguen. In fact, Chudleigh was secretary in France, Spain, Italy, Cologne, and Nimeguen (*The Bulstrode Papers: The Collection of Autograph Letters and Historical Documents Formed by Alfred Morrison*, 2 vols. [London, 1897], I, 203; *C.S.P.D.* 1671, p. 503; 1673, pp. 105, 212; 1675–1676, p. 423; 1678, p. 531; 1680–1681, p. 53; *C.T.B.* III, 1122, 1289, 1360; IV, 147, 474, 636).

5 Caroline Robbins, "Carlisle and Marvell in Russia, Sweden, and Denmark, 1663–1664," *The History of Ideas Newsletter*, III:1 (January, 1957), 8–17.

[6] *C.S.P.D.* 1668–1669, p. 79; H.M.C. *Buccleuch MSS.* I, 425.

[7] Gertrude Ann Jacobsen, *William Blathwayt, a Late Seventeenth Century English Administrator* (New Haven, 1932), pp. 66–77.

[8] References to Ross, twice in Stockholm, once in Denmark, are in Longleat, MSS. of the Marquis of Bath, Coventry Papers, XXVI, f. 11; *Bulstrode Papers,* p. 194; Thomas Brown, ed. *Miscellanea Aulica: Or, A Collection of State-Treatises, Never before Published* (London, 1702), p. 70; *C.T.B.* III, 197; IV, 567, 573. Article in *D.N.B.* omits his later employments.

[9] Service three times in France, at the Congress of Cologne, and Vienna (P.R.O. S.P. 78/118; 78/126; *C.S.P.D.* 1663–1664, p. 266; 1660–1670, *Addenda,* p. 49; 1672, pp. 303, 304, 312; 1673, pp. 420, 435, 567; 1673–1675, pp. 110, 562–63; *C.T.B.* IV, 314, 739; V, 880, 1424).

[10] Thomas Plott and Thomas Chudleigh, *The Despatches of Thomas Plott (1681–1682) and Thomas Chudleigh (1682–1685), English Envoys at The Hague,* ed. Frederick Arnold Middlebush (The Hague, 1926), p. 134; see also Henry Sidney, earl of Romney, *Diary of the Times of Charles the Second,* ed. R. W. Blencowe, 2 vols. (London, 1843), I, 61, 305; II, 183.

[11] H.M.C. *Various Collections* II, "Wombwell MSS.," 156–57.

[12] *C.S.P.D.* 1660–1670, *Addenda,* p. 357; 1673–1675, p. 397; 1676–1677, pp. 204, 280; 1677–1678, p. 404.

[13] John Evelyn, *Diary,* ed. E. S. De Beer, 6 vols. (Oxford, 1955), IV, 447–48.

[14] P.R.O. S.P., 78/120, f. 136.

[15] Henry Hyde, *The Correspondence of Henry Hyde, Earl of Clarendon, and of His Brother Laurence Hyde, Earl of Rochester . . . and the Diary of Lord Rochester during His Embassy to Poland in 1676,* ed. Samuel Weller Singer, 2 vols. (London, 1828), I, xv.

[16] B.M. Add. MSS. 37,984, f. 75.

[17] During the mission of William Swann, the Hamburg Company was employing an unorthodox divine, Dr. Elborrow. Swann's instructions required him to make sure that Elborrow adjured the Covenant and accepted the Book of Common Prayer (*C.S.P.D.* 1661–1662, p. 478).

[18] John Batteridge Pearson, *A Biographical Sketch of the Chaplains to the Levant Company Maintained at Constantinople, Aleppo and Smyrna, 1611–1706* (Cambridge, 1883), pp. 8–9, 51–52. In 1682, 380 lyon dollars brought £100; H.M.C. *Finch MSS.* I, 380; *C.S.P.D.* 1660–1670, *Addenda,* p. 414.

[19] E.g., Lady Anne Fanshawe, *Memoirs* (London, 1905), p. 229; H.M.C. *Downshire MSS.* I, part 1, 228; Thomas Peregrine Courtenay, *Memoirs of the Life, Works, and Correspondence of Sir William Temple,*

Bart., 2 vols. (London, 1836), I, 115; Longleat, MSS. of the Marquis of Bath, Coventry Papers, XXV, f. 99.

20 P.R.O. S.P. 91/3, f. 213; *C.S.P.D.* 1664–1665, p. 29.

21 Sir George Etherege, *Letterbook,* ed. and introd. Sybil Rosenfeld (London, 1928), p. 403; *C.S.P.D.* 1660–1670, *Addenda,* pp. 466–67.

22 I have not been able to locate a reference to wages paid interpreters to English embassies. An interpreter for the Portuguese ambassador in England received 40 shillings per month (*C.S.P.D.* 1680–1681, p. 333).

23 Longleat, MSS. of the Marquis of Bath, Thynne Papers, LXVIII, f. 15; LXXXIII, f. 131; HM. Stowe MSS. (Dodington to Richard Temple, 21 November 1670).

24 P.R.O. S.P. 82/11, f. 16; H.M.C. *Downshire MSS.* I, part 1, 89; H.M.C. *Heathcote MSS.,* p. 159.

25 Etherege, *Letterbook,* p. 18; Christopher Lindenov, *The First Triple Alliance: The Letters of Christopher Lindenov, Danish Envoy to London, 1668–1672,* ed., trans. and introd. Waldemar Westergaard (New Haven, 1947), p. 133; H.M.C. *Twelfth Report,* Appendix, part 7, "Le Fleming MSS.," p. 65.

26 Narcissus Luttrell, *A Brief Historical Relation of State Affairs from September 1678 to April 1714,* 6 vols. (Oxford, 1857), I, 371; F. R. Harris, *The Life of Edward Montagu, K.G., First Earl of Sandwich (1625–1672),* 2 vols. (London, 1912), II, 51. The names and status of those in Sandwich's group are given in Lady Anne Fanshawe, *Memoirs,* pp. 232–33.

27 Patrick Gordon, *Passages from the Diary of General Patrick Gordon of Auchleuchreis, A.D. 1635–A.D. 1699* (Aberdeen, 1859), p. 56.

28 Guy Miège, *A Relation of Three Embassies from His Sacred Majestie Charles II to the Great Duke of Muscovie, the King of Sweden, and the King of Denmark* (London, 1669), pp. 4, 99; H.M.C. *Twelfth Report,* part 7, "Le Fleming MSS.," p. 30.

29 P.R.O. S.P. 105/49 (Southwell to Sunderland, 15 April 1680); Abel Boyer, *Memoirs of the Life and Negotiations of Sir William Temple . . . 1665 to . . . 1681* (London, 1714), p. 70; *C.S.P.D.* 1680–1681, p. 685; Lady Anne Fanshawe, *Memoirs,* pp. 164, 227; *C.S.P.D.* 1683–1684, p. 188; P.R.O. S.P. 78/149, f. 70; J. J. Jusserand, *A French Ambassador at the Court of Charles II, Le Comte de Comenges, from His Unpublished Correspondence* (New York, 1892), pp. 165–66.

30 George F. Abbott, *Under the Turk in Constantinople* (London, 1920), p. 47; H.M.C. *Downshire MSS.* I, part 1, 258; Evelyn, *Diary,* IV, 547, and note.

31 H.M.C. *Downshire MSS.* I, part 1, 223–24.

32 H.M.C. *Downshire MSS.* I, part 1, 223–24.

[33] Also called druggermen, both words being a corruption of the Arabic *targuman*.

[34] Camille G. Picavet, *La Diplomatie en France au temps de Louis XIV (1661–1706)* (Paris, 1930), pp. 267, 298.

[35] Sir Paul Rycaut, *The Present State of the Ottoman Empire, Containing the Maxims of the Turkish Polities, the Most Material Points of the Mahometan Religions . . . Their Military Discipline . . . in Three Books* (London, 1668), p. 90.

[36] *C.S.P.V.* XXXIII, 50–51.

[37] *C.S.P.D.* 1665–1666, p. 248; B.M. Stowe MSS. 219, f. 11; H.M.C. *Finch MSS.* I, 380, 418; John Covel, *Extracts from the Diaries of Dr. John Covel, 1670–1679*, ed. T. Theodore Bent (London, 1893), p. 146.

[38] B.M. Egerton MSS. 2071, f. 80; *Bulstrode Papers*, pp. 54, 119, 168; H.M.C. *Twelfth Report*, part 7, "Le Fleming MSS.," p. 46; *C.S.P.V.* XXXIII, 217; XXXV, 246, and notes; XXXVII, 15; Jusserand, *A French Ambassador*, pp. 21, 82, 85; Henry Benjamin Wheatley, *London, Past and Present*, 3 vols. (London, 1891), II, 299; III, 539.

[39] *A Narrative or Journal of the Procedings of . . . Lord Holles and Lord Coventry . . . Plenipotentiaries for the Treaty Held at Breda with the Ambassadors of the French King, the King of Denmark, and . . . the United Provinces*, By a Person of Quality, Concerned in this Ambassy (London, 1667), p. 7; Samuel Pepys, *Diary*, ed. Henry B. Wheatley, 9 vols. (London, 1910), III, 301.

[40] William Wynne, *The Life of Sir Leoline Jenkins*, 2 vols. (London, 1724), I, 363, 418, 503; P.R.O. S.P. 78/141, f. 11; Courtenay, *Temple*, I, 457; *C.T.B.* IV, 506; 723–24, 1075. Amounts in pounds are approximate. Rent at Cologne was given as 2,532 guilders, at Nimeguen as 2,850 guilders. Ten guilders plus 10 stivers equalled one pound. These amounts are known because the delegates tried to secure reimbursement for rent, since charges at the congresses were excessively high. They were not successful.

[41] HM. Stowe MSS. (Dodington to Richard Temple 31 October 1670).

[42] P.R.O. S.P. 101/13 (Newsletter from Paris, 7 August 1663); 78/126, f. 63; B.M. Add. MSS. 23,894, ff. 1–2, 14; *C.S.P.V.* XXXII, 242; H.M.C. *Downshire MSS.* I, part 1, 50, 55; *Seventh Report*, part 1, p. 293; Ruth Clark, *Sir William Trumbull in Paris, 1685–86* (Cambridge, 1938), pp. 164–65.

[43] P.R.O. S.P. 84/184, f. 62; Boyer, *Temple*, p. 189; Courtenay, *Temple*, I, 354; Plott and Chudleigh, *Despatches*, pp. 4–5.

[44] Miège, *Relation*, pp. 5, 139–40; Baroness Sophie Buxhoeveden, *A Cavalier in Muscovy* (London, 1932), pp. 94–95. This book contains a picture of Carlisle's house in Moscow, from a drawing done in 1662.

45 Harris, *Sandwich*, II, 53, 60, 89, 90; Sir Richard Fanshawe et al., *Original Letters and Negotiations of Sir Richard Fanshawe, the Earl of Sandwich, the Earl of Sunderland and Sir William Godolphin, Wherein Divers Matters between the Three Crowns of England, Spain and Portugal from 1663 to 1678 Are Set in a Clearer Light Than Is Anywhere Else Extant*, 2 vols. (London, 1724), I, 37, 129; Lady Anne Fanshawe, *Memoirs*, pp. 167–68, 194, 270–71; Edward Montagu, earl of Sandwich, *Hispania Illustrata . . . in Letters from . . . the Earl of Sandwich, the Earl of Sunderland, and Sir William Godolphin during Their Embassies in Spain* (London, 1703), p. 142; *C.S.P.V.* XXXIV, 19 and note, 22.

46 *C.T.B.* V, 547, 872, 1075.

47 Abbott, *Under the Turk*, p. 35; Covel, *Diary*, pp. 189–90; H.M.C. *Finch MSS.* I, 103; *C.S.P.V.* XXXIII, 260; XXXIV, 4.

V. REMUNERATION

1 England had no statute which fixed diplomatic salaries until the nineteenth century (R. H. Feller and Manley O. Hudson, eds. *A Collection of the Diplomatic and Consular Laws and Regulations of Various Countries*, 2 vols. [Washington, 1933], I, 168).

2 P.R.O. S.P. 9/166, f. 75; *C.S.P.D.* 1663–1664, p. 306; H.M.C. *Heathcote MSS.*, p. 132.

3 For example, Temple's salary for his mission to Brussels was settled at a conference between Arlington and the Lord Treasurer Henry Bennet, earl of Arlington, *The Right Honourable the Earl of Arlington's Letters to Sir William Temple, Bart.*, 2 vols. (London, 1701), I, 3.

4 *C.S.P.D.* 1663–1664, p. 306; W. L. Grant, "A Puritan at the Court of Louis XIV," *Bulletin of the Departments of History and Political and Economic Sciences in Queen's University*, VIII (July, 1913), 5; H.M.C. *Buccleuch MSS.* I, 420.

5 Samuel Pepys, *Diary*, ed. Henry B. Wheatley, 9 vols. (London, 1910), VII, 125–26; VIII, 110.

6 *C.T.B.* II, 4, 43, 45, 144.

7 *C.S.P.D.* 1669, pp. 265, 612.

8 Abel Boyer, *Memoirs of the Life and Negotiations of Sir William Temple . . . 1665 to . . . 1681* (London, 1714), p. 83; P.R.O. S.P. 82/11, f. 46.

9 P.R.O. S.P. 78/123, f. 435: "Les Appointmens que le Roy de France donne à ses Ambassadeurs et Ministres (1667)." French diplomats were reimbursed in this descending order: first, ambassadors in Rome; second, ambassadors in Holland and Sweden; third, ambassadors in Venice, Savoy, Switzerland, Spain, England, Denmark, Poland;

fourth, residents in Vienna; fifth, residents in Genoa, Florence, German states, Portugal.

10 *C.S.P.V.* XXXII, 166–67. I use the rate of exchange mentioned in 1668 (*C.S.P.V.* XXXV, 240): £400 equals 2,400 ducats.

11 *C.T.B.* III, 287.

12 Margery Lane, "The Diplomatic Service under William III," *Trans. R.H.S.*, 4th series, X (1927), 94–95; David Baynes Horn, *The British Diplomatic Service, 1689–1789* (Oxford, 1961), pp. 48 ff.

13 *C.T.B.* VIII, 453, 1223.

14 *C.T.B.* I, 644; II, 470, 1246; III, 712; IV, 321, 430, 537, 657; V, 696, 1022, 1029.

15 *C.S.P.D.* 1671, p. 503; *C.T.B.* II, 160, 270; III, 1122, 1359; IV, 81.

16 *C.T.B.* II, 371, 444, 470; III, 225.

17 Henry Sidney, earl of Romney, *Diary of the Times of Charles the Second,* ed. R. W. Blencowe, 2 vols. (London, 1843), I, 1–2.

18 *C.T.B.* III, 1291.

19 *Ibid.,* III, 1165.

20 The sources do not describe the cloth of state. The cloth of state which hung in the House of Lords pictured a unicorn, and members bowed when they approached it.

21 Lady Anne Fanshawe, *Memoirs* (London, 1905), p. 137.

22 *C.S.P.D.* 1669, p. 612.

23 *C.T.B.* V, 893–94.

24 *Ibid.,* V, 547; VIII, 2071.

25 P.R.O. S.P. 78/150, f. 25; *C.T.B.* VI, 135; VII, 1291, 1886.

26 To give but two examples: Poley, who had a bill for £33 5s. 00d. passed quickly, admitted to a friend that he would have claimed more if he had known he would have had so little trouble getting his account passed (B.M. Add. MSS. 37,986, f. 135). Etherege estimated his expenses for intelligence and express postage, and then more than tripled them before submitting the accounts to Middleton (Sir George Etherege, *Letterbook,* ed. and introd. Sybil Rosenfeld [London, 1928], pp. 365–66 and notes).

27 HM. Stowe MSS. (Dodington to Temple, 10 April 1671); Stephen B. Baxter, *The Development of the Treasury, 1660–1702* (Cambridge, 1957), pp. 55, 72; Horn, *British Diplomatic Service,* p. 49; *C.T.B.* VIII, 1903, 1887, 2054. Carl Brinkmann ("The Relations Between England and Germany, 1660–1688," *E.H.R.,* XXXIV:94 [April, 1909], part I, 247–77), citing Middleton's directive to Etherege to limit his extraordinaries to £50 per quarter (*Letterbook,* p. 394), errs in the assertion that his order limited all diplomats to that sum after 1687. See *C.T.B.* VIII, 1900, 1904, for higher extraordinary bills allowed through 1688.

[28] H.M.C. *Finch MSS.* I, 342; *Downshire MSS.* I, part 1, 210, 215.

[29] P.R.O. S.P. 105/175, f. 241; H.M.C. *Downshire MSS.* I, part 1, 215; *Finch MSS.* II, 76; P.R.O. S.P. 105/155, ff. 13, 65; *C.T.B.* I, 63; II, 327; VIII, 983; H.M.C. *Finch MSS.* I, 97, 133, 160, 187.

[30] H.M.C. *Finch MSS.* I, 139. In fact, the French ambassador received 6,000 dollars from the Turkey Company and, in theory, another 12,000 from the King. In 1676 the latter salary had not been paid for several years. Pompone's remedy was to order the ambassador to take his arrears due from the crown from the merchants, and give them bills upon the court. When the merchants objected, an embargo was placed on all French merchant shipping in the Levant until they accepted these terms (Longleat, MSS. of the Marquis of Bath, Coventry Papers, LIX, ff. 130–299).

[31] *C.T.B.* I, 532, 535; II, 162; VIII, 1095; Guy Miège, *A Relation of Three Embassies from His Sacred Majestie Charles II to the Great Duke of Muscovie, the King of Sweden, and the King of Denmark* (London, 1669), p. 5.

[32] J. Heringa, *De Eer en Hoogheid van de Staat* (Groningen, 1961), pp. 478–79.

[33] P.R.O. L.C. 5/2, ff. 22–23; E. 403/2609, ff. 109, 122, 125; *C.T.B.* VIII, 1771; H.M.C. *Second Report*, Appendix, "Cottrell Dormer MSS.," pp. 82–84.

[34] In the years 1660 to 1662 and 1685 to 1688 amounts ranged between £2,150 and £18,527 (*C.T.B.* I, xxxii; VIII, xxxix; V, xv).

[35] Edward Montagu, earl of Sandwich, *Hispania Illustrata . . . in Letters from . . . the Earl of Sandwich, the Earl of Sunderland, and Sir William Godolphin during Their Embassies in Spain* (London, 1703), p. 169.

[36] Abraham de Wicquefort, *The Embassador and His Functions*, trans. John Digby (London, 1716), p. 206.

[37] *C.S.P.D.* 1665–1666, pp. 127–28.

[38] *C.T.B.* III, 1177; IV, 440–41; V, 117; VII, 1653; Browning, *Danby*, I, 130, 186–87, 324; III, 14, 22–23.

[39] P.R.O. S.P. 78/141, f. 132; 78/146, f. 116; *C.T.B.,* I, 716; IV, 814; VI, 115, 426, 484; VII, 372, 373, 459, 835; H.M.C. *Seventh Report*, part I, "Graham MSS.," p. 340; Sir William Temple, *Letters . . . Containing an Account of the Most Important Transactions . . . in Christendom from 1665 to 1672*, 2 vols. (London, 1700), I, 194–95; Romney, *Diary*, II, 181.

[40] H.M.C. *Montagu Bertie MSS.*, p. 97; *C.S.P.D.* 1685, pp. 106, 281.

[41] Violet Barbour, *Henry Bennet, Earl of Arlington* (Washington, 1914), pp. 39–40. *Recueil des instructions donneés aux ambassadeurs et ministres de France depuis les traités de Westphalie jusqu'à la Révolution*

Française . . . Angleterre, ed. and introd. J. J. Jusserand, 2 vols. (Paris, 1929), II, 265–66; Sir John Dalrymple, *Memoirs of Great Britain and Ireland,* 2nd ed., 3 vols. (London, 1771), I, 199 and note.
42 Baxter, *Treasury,* p. 248.
43 Examples of ministers who relied on private credit to maintain themselves abroad: Poley (B.M. Add. MSS. 37,986, ff. 100, 273, 293), Sidney Godolphin (P.R.O. S.P. 78/146, f. 175), Paull (Longleat, MSS. of the Marquis of Bath, Coventry Papers, XXVI, ff. 69–70), Sunderland (Browning, *Danby,* II, 527), and Holles (B.M. Add. MSS. 32,679, f. 14).
44 Selling tallies at a discount was a fairly common procedure for all employees of the crown (Baxter, *Treasury,* p. 76). Lady Anne Fanshawe, *Memoirs,* p. 248; *C.S.P.D.* 1667, p. 494.

VI. PROTOCOL

1 *C.S.P.V.* XXXIII, 19.
2 P.R.O. L.C. 5/2, "The Notebooks of Sir Charles Cotterell," f. 39; John Finet, *Finetti Philoxensis: Som Choice Observations of Sir John Finet . . . Touching the Reception, and Precedence, the Treatment and Audience, the Puntillios and Contests of Forren Ambassadors in England,* ed. James Howell (London, 1656), pp. 228 ff.; John Evelyn, *Diary,* ed. E. S. De Beer, 6 vols. (Oxford, 1955), III, 515, gives an eye witness account of an exceptionally colorful Venetian entry also reported in *C.S.P.V.* XXXV, 273–75.
3 *C.T.B.* I, 57, 72; II, 172; IV, 442, 448; VI, 43, 102, 186, 192, 593, 595; VII, part 1, 141.
4 Christopher Lindenov, *The First Triple Alliance: The Letters of Christopher Lindenov, Danish Envoy to London, 1668–1672,* ed., trans., and introd. Waldemar Westergaard (New Haven, 1947), pp. 8, 19–20; *C.S.P.V.* XXXII, 191; XXXIII, 217; *The Bulstrode Papers: The Collection of Autograph Letters and Historical Documents Formed by Alfred Morrison,* 2 vols. (London, 1897), I, 354–55.
5 Abraham de Wicquefort, *The Embassador and His Functions,* trans. John Digby (London, 1716), p. 137; *C.S.P.V.* XXXIII, 97.
6 Wicquefort, *Embassador,* p. 127; P.R.O. L.C. 5/2, "Manière de la réception des ambassadeurs étrangers en France."
7 H.M.C. *Downshire MSS.* I, part 1, 88–90.
8 P.R.O. L.C. 5/2.
9 Longleat, MSS. of the Marquis of Bath, Coventry Papers, LX, ff. 287, 311; Sir Richard Fanshawe et al., *Original Letters and Negotiations of Sir Richard Fanshawe, the Earl of Sunderland and Sir William Godolphin, Wherein Divers Matters between the Three Crowns*

of England, Spain and Portugal from 1663 to 1678 Are Set in a Clearer Light Than Is Anywhere Else Extant, 2 vols. (London, 1724), I, 107–109; F. R. Harris, *The Life of Edward Montagu, K.G., First Earl of Sandwich (1625–1672),* 2 vols. (London, 1912), II, 63; *Bulstrode Papers,* I, 217; B.M. Add. MSS. 35,100, f. 11.

10 H.M.C. *Various Collections* II, "Wombwell MSS.," 217–18; *C.S.P.V.* XXXVI, 227; Wicquefort, *Embassador,* p. 141.

11 P.R.O. S.P. 98/11, f. 150, "An Account of yᵉ manner of entertaining Ambʳˢ in the States of the Gr. Duke of Tuscanie"; P.R.O. S.P. 98/5 (Finch to Arlington, 3 June 1665); H.M.C. *Downshire MSS.* I, part 1, 235.

12 Wicquefort, *Embassador,* p. 142; B. M. Sloane MSS. 3660, f. 93.

13 P.R.O. S.P. 84/187, f. 190.

14 J. Heringa, *De Eer en Hoogheid van de Staat* (Gromingen, 1961), pp. 395–96.

15 *A Narrative or Journal of the Procedings of . . . Lord Holles and Lord Coventry . . . Plenipotentiaries for the Treaty Held at Breda with the Ambassadors of the French King, the King of Denmark, and . . . the United Provinces,* By a Person of Quality, Concerned in this Ambassy (London, 1667), pp. 7–13.

16 Sir Bernard Gascoigne, "A Description of Germany Sent to Charles II from Vienna in 1672," in Thomas Brown, ed., *Miscellanea Aulica: Or, A Collection of State-Treatises, Never before Published* (London, 1702), pp. 40–41.

17 Guy Miège, *A Relation of Three Embassies from His Sacred Majestie Charles II to the Great Duke of Muscovie, the King of Sweden, and the King of Denmark* (London, 1669), pp. 112–35. The house in Stockholm used for lodging ambassadors belonged to General Wrangels. Carlisle stayed there again for three days in 1669 (*Bulstrode Papers,* I, 111).

18 *Ibid.,* p. 407.

19 Heneage Finch, earl of Winchilsea, *A Narrative of the Success of the Voyage of . . . Heneage Finch . . . His Majesties Ambassadour Extraordinary to the High and Mighty Prince Sultan Mamet Han* (London, 1661), pp. 3–6.

20 Wicquefort, *Embassador,* pp. 148–49.

21 *Bulstrode Papers,* I, 8, 201.

22 P.R.O. L.C. 5/2, "Notebooks of Sir Charles Cotterell."

23 *C.S.P.V.* XXXII, 174.

24 P.R.O. L.C. 5/2, "Manière de la réception."

25 H.M.C. *Seventh Report,* part I, "Graham MSS.," p. 271; P.R.O. S.P. 78/118, f. 193.

26 Miège, *Relation,* pp. 143–52.

27 Longleat, MSS. of the Marquis of Bath, Coventry Papers, LX, f. 321; Miège, *Relation*, p. 353.

28 P.R.O. S.P. 105/49 (Southwell to Sunderland, 5 April 1680).

29 Henry Sidney, earl of Romney, *Diary of the Times of Charles the Second*, ed. R. W. Blencowe, 2 vols. (London, 1843), I, 56–57.

30 *C.S.P.V.* XXXV, 29.

31 Holles to Arlington, 9 March 1662, letter printed in W. L. Grant, "A Puritan at the Court of Louis XIV," *Bulletin of the Departments of History and Political and Economic Sciences in Queen's University*, VIII (July, 1913), 80.

32 A formal order of precedence drawn up in 1504 by Pope Julius II fixed the order as: German Emperor, King of the Romans, King of France, King of Spain. England ranked seventh in this list, after Aragon and Portugal. The order was never accepted without quarrels, especially after 1556, when Philip II succeeded to the Hapsburg lands but not the imperial title. France and Spain then entered a long series of disputes for second place. The criterion for determining precedency in a new list drawn up in 1564 was the comparative antiquity of royal title. After the Pope and the Holy Roman Emperor came France (A.D. 481), Spain (718), England (827). (Sir Ernest Satow, *A Guide to Diplomatic Practise*, 2 vols. [London, 1917], I, 13–16; Garrett Mattingly, *Renaissance Diplomacy* [London, 1955], p. 252.)

33 *Diary*, ed. Henry B. Wheatley, 9 vols. (London, 1910), II, 104–06.

34 Evelyn, *Diary*, III, 297–300 and notes; *C.S.P.D.* 1661, p. 104; 1663, pp. 41–42; Fanshawe, *Original Letters*, I, 107–09; P.R.O. S.P. 78/115, f. 261.

35 Robert Cotton, *A Briefe Abstract of the Questions of Precedency, betweene England and Spain* (London, 1643), pp. 2–7; *C.S.P.D.* 1667–1668, pp. 457–58.

36 Heringa, *Hoogheid*, p. 496.

37 P.R.O. S.P. 78/117, ff. 158, 161, 204, 210, 220, 224, 228, 244; 78/118, ff. 1, 32, 53, 58, 93, 110, 115, 117.

38 H.M.C. *Finch MSS.* I, 303. This was the official position. Pepys considered it "most dishonourable" to England and said Charles II vowed "he would not be hectored out of his rights and preeminencys by the King of France, as great as he was." (*Diary*, IV, 49.)

39 P.R.O. S.P. 78/126, ff. 71–72, 139, 150; B.M. Add. MSS. 23,894, ff. 1, 11.

40 Abel Boyer, *The History of the Reign of Queen Anne Drafted into Annals*, 11 vols. (London, 1710), VIII, 366–67; *Recueil des instructions donneés aux ambassadeurs et ministres de France depuis les traités de Westphalie jusqu'à la Révolution Française . . . Angleterre*,

ed. and introd. J. J. Jusserand, 2 vols. (Paris, 1920), II, 229–30, to Barillon (6 August 1677): "Il serait à craindre qu'une plus longue suite d'éviter ces cérémonies n'abolit insensiblement une coutume que Sa Majesté juge important de maintenir." H.M.C. *Ormonde MSS.* IV, 338.

41 Wicquefort, *Embassador*, pp. 184–92.

42 Examples of this point are in H.M.C. "Le Fleming MSS.," p. 59; Plott and Chudleigh, *Despatches*, pp. 59–60.

43 P.R.O. S.P. 9/166, f. 327; Abel Boyer, *Memoirs of the Life and Negotiations of Sir William Temple . . . 1665 to 1681* (London, 1714), pp. 101, 198; Thomas Peregrine Courtenay, *Memoirs of the Life, Works, and Correspondence of Sir William Temple, Bart.,* 2 vols. (London, 1836), I, 272–76.

44 B.M. Harl. MSS. 1516, f. 12.

45 *C.S.P.D.* 1675–1676, pp. 503–504; Harl. MSS. 1515, ff. 76–77.

46 B.M. Sloane MSS. 3660, f. 90, and Harl. MSS. 1517, f. 8, show how this was done at the Treaty of Breda, Sweden mediating between England and the United Provinces; Satow, *Diplomatic Practise*, I, 22.

47 B.M. Stowe MSS. 193, f. 7; *Bulstrode Papers*, I, 42; Courtenay, *Temple*, I, 223.

48 Camille A. Picavet, "Française et les langues étrangères dans la diplomatie," *Revue des Sciences Politiques*, LI (1928), 578–629. Comenges, of the Célèbre Ambassade, was an exception. He knew Latin well enough to negotiate in it, but knew no English.

49 For example, St. Albans received his written instructions in English, but another copy, in Latin, is deposited among the State Papers Foreign. Collections of instructions are so fragmentary it is impossible to tell whether this was regular procedure or not (P.R.O. S.P. 78/115, ff. 193–95).

50 B.M. Stowe MSS. 195, "A Collection of State Documents," *passim;* Lindenov, *Letters*, pp. 223–24; *C.S.P.V.* XXXII, 155, 174.

51 Bodleian, Carte MSS. 72, f. 54; P.R.O. S.P. 78/118, f. 110; Fanshawe, *Original Letters*, I, 117; *C.S.P.V.* XXXIV, 286; P.R.O. S.P. 81/56, f. 274; *C.S.P.V.* XXXVIII, 289; Heringa, *Hoogheid*, p. 462; H.M.C. *Montagu-Bertie MSS.*, pp. 196–98; Miège, *Relation*, pp. 153–63.

52 Longleat, MSS. of the Marquis of Bath, Coventry Papers, XXVI, *passim;* The Hague, Algemeen Rijksarchief: Staaten-General, Engeland 6917–6928; P.R.O. S.P. 105/49 (Southwell to Sunderland, 3 October 1680); S.P. 91/3, f. 245; Sir Patrick Gordon, *Passages from the Diary of General Patrick Gordon of Auchleuchries, A.D. 1635– A.D. 1699* (Aberdeen, 1859), p. 162.

53 Sir William Temple, *Letters . . . Containing an Account of the Most Important Transactions . . . in Christendom from 1665 to 1672,* 2

vols. (London, 1700), I, 144; Jean Du Mont, *Corps universel diplomatique du droit des gens,* 8 vols. (Amsterdam, 1726 ff.), VI, VII; William Wynne, *The Life of Sir Leoline Jenkins,* 2 vols. (London, 1724), II, 39–42.

54 Gilbert Burnet, *History of My Own Time,* ed. Osmund Airy, 2 vols. (Oxford, 1897, 1900), II, 284.

VII. EXTERRITORIALITY

1 Percy E. Corbett, *Law in Diplomacy* (Princeton, 1959), pp. 20–23.

2 Gentili was born in Italy and studied at the University of Perugia. He converted to Protestantism and fled from the Inquisition to England, where he became lecturer in civil law at Oxford.

3 *De legationibus libri tres,* trans. Gordon J. Laing, introd. Ernest Nys (New York, 1924), pp. 111–14. The decision marked a reversal from a position taken in the case against John Leslie, bishop of Ross, ambassador from Mary Queen of Scots to Queen Elizabeth, who was convicted of conspiracy in 1571. The earlier decision, now held to be wrong, stated: "An Embassador procuringe an Insurrection or Rebellion in the Prince's Cowntrey towards whom he is Embassador, ought not, Jure Gentium et Civile Romanor, to enjoye the Privileges otherwise dew to an Embassador; but that he maye notwithstandinge be ponished for the same" ("The Opinion of the Doctors to the Articles," *International Law Opinions Selected and Annotated,* ed. Lord McNair, 2 vols. [Cambridge, 1956], I, 186).

4 Gentili, *De legationibus,* pp. 72, 90–91.

5 Gentili, *De legationibus,* pp. 96–97.

6 Hotman was born in Lausanne and studied jurisprudence in France. From 1580 to 1585 he was in England in the service of Robert Dudley, earl of Leicester. He returned to France in 1585, where the King made him master of requests.

7 London, 1603. This edition is a translation of the original, *De la charge et dignité de l'ambassadeur,* of which the first edition is no longer extant. A second French edition appeared in Paris in 1604.

8 Hotman, *The Ambassadors,* p. 98.

9 Grotius was born in Delft and educated at the University of Leyden. He gained diplomatic experience as a member of the Dutch embassy in France in 1598, and in England in 1613, and as the Swedish ambassador to France in 1634. Prince Maurice of Orange sentenced Grotius to life imprisonment in 1619 for supporting the Arminians against the Orthodox Calvinists. He escaped four years later and fled to France, where he wrote *De jure belli ac pacis libri tres* in 1623.

10 Hugo Grotius, *De jure belli ac pacis libri tres,* trans. Francis M. Kelsey et al., introd. James Brown Scott, 2 vols. (Oxford, 1925), II, 443.

11 E. R. Adair, *The Exterritoriality of Ambassadors in the Sixteenth and Seventeenth Centuries* (London, 1929), pp. 5–6, 28.

12 Grotius, *De jure,* II, 444–47.

13 Zouche was educated at New College and attained the Regius professorship in 1620. He became judge of the High Court of Admiralty in 1641. Although of Royalist sympathies he won the admiration of Cromwell, who appointed him to a special commission of oyer and terminer in 1654. After the Restoration he was restored to his judgeship of the Admiralty.

14 Adair, *Exterritoriality,* pp. 29–30; Richard Zouche, *An Exposition of Fecial Law and Procedure, and of Law between Nations, and Questions Concerning the Same,* ed. Thomas Erskine Holland, trans. J. L. Brierly, 2 vols. (Washington, 1911), II, 29–30, 98–100.

15 Pufendorf was born in Germany and educated at Leipzig and Jena. He served in the Swedish embassy at Copenhagen in 1658. The Danes imprisoned him when war broke out between Sweden and Denmark. In prison he wrote *Elementorum jurisprudentiae universalis, libri duo* (The Hague, 1660). In 1661 the Elector Palatine appointed him the first holder of the new chair in the Law of Nature and Nations in Heidelberg with the obligations to teach the writings of Grotius. In 1670 he obtained a professorship at the University of Lund. *De jure naturae et gentium, libri Octo* appeared in 1672, and in an abridged version the following year under the title *De officio hominis et civis, libri duo.*

16 Rachel was born in Holstein and educated at the universities of Rostock and Jena. He became Professor of the Law of Nature and Nations at the University of Kiel. Rachel published *De jure gentium dissertatio* in 1676. He served in the diplomatic corps of the Duke of Schleswig-Holstein at Nimeguen, Dresden, Regensburg, and Nuremberg.

17 Samuel Pufendorf, *De jure naturae et gentium, libri octo,* trans. C. H. and W. A. Oldfather, 2 vols. (Oxford, 1934), II, 28.

18 Pufendorf, *De jure naturae,* pp. 228–29.

19 Samuel Rachel, *Dissertations on the Law of Nature and Nations,* trans. John Pawley Bate, introd. Ludwig von Bar, 2 vols. (Washington, 1916), II, 196, 215.

20 Gentili, *De legationibus,* pp. 106–08.

21 Hotman, *Ambassadors,* pp. 138–39.

22 Grotius, *De jure,* II, 448–49; Garrett Mattingly, *Renaissance Diplomacy* (London, 1955), pp. 272–73.

23 Gentili, *De legationibus,* pp. 103–04; Hotman, *Ambassadors,* pp. 131–33.

24 Grotius, *De jure,* II, 447–48.

25 Rachel, *Dissertations,* II, 198.

26 Zouche, *Exposition,* p. 99.

27 *"Frustra auxilium legis invocat qui in legem committit.* Murder is an offense against the law of nations, whilst an offense against the municipal laws is only *crimen prohibitum,* and not *malum in se"* (McNair, ed., *International Law Opinions,* I, 188).

28 Hale was educated at Oxford and Lincoln's Inn. Cromwell made him a justice of the Common Pleas. After the Restoration he was appointed to the commission to try the regicides, and became Chief Justice of the King's Bench in 1671.

29 Sir Matthew Hale, *The History of the Pleas of the Crown,* new ed., 2 vols. (London, 1800), I, 99. This book was not published until two years after Hale's death, and went through seven editions by 1773.

30 Hale, *Pleas of the Crown,* I, 97.

31 Adair, *Exterritoriality,* pp. 38–39. Adair's examination of specific cases ends with 1660.

32 *Mémoires touchant les ambassadeurs et les ministres publics,* par L[e] M[inistre] P[risonnier], (Cologne, 1677). This book appeared under the initials L.M.P. ("le ministre prisonnier") and is credited by all authorities to Wicquefort. "Il est vray, qu'un Souverain n'est pas obligé de recevoir indistinctement tous ceux qu'un Prince estranger lui veut envoyer . . . mais après qu'il l'a admis & reconnu en cette qualité il ne le peut pas empescher de jouir du bénéfice du droit des gens, en toute son estendue; Sans que la Justice du lieu, ny mesmes l'Autorité du Souverain, auprès duquel il réside, puisse faire exercer sur la personne du Ministre une Jurisdiction, qu'il a cedée à un autre Prince, en permettant à son sujet de lui faire le serment de fidelité" (p. 34).

33 The Hague, 1681. A German translation appeared in 1689.

34 *Mémoires,* p. 134; Abraham de Wicquefort, *The Embassador and His Functions,* trans. John Digby (London, 1716), pp. 251–53.

35 William Wynne, *The Life of Sir Leoline Jenkins,* 2 vols. (London, 1724), I, xxiii–iv, 280–86; *C.S.P.V.* XXXVIII, 244, 482, 492. Louis XIV made Fürstenberg bishop of Strasbourg in 1682, and secured a cardinalate for him in 1686.

36 *C.S.P.D.* 1677–78, pp. 14–15, 30, 58, 82, 346–47, 542; Anchitell Grey, *Debates of the House of Commons from the Year 1667 to the Year 1694,* 10 vols. (London, 1763), IV, 132–33, 259, 261–62, 269, 281.

37 *C.S.P.D.* 1677–1678, p. 82. Williamson's notes, which consist of a list of cases taken from Wicquefort's second book, are in P.R.O. S.P.

9/166. The cases are outlined without reference to Salinas, but it
seems probable that they were compiled at this time.

[38] Longleat, MSS. of the Marquis of Bath, Coventry Papers, LX, ff. 28,
45, 81.

[39] Cornelius van Bynkershoek, *De foro legatorum,* trans. Gordon J.
Laing, introd. Jan de Louter (Oxford, 1946), p. 28; John Beresford,
The Godfather of Downing Street: Sir George Downing, 1623–1684
(Boston, 1925), p. 194; Thomas Peregrine Courtenay, *Memoirs of the
Life, Works, and Correspondence of Sir William Temple, Bart.,* 2
vols. (London, 1836), I, 113–15.

[40] *C.S.P.V.* XXXIV, 214; Thomas Brown, ed., *Miscellanea Aulica: Or,
A Collection of State-Treatises, Never before Published* (London,
1702), p. 43; Wynne, *Jenkins,* II, 409–10; P.R.O. S.P. 91/3, ff. 285–86.

[41] *C.S.P.V.* XXXIV, 214, 221, 229.

[42] Guy Miège, *A Relation of Three Embassies from His Sacred Majestie
Charles II to the Great Duke of Muscovie, the King of Sweden, and
the King of Denmark* (London, 1669), p. 160; *C.S.P.V.* XXIV, 90.
A false rumor reached England that Carlisle was almost put to death
but was saved by three votes; P.R.O. S.P. 91/3, ff. 258–92.

[43] P.R.O. S.P. 78/126, f. 13; B.M. Add. MSS. 23,894, ff. 2, 13.

[44] Wicquefort, *Mémoires,* pp. 57–60. The quotation is taken from a translation of fragments of the book in B. M. Sloane MSS. 3660, f. 78.

[45] Oudart was born in the Spanish Netherlands, served as secretary to
William Boswell, resident of Charles I in the Netherlands, and sub-
sequently became an English subject before he returned to The Hague
in Downing's suite.

[46] The Hague: Algemeen Rijksarchief: Staaten-Generaal, Engeland 6920
(14, 17 July, 10, 13, 19 August 1665); *C.S.P.D.* 1664–1665, p. 486. The
affair was reported fully in France (P.R.O. S.P. 78/121, ff. 53 ff.).
Oudart was out of prison a year later, and Arlington rewarded him
for his pains by making him Latin secretary (H.M.C. *Finch MSS.*
I, 431).

[47] Cases of success and failure in securing asylum in embassies in London are in J. J. Jusserand, *A French Ambassador at the Court of
Charles II, Le Comte de Comenges, from His Unpublished Corre
spondence* (New York, 1892), pp. 146–47; W. W. Christie, ed., *Letters
Addressed from London to Sir Joseph Williamson While Plenipotentiary at the Congress of Cologne, in the Years 1673 and 1674,* 2 vols.
(London, 1874), I, 187.

[48] Bynkershoek, *De foro,* p. 116.

[49] *C.S.P.V.* XXXVII, 97, 129–30.

[50] Mattingly, *Renaissance Diplomacy,* p. 279; F. R. Harris, *The Life of
Edward Montagu, K.G., First Earl of Sandwich (1625–1672),* 2 vols.

(London, 1912), II, 81–88; Lady Anne Fanshawe, *Memoirs* (London, 1905), pp. 205–08.

51 *C.S.P.D.* 1682, p. 401; H.M.C. *Downshire MSS.* I, part 1, 14–15; H.M.C. *Seventh Report*, part 1, "Graham MSS.," pp. 279, 346, 361; Charles A. Goodricke, *History of the Goodricke Family*, rev. ed. (London, 1897), pp. 29–30.

52 *Embassador*, p. 268. Adair explains the general absence of comment on *droit du chapel* by the proposition that this freedom was implicit in the concept of exterritoriality: *cuius regio eius religio* (*Exterritoriality*, pp. 177–78).

53 *C.S.P.D.* 1661–1662, p. 451; 1667, p. 457; *Tudor and Stuart Proclamations, 1485–1714*, ed. Robert Steele, vol. I. *England and Wales* (Oxford, 1910); *C.S.P.V.* XXXII, 140, 279; XXXIII, 131–32.

54 Jusserand, *A French Ambassador*, pp. 118–19. The word Jusserand used was "communions," but he was obviously referring to the number of people attending services.

55 *C.S.P.V.* XXXVI, 133; XXXVII, 62.

56 *C.S.P.D.* 1676–1677, p. 349.

57 *C.S.P.V.* XXXVIII, 287–88, 293, 303, 307.

58 *C.S.P.V.* XXXVIII, 333, 338, 343, 392; *C.S.P.D.* 1673–1675, p. 466; 1675–1676, pp. 12, 13. William Raleigh Trimble, "The Embassy Chapel Question, 1625–1660," *Journal of Modern History*, XVIII:2 (June, 1946), 97–107, shows that conditions before the Restoration were much the same. During periods of unrest, such as Cromwell's war with Spain, attendance at Catholic chapels was restricted and English priests were denied immunity.

59 B.M. Stowe MSS. 195, f. 57.

60 *C.S.P.D.* 1678, p. 557.

61 P.R.O. S.P. 78/150, f. 99. Several of Trumbull's letters are cited by Ruth Clark, *Sir William Trumbull in Paris, 1685–86* (Cambridge, 1938), pp. 135–43.

62 *C.S.P.D.* 1667, p. 260; HM. Stowe MSS. (Dodington to Temple, 21 June, 5 July, 8, 15 August 1670); H.M.C. *Various Collections* II, "Wombwell MSS.," 135–36, 139, 140, 153.

63 Miège, *Relation*, pp. 140–41; Christopher Lindenov, *The First Triple Alliance: The Letters of Christopher Lindenov, Danish Envoy to London, 1668–1672*, ed. and introd. Waldemar Westergaard (New Haven, 1947), p. 145. England had similar restrictions during the Protectorate. No member of Parliament was allowed to have an interview with a foreign minister without formal permission. If he did, he lost his seat (O. Krauske, *Die Entwickelung der ständigen Diplomatie vom 15. Jahrhundert bis zu den Beschlüssen von 1815–18, in*

staats- und sozialwissenschaftliche Forschungen, ed. Gustav Schmoller, vol. III [Leipzig, 1885], p. 19).

64 Bynkershoek, *De foro,* p. 47. The States granted the immunity by an edict of 1679. England's first act granting diplomats immunity from arrest came in 1709 as a result of a complaint growing out of the arrest, for debt, of the Russian ambassador in London the year before. This Act, 7 Anne c. 2, incorporated generally accepted theory into law, so as to make prerogative action by the King and Privy Council unnecessary (E. R. Adair, "The Law of Nations and the Common Law of England," *Cambridge Historical Journal,* II [1926–1928], 290–97.

65 B.M. Add. MSS. 37,982, f. 231.

66 George F. Abbott, *Under the Turk in Constantinople* (London, 1920), pp. 301–11; H.M.C. *Finch MSS.* II, 69–73.

67 Sir Paul Rycaut, *The Capitulations and Articles of Peace . . . betweene . . . the King of England . . . and the Sultan . . . Which Serve towards the Maintenance of a Well Grounded Peace & Security of the Trade & Trafficke of His Majestie's Subjects in the Levant* (n.p., 1663).

68 *C.T.B.* I, 155, 206, 228, 243, 269, 353, 362, 376, 381, 447, 523, 525, 579, 580, 601, 666, 721, 722, 736; II, 457; *C.S.P.D.* 1660–1661, p. 467; *C.S.P.V.* XXXIII, 197–98, 201–02.

69 12 Car. II c. 19, *Statutes of the Realm* V, 250; 14 Car. II c. 11, V, 393–400; 22 Car. II c. 4, V, 656; 30 Car. II c. 2, V, 883–84; 1 Jac. II c. 3, VI, 2–3; 1 Jac. II c. 4, 3–5; 1 Jac. II c. 5, VI, 7–9.

70 Elizabeth Evelynola Hoon, *Organization of the English Customs System, 1696–1786* (New York, 1938), p. 26; *C.S.P.D.* 1670, p. 553; *C.S.P.D.* 1678, pp. 96, 105, 106.

71 P.R.O. S.P. 78/117, ff. 158, 193; *C.T.B.* I, 243, 523, 579, 580, 626.

72 William Perwich, *The Despatches of William Perwich, English Agent in Paris, 1669–1677,* ed. M. Beryl Curran (London, 1903), pp. 23–24; Clark, *Trumbull,* pp. 92–93.

73 Memorial of Downing to the States of Holland (11 January 1671), Algemeen Rijksarchief: Staaten-Generaal, Engeland 6922. The same complaint that English ministers had to pay taxes no other ministers paid appears in the correspondence of Thomas Chudleigh (Thomas Plott and Thomas Chudleigh, *The Despatches of Thomas Plott (1681–1682) and Thomas Chudleigh (1682–1685), English Envoys at The Hague,* ed. Frederick Arnold Middlebush [The Hague, 1926], p. 14).

VIII. WRITINGS

1 Almost nothing is known of Aglionby's early life or travels abroad before 1678. G. N. Clark ("Dr. William Aglionby, F.R.S.," *Notes and Queries,* 12th series, IX [August, 1921], 141–43) tells what is known of his career.

2 John Batteridge Pearson, *A Biographical Sketch of the Chaplains to the Levant Company Maintained at Constantinople, Aleppo and Smyrna, 1611–1706* (Cambridge, 1883), p. 16.

3 See *D.N.B.* s.v. "Rycaut"; Clyde Leclare Grose, *A Select Bibliography of British History, 1660–1760* (Chicago, 1939), p. 275; David Baynes Horn, *The British Diplomatic Service, 1689–1789* (Oxford, 1961), p. 290.

4 Samuel Pepys, *Diary,* ed. Henry B. Wheatley, 9 vols. (London, 1910), VI, 21–22, 218.

5 Pepys, *Diary,* VI, 248.

6 For this information I am indebted to Professor R. C. Latham of the University of London. Professor Latham thinks that the edition which came out before the Fire was probably dated 1666, although it was common custom to date books published in the latter months of any year by the date of the following year. The first date for the work in Donald Wing, *Short Title Catalog of Books Printed in England . . . and English Books Printed in Other Countries, 1641–1700,* 3 vols. (New York, 1945), is 1667. The book was soon translated into French (1670), Polish (1678), and German (1684).

7 Epistle Dedicatory.

8 London, 1679. A German translation appeared in 1700.

9 London, 1680.

10 London, 1603. The fifth edition of Knolles (1638) contained new material collected from the diplomatic correspondence of Sir Peter Wyche, ambassador at Constantinople 1627–1641, and father of the Peter Wyche who was a diplomat of Charles II and James II. The sixth edition of Knolles (3 vols. [London, 1687–1700]) incorporated the histories of Knolles and Rycaut, a continuation by Rycaut of Turkish history up to the Treaty of Carlowitz (1699), and Rycaut's *Present State of the Ottoman Empire.* John Savage abridged this work to a two volume edition in 1701. Rycaut was so pleased with Savage's abridgement he wanted to write the introduction himself, but he died before completing it. Rycaut's *History* was translated into French in 1709.

11 Before the *History* was published, Rycaut sent Evelyn material he collected on Shabettai Zebi, a messianic pretender. Evelyn used the

information in his *History of the Three Late Famous Imposters* (*Diary*, ed. E. S. De Beer, 10 vols. [London, 1910], III, 522 and note).

[12] Rycaut was also responsible for the translation of three works by other authors: *The Lives of the Popes* (London, 1685), from the Latin of Baptista Platina, to which he added his own continuation; *The Critick* (London, 1681), from the Spanish of Lorenzo Gracián; and *The Royal Commentaries of Peru* (London, 1688), from the Spanish of Garcilaso de la Vega.

[13] Roger North, *The Lives of the Right Hon. Francis North, Baron Guilford, the Hon. Sir Dudley North, and the Hon. and Rev. Dr. John North*, ed. Augustus Jessopp, 3 vols. (London, 1890), II, 156–57. North left some observations on Turkish law which are more explicit, although not in contradiction to Rycaut's statement on the subject (*ibid.*, II, 58–64; cf. Rycaut, *Present State*, pp. 106–107).

[14] Lady Mary Wortley Montagu, *Letters*, introd. R. Brimley Johnson (London, 1934), p. 108.

[15] Edwin Pears, Review of *Mémoire historique sur l'ambassade de France à Constantinople*, by Marquis de Bonnac (Paris, 1894), *E.H.R.*, XI (1896), 167–70.

[16] [John Trenchard], *Cato's Letters*, 3rd ed. 4 vols. (London, 1733), I, 177.

[17] H.M.C. *Finch MSS.*, I, 521–23. On his journey home from the Levant Winchilsea witnessed a destructive eruption of Mt. Aetna. His vivid letter to the King was published as *A True and Exact Relation of the Late Prodigious Earthquake and Eruption of Mount Aetna* (London, 1669).

[18] See Appendix III.

[19] London, 1677.

[20] Smith, *Remarks*, pp. 1–4, 121.

[21] London, 1684.

[22] Some years before he left England for the Republic Higgons translated in verse *A Prospective of the Naval Triumph of the Venetians over the Turk* (London, 1658), from the Italian of Giovanni Francesco Busenello. Higgons received the original poem from the Venetian ambassador in England, with whom he had struck up a friendship. He presented the work to Peterborough because of his interest in Venetian affairs.

[23] *Relation*, pp. 48–49, 57–64.

[24] Miège, *Relation*, p. 398.

[25] Gilbert Burnet, *History of My Own Time*, ed. Osmund Airy, 2 vols. (Oxford, 1897, 1900).

[26] London, 1683.

[27] Dedication and Preface.

[28] Miège, *Denmark*, pp. 60–98.

[29] [Robert Molesworth], *An Account of Denmark as It Was in the Year 1692*, 3rd ed. (London, 1694), p. 67. Molesworth's political philosophy and ideas on education and their influence on thinkers of the Enlightenment are discussed by Caroline Robbins, *The Eighteenth-Century Commonwealthman: Studies in the Transmission, Development and Circumstance of English Liberal Thought from the Restoration of Charles II to the War with the Thirteen Colonies* (Cambridge, 1959), pp. 98–102.

[30] Horn, *British Diplomatic Service*, pp. 286–88.

[31] John Robinson, *An Account of Sueden Together with an Extract of the History of That Kingdom*, 2nd ed. (London, 1711), pp. 29–30, 70 ff.

[32] London, 1669.

[33] Aglionby, *Present State*, p. 174.

[34] *Ibid.*, p. 251.

[35] Printed in Sir William Temple, *Works*, new ed., 4 vols. (London, 1757), I, 58–222. The "Observations" were translated into Dutch (1673) and French (1685).

[36] Homer E. Woodbridge, *Sir William Temple, the Man and His Work* (New York, 1940), pp. 126–28.

[37] Temple, *Works*, I, 137.

[38] Aglionby, *Present State*, p. 251; Temple, *Works*, I, 167.

[39] Temple, *Works*, I, 181.

[40] Woodbridge, *Temple*, pp. 128–31.

[41] In Temple, *Miscellanea*, 5th ed. (London, 1697), pp. 1–44.

[42] Printed in Thomas Brown, ed., *Miscellanea Aulica: Or, A Collection of State-Treatises, Never before Published* (London, 1702).

[43] *The Present State of Germany*, by a Person of Quality (London, 1690), pp. 52, 84.

[44] Savoy, 1688.

[45] Thomas Birch, *The History of the Royal Society of London*, 2 vols. (London, 1756), II, 132, 266–70.

[46] H.M.C. *Finch MSS.* II, 140 ff.

[47] Royal Society, *Philosophical Transactions*, part I, XIII:152 (1683), 335–46; part II, XIV:155 (1683/4), 431–54.

[48] *Ibid.*, XIV:230 (1697), 597–619.

[49] Sir Richard Fanshawe, et al., *Original Letters and Negotiations of Sir Richard Fanshawe, the Earl of Sandwich, the Earl of Sunderland and Sir William Godolphin, Wherein Divers Matters between the Three Crowns of England, Spain and Portugal from 1663 to 1678 Are Set in a Clearer Light Than Is Anywhere Else Extant*, 2 vols. (London, 1724), II, 48; Birch, *Royal Society*, II, 119.

[50] London, 1670. The original appeared in 1640.

[51] Birch, *Royal Society*, II, 151, 323.

[52] *Ibid.*, 444–46. Wyche was a man of many interests. He fashioned cards representing several countries of the world to be used for teaching geography, for which he received a copyright in 1676 (*C.S.P.D.* 1675–1676, pp. 524, 527). He also translated Jacinto Freire de Andrada's *Life of Dom John de Castro, the Fourth Vice-Roy of India* (London, 1664), to glorify the Queen's native land. He received help in obtaining maps for the book from Francesco de Melo, marquis de Sande, Portuguese ambassador in England.

[53] Birch, *Royal Society*, II, 256, 397.

[54] Royal Society, *Philosophical Transactions*, I:21 (1666), 375–76.

[55] Birch, *Royal Society*, II, 194–95.

[56] Royal Society, *Philosophical Transactions*, VII:83 (1672), 4067–68.

CONCLUSIONS

[1] David Baynes Horn, *The British Diplomatic Service, 1689–1789* (Oxford, 1961), pp. 14–16. Munich, Cologne, Dresden, Naples, Florence, Venice, Warsaw, and St. Petersburg became regular posts, and six others were upgraded during the eighteenth century.

[2] Samuel Pepys, *Diary*, ed. Henry B. Wheatley, 9 vols. (London, 1910), VII, 300–01; Anchitell Grey, *Debates of the House of Commons, from the Year 1667 to the Year 1694*, 10 vols. (London, 1763), I, 70 ff.; *C.J.* IX, 49–51.

[3] Florence May Greir Higham (Evans), *The Principal Secretary of State: A Survey of the Office from 1558 to 1680* (London, 1923), pp. 112–13, 128–29. Evans shows that Thurloe never had a regular allowance for intelligence, and constantly disbursed more than he received, but his system of spies and informers worked well.

[4] Horn, *British Diplomatic Service*, pp. 282–83.

[5] Garrett Mattingly, *Renaissance Diplomacy* (London, 1955), pp. 233–36.

[6] Mattingly, *Renaissance Diplomacy*, p. 234.

[7] Horn, *British Diplomatic Service*, pp. 47, 53–54.

[8] Mattingly, *Renaissance Diplomacy*, pp. 103, 240–41.

[9] Horn, *British Diplomatic Service*, p. 46.

Bibliographical Note

No attempt is made here to list every reference used in the body of the text. All this information is cited in the footnotes. Material for the chapter on literature, which is itself a bibliographical essay, is omitted from this section.

Bibliographies and Guides

English diplomatic papers for the years of the Restoration have been neglected. C. H. Firth and Sophie C. Lomas, eds., *Notes on the Diplomatic Relations of England and France, 1603–1688* (Oxford, 1906), contains a complete list of English ministers to France which indicates the location of the instructions and correspondence of each diplomat. F. G. Davenport, ed., "Materials for English Diplomatic History, 1509–1783, Calendared in the Reports of the Historical

Manuscripts Commission, with References to Similar Materials in the British Museum," *Eighteenth Report of the Royal Commission on Historical Manuscripts* (London, 1917), indicates the correspondence listed by diplomat and year. David Baynes Horn, ed., *British Diplomatic Representatives, 1689–1789* (London, 1932), while concerned with a later period, has some information on Restoration diplomats who continued in the service under William III. For the complete list of accredited diplomats one must consult L. Bittner and L. Gross, eds., *Repertorium der diplomatischen Vertreter aller Länder seit dem westfälischen Frieden (1648)* (Berlin, 1936).

The author wishes to acknowledge her general debt to the work of Garrett Mattingly, *Renaissance Diplomacy* (London, 1955), and David Baynes Horn, *The British Diplomatic Service, 1689–1789* (Oxford, 1961). Although concerned with different periods of time, both were exceedingly helpful in presenting the nature of the problems connected with an institutional study of this type, and in serving as a guide to the kind of material available for such a study. Camille G. Picavet, *La Diplomatie en France au temps de Louis XIV (1661–1715)* (Paris, 1930), was also a useful model, although concerned with foreign policy almost as much as with the diplomatic corps itself.

Manuscripts

The most important body of source material for this study has been the correspondence between the ministers and the Secretaries of State, of which only a relatively small part has been published. The great mass of diplomatic papers remains, uncalendared, in the State Papers, Foreign, at the Public Record Office in London. Other pertinent collections at the Public Record Office are the Minutes of the Board of Trade, concerned with commercial missions, and the Records of the Lord Chamberlain's Office, for information on protocol and wages.

The men of the seventeenth century were careless record keepers. Neither diplomats nor Secretaries always distinguished clearly between public documents and personal papers. A man who left office might destroy correspondence relating to his official duties, or he might take it into his own possession. These letters, if they are to be found at all, may appear in private libraries such as the collection of the Marquis of Bath at Longleat, which contains the Coventry and Thynne papers; in the calendars of the Historical Manuscripts Commission, which include for this period the Finch correspondence from Turkey and the Preston letters from France; or in the repository of manuscripts in the British Museum, where a considerable amount of correspondence relating to the international congresses is preserved. A large number of letters concerned with English missions are to be found in the Temple correspondence in the uncalendared Stowe MSS. at the Huntingdon Library, San Marino, California.

Printed Diplomatic Correspondence, Diaries, Memoirs

The largest collections of printed letters are those of Arlington and Temple: for the former, *The Right Honourable the Earl of Arlington's Letters to Sir William Temple, Bart.*, 2 vols. (London, 1701); and, by Arlington and Henry Coventry, et al., *Letters from the Secretaries of State, and Other Persons, in the Reign of King Charles the Second, to Francis Parry, esq., English Envoy in Portugal* (London, 1817). Sir William Temple, *Letters . . . Containing an Account of the Most Important Transactions . . . in Christendom from 1665 to 1672*, 2 vols. (London, 1700), was the earliest collection of Restoration diplomatic papers to be printed. Sir Richard Fanshawe, et al., *Original Letters and Negotiations of Sir Richard Fanshawe, the Earl of Sandwich, the Earl of Sunderland and Sir William Godolphin, Wherein Divers Matters between the Three Crowns of England, Spain and Portugal from 1663 to 1678 Are Set in a Clearer Light Than Is Anywhere Else Extant*, 2 vols. (London, 1724), amplifies the material found in Arlington and Coventry's letters to Parry.

Newsletters sent out from London have been used extensively. *The Bulstrode Papers: The Collection of Autograph Letters and Historical Documents Formed by Alfred Morrison*, 2 vols. (London, 1897), and W. D. Christie, ed., *Letters Addressed from London to Sir Joseph Williamson While Plenipotentiary at the Congress of Cologne, in the Years 1673 and 1674*, 2 vols. (London, 1874), show the kind of information generally available to the diplomat during his service abroad. Christopher Lindenov, *The First Triple*

Alliance: The Letters of Christopher Lindenov, Danish Envoy to London, 1668–1672, ed., trans., and introd. Waldemar Westergaard (New Haven, 1947), tells a great deal about the diplomatic scene as it looked from London. *Calendar of State Papers and Manuscripts Relating to English Affairs Existing in the Archives and Collections of Venice, and in Other Libraries of Northern Italy*, vols. XXXII-XXXVIII, ed. Allen B. Hinds (London, 1931–1947), presents the Venetian view of English diplomatic activity in London and the other principal capitals of Europe.

The best diplomatic reporting, indeed the ideal from the point of view of the government to which it was directed, was terse, impersonal, and concerned exclusively with the business at hand, which was current developments in matters of policy. The most capable ministers, therefore, often tell us the least about the subjects to which this book is devoted. They say little of the daily problems that the minister encountered, such as the management of his household or his reaction to the way the government managed the foreign service. One must therefore depend on the more candid sentiments expressed to friends and family in letters from abroad, in memoirs and diaries, or in the official correspondence of the important ministers. These papers are characterized by a chattiness, which is not found in the letters of a William Temple, about everyday life in an embassy. Notable in this type of source material are Sir George Etherege, *Letterbook*, ed. and introd. Sybil Rosenfeld (London, 1928); Lady Anne Fanshawe, *Memoirs* (London, 1905); William Perwich, *The Despatches of William Perwich, English Agent in Paris, 1669–1677*, ed. M. Beryl Curran (London, 1903); Thomas Plott and Thomas Chudleigh, *The Despatches of Thomas Plott (1681–1682) and Thomas Chudleigh (1682–1685), English Envoys at The Hague*, ed. Frederick Arnold Middlebush (The Hague, 1926); and Sir Henry Savile, *Letters to and from Henry Savile, esq. Envoy at Paris*, ed. William Durrant Cooper, Camden Society, series I, vol. 71 (London, 1858).

Printed Works on Special Topics

Duties and Responsibilities: Sets of official instructions, like the diplomatic correspondence for this period, are scattered and incomplete. Relatively few are in the State Papers, Foreign; of these, some are rough drafts with marginal emendations, making it difficult to ascertain whether the document is in the same form in which the diplomat finally received it. A clear picture of what was expected of the ministers serving Louis XIV emerges in *Recueil des instructions donneés aux ambassadeurs et ministres de France depuis les traités de Westphalie jusqu'à la Révolution Française . . . Angleterre,* ed. and introd. J. J. Jusserand, 2 vols. (Paris, 1929). The *Calendar of State Papers, Domestic Series, 1660–1685,* ed. Mary Anne Everett Green, et al. (London, 1860ff.), has occasional references to the official responsibilities of departing ministers. Peter Fraser, *The Intelligence of the Secretaries of State and Their Monopoly of Licensed News, 1660–1688* (New York, 1956), is an excellent analysis of the Restoration news service.

Personnel and Household: In addition to the classic mines of information in John Evelyn, *Diary,* ed. E. S. De Beer, 6 vols. (Oxford, 1955), and Samuel Pepys, *Diary,* ed. Henry B. Wheatley, 9 vols. (London, 1910), some other contemporary memoirs and diaries proved to be useful guides to diplomatic skills and methods of recruiting members to the service. The most rewarding in this regard were Sir Richard Bulstrode, *Memoirs and Reflections upon the Reign and Government of King Charles the 1st and K. Charles the IInd* (London, 1721); Gilbert Burnet, *History of My Own Time,* ed. Osmund Airy, 2 vols. (Oxford, 1897); Edward Hyde, earl of Clarendon, *The Life of Edward Earl of Clarendon . . . in Which Is Included, a Continuation of His History of the Grand Rebellion,* 2 vols. (Oxford, 1857); Sir John Reresby, *Memoirs,* ed. and introd. Andrew Browning (Glasgow, 1936); and Henry Sidney, earl of Romney, *Diary of the Times of Charles the Second,* ed. R. W. Blencowe, 2 vols. (London, 1843).

Biographical studies which deserve special mention are Violet Barbour, *Henry Bennet, Earl of Arlington* (Washington, 1914), excellent on Arlington the man and on the offices of the secretary of state; Andrew Browning, *Thomas Osborne, Earl of Danby and Duke of Leeds, 1632–1712,* 3 vols. (Glasgow, 1951), which tells about the selection of ministers and the problems of payment; John Beresford, *The Godfather of Downing Street:* Sir George Downing, *1623–1684* (Boston, 1925), has interesting comments on contemporary opinion of the minister to the United Provinces. For the embassy staff, Gertrude Ann Jacobsen *William Blathwayt, a Late*

Seventeenth Century English Administrator (New Haven, 1932), and John Batteridge Pearson, *A Biographical Sketch of the Chaplains to the Levant Company Maintained at Constantinople, Aleppo and Smyrna, 1611–1706* (Cambridge, 1883), were the most informative books.

Remuneration: The *Calendar of Treasury Books,* ed. William A. Shaw, 32 vols. (London, 1904–1923), vols. I-VIII, is the fundamental reference. Stephen B. Baxter, *The Development of the Treasury, 1660–1702* (Cambridge, 1957), is a first rate institutional study which explains the difficulty the ministers experienced in collecting their salaries. John Yonge Akerman, ed., *Moneys Received and Paid for Secret Services of Charles II and James II from 30th March, 1679 to 25 December, 1688* (London, 1851), and James Walker, "The Secret Service under Charles II and James II," *Transactions of the Royal Historical Society,* 4th series, XV (1932), 211–42, throw light on some of the subsidiary expenses connected with the foreign service.

Protocol: Since matters of etiquette were of such concern in the seventeenth century, almost every collection mentioned in this study has some reference to the general topic of protocol. Special contemporary works on this specific subject are John Finet, *Finetti Philoxensis: Som Choice Observations of Sir John Finet . . . Touching the Reception, and Precedence, the Treatment and Audience, the Puntillios and Contests of Forren Ambassadors in England,* ed. James Howell (London, 1656); James Howell, *A Discourse Concerning the Precedency of Kings, Wherein the Reasons and Arguments of the Three Greatest Monarks of Christendom, Who Claim a Several Right Thereunto, Are Faithfully Collected and Render'd, Whereunto Is Also Adjoyn'd a . . . Treatise of Ambassadors, etc.* (London, 1664); and Abraham de Wicquefort, *The Embassador and His Functions,* trans. John Digby (London, 1716). Wicquefort's book is also important for the general topics of personnel and exterritoriality.

J. Heringa, *De Eer en Hoogheid van de Staat* (Groningen, 1961), is excellent on Dutch practises in general and on special forms observed with England both under the Protectorate and the restored monarchy. The book of Picavet, mentioned above, tells about French protocol. Usages in Russia and the northern countries are best described in Guy Miège, *A Relation of Three Embassies from*

His Sacred Majestie Charles II to the Great Duke of Muscovie, the King of Sweden, and the King of Denmark (London, 1669), and Caroline Robbins, "Carlisle and Marvell in Russia, Sweden, and Denmark, 1663–1664," *The History of Ideas Newsletter,* III:1 (1957), 8–17.

Exterritoriality: The writings of the theorists themselves form the basis of this chapter: Alberico Gentili, *De legationibus libri tres,* trans. Gordon J. Laing, introd. Ernest Nys (New York, 1924); Jean Hotman, *The Ambassadors* (London, 1603); Samuel Pufendorf, *De jure naturae et gentium libri octo,* trans. C. H. and W. A. Old-father (Oxford, 1934); Samuel Rachel, *Dissertations on the Law of Nature and Nations,* trans. John Pawley Bate, introd. Ludwig von Bar (Washington, 1916); Richard Zouche, *An Exposition of Fecial Law and Procedure, and of Law between Nations, and Questions Concerning the Same,* ed. Thomas Erskine Holland, trans. J. L. Brierly, 2 vols. (Washington, 1911).

The most exhaustive secondary study is that of E. R. Adair, *The Exterritoriality of Ambassadors in the Sixteenth and Seventeenth Centuries* (London, 1929), but it does not cover the reigns of Charles II and James II.

Index

About the Author

Phyllis S. Lachs did her undergraduate work at Wellesley College and the University of Pennsylvania and received her M.A. and Ph.D. degrees from Bryn Mawr College. She joined the faculty of Rutgers College of South Jersey in 1963. Part of the research for this book was done with the aid of a fellowship from the American Association of University Women.